MAQĀṢID AL-SHARĪʿAH: A CIVILIZATIONAL PERSPECTIVE

MAQĀṢID AL-SHARĪʿAH : A CIVILIZATIONAL PERSPECTIVE

MAZEN HASHEM

LONDON · WASHINGTON

IIIT, P.O. Box 669, Herndon, VA 20172, USA • www.iiit.org
P.O. Box 126, Richmond, Surrey, TW9 2UD, UK • www.iiituk.com

Library of Congress Cataloging-in-Publication Data
Names: Hashem, Mazen, author.
Title: Maqāṣid al-Sharīʿah: a civilizational perspective / Mazen Hashem.
Description: Herndon : The International Institute of Islamic Thought IIIT, 2023. | Includes bibliographical references.
Identifiers: LCCN 2023032589 (print) | LCCN 2023032590 (ebook) ISBN 9781642059038 (hardback) | ISBN 9781642059045 (paperback) | ISBN 9781642059052 (ebook)
Subjects: LCSH: Maqāṣid (Islamic law) | Islamic law—Interpretation and construction.
Classification: LCC KBP442 .H3765 2023 (print) | LCC KBP442 (ebook) | DDC 340.5/9--dc23/eng/20230817
LC record available at https://lccn.loc.gov/2023032589
LC ebook record available at https://lccn.loc.gov/2023032590

Typesetting Wordzworth www.wordzworth.com
Cover design Shiraz Khan

Printed in the USA

Contents

Introduction

This book, titled *Maqāṣid al-Sharīʿah: An ʿUmrānī Perspective*, is a translation of this author's original Arabic work titled *Mukhtaṣar Maqāṣid al-Sharīʿah al-Islāmiyyah: Mudkhal ʿUmrānī* and is a modest treatment of the subject matter in which some detailed scholarly discussions from the original have been omitted, while having also added certain clarifying or elaborating points to the original that this author deemed appropriate for an English reading audience. However, the major contributions remain. The book aims to contribute to the development of *maqāṣid al-Sharīʿah* (the aims of Shariʿah) theory by offering an *ʿumrānī* (civilizational) perspective on the matter. Such a perspective hopes to advance the discipline of *maqāṣid al-Sharīʿah* to new horizons and make it more relevant to a public discourse; a discourse that is not limited to the juristic derivation of rulings, the fatwa of the mufti, or the legal theorizing of the *uṣūlī*. The *ʿumrānī* approach allows *maqāṣid* theory to be more comprehensive and to better serve the circumstances and needs of the diverse peoples and communities of the Ummah and beyond.

The subject of the book is entrenched in Islamic legacy literature that has a special style and utilizes specialized terms, and such terms have developed within a specific intellectual milieu in a language that has its own internal logic. All of that poses a challenge for translation, lest distortions seep into the original meanings and intent, or shades of incompatible meanings impinged upon us by modern sensibilities cloud our understanding. Therefore, this introduction will clarify key Islamic terminology to ensure the proper understanding of this subject.

The aforementioned concerns made us keen to use the following original Arabic-Islamic terminology, especially when quoting. Yet, to enhance readability we included some commonly used English approximations, in the hopes that the reader will resurrect the Islamic framework within which the original terms operate.

Shari'ah (Variants: *Sharī'ah*, Shariah, Sharia)

Since the term Shari'ah is pivotal and appears in the title of the book, we will elaborate on it in somewhat lengthy discussion. It is worth mentioning that Muslim scholars throughout history considered the term Shari'ah as self-explanatory and did not feel the urge to define it.

In the context of politics, Gurdun Krämer notes,

> No sharp distinction is usually made between Islam and the shari'a, and as a rule both terms are used interchangeably. In accordance with what might be called the functional theory of government, which sees the shari'a as the cornerstone of an Islamic order and government as merely the executive of God's law, the debate has shifted as to how the shari'a is to be defined—whether as a comprehensive set of norms and values regulating human life down to the minutest detail, or as a set of general rules of good life and moral behavior aiming at people's welfare on earth and their salvation in the hereafter (which still leaves room for human interpretation).[1]

Safi provides a definition that stresses the comprehensiveness of the term: "Shari'ah, or Islamic law, is a comprehensive system encompassing the whole field of human experience. It is not simply a legal system, but rather a composite system of law and morality. That is, Islamic law aspires to regulate all aspects of human activities, not only those that may entail legal consequences."[2]

Barazangi warns against a common pitfall in considering Shari'ah as law:

> Note that the Arabic term *shar'* or *shar'i* is often confused when making reference to what is known as "Islamic law." The constructs "Islamic law" and "*shari'a* laws" do not represent the Qur'anic *Shari'a* (with a capital *S*), meaning the collective guidelines of the Qur'an that encompass an intertwined moral and legal bind once the individual accepts the guidelines as his or her belief system, nor do they represent the Qur'an's principles. "Islamic law" or "*shari'a* laws" (with lowercase *s*) are mainly used by Orientalists in reference to jurisprudence opinions, documented in books of *fiqh* (jurisprudence) and supported by some

Qur'anic verses and Hadith narratives. By giving those opinions a legal character known in the West as "law," Orientalists and most contemporary Muslims have confused the Qur'anic *Shari'a* (guidelines) with other legislation or canonized laws.[3]

Regarding the special position of Shari'ah in the life of Muslims, Abou El Fadl states the following:

The *Shari'a*—as a symbol to the Divine path and as the representative of the collective effort of Muslims at understanding what God wants from human beings—functioned like the symbolic glue that held the diverse Muslim nation together, despite its many different ethnicities, nationalities, and political entities. *Shari'a* became a symbol of unity and commonality for Muslims around the world, and jurists were the *Shari'a's* guardians and protectors.[4]

Elsewhere, I noted the misuse of the term:

The term Shari'ah is uncritically invoked by both Muslims and non-Muslims. Outside the Islamic realm, it is often mentioned as an archaic religious system of laws that are anti-modern and manipulated by male clerics. Yet, properly understood, the Shari'ah stands as a comprehensive body of generative principles and directives that reflect Islam's moral outlook, social philosophy, and legal precepts.[5]

In an attempt to produce a short definition of Shari'ah, I've previously stated the following: "Shari'ah stands for 'the overall socio-religious mandates of Islam.'"[6] To simplify the matter, I often present the following formula: Shari'ah = Islamic moral outlook + Islamic system principles + Regulations for the virtuous life.

By the expression "Islamic system," which this book frequently uses, we wish to emphasize the integrative nature of the Islamic perspective toward life and the dynamic interactions among its components. Therefore, approaching social matters is a constructive process (*iṣlāḥ*) that is not divorced from economic and political matters. Moreover, the macro-level is, by default, mindful of the miso level (such as organizations) and of the individual micro level. That relates to the very idea of *maqāṣid* and that Shari'ah is not simply a collection of direct commands.

We further note the term *nuṣūṣ* (literally texts) that is commonly used in Islamic literature refers exclusively to the texts of the Qur'an and Sunnah, not including the texts of Muslim intellectual legacy (*turāth*) that is the production of scholars' work; for that reason, this book uses the term "Shari'ah Texts," with capitals. We did not feel comfortable using the term "sacred texts," lest be thought that they are not open to rational understanding. Lastly, this book will not use the term *naṣ* (the singular form of *nuṣūṣ*) because it has different meanings in the usage of fiqh compared to that of *uṣūl al-fiqh*—in fiqh the term *naṣ* means a text of the Qur'an or Sunnah, while in *uṣūl al-fiqh* it is the text with a definite meaning not open to other possible interpretations.

Shāri', Shar'ī, and *Tashrī'*

The terms *shāri', shar'ī,* and *tashrī'* are derivatives from the same root of which Shari'ah is. Ultimately, the *Shāri'* is Allah, Who bestowed guidance to humanity through the Qur'an as well as the Sunnah of Prophet Muhammad (ṢAAS – *Ṣallā Allāhu `alayhi wa sallam.* May the peace and blessings of God be upon him. Said whenever the name of Prophet Muhammad is mentioned). Hadith represents the verbal reports of what Prophet Muhammad said, did, or condoned; thus, the term "Sunnah" is more general than hadith as the former points to the overall way of Prophet Muhammad.

In the writings of *uṣūl* in particular, but also in fiqh, the term *Shāri',* not Allah, is customarily invoked when discussing what the Shari'ah says. Such a use is to denote the intent of Allah in commanding specific guidance and regulations. The term *shar'ī* is an adjective, denoting that something is compatible with Shari'ah or falls within its domain.

Tashrī' is the content of the commands of Allah the *Shāri',* whether it is explicit or implicit. Therefore, the term "legislation" is out of scope, for *tashrī'* stands for the Shari'ah's precepts regarding the regulations of life, which nevertheless are captured and elaborated on in the work of scholars. Again, legislation does not stand for *tashrī',* as the latter is specifically connected to the Will of Allah. Thus, the scholars are not agents of *tashrī',* rather, they are interpreters of it. Therefore, invoking the concept of *tashrīʿ* in fiqh and *uṣūl al-fiqh* is qualitatively different from the modern use in the sense of legislation that legislative governmental bodies produce. That does not mean that there could be no legislation in an Islamic system; rather, such legislation operates at a different level—at the level of organizing ordinary life matters, the *ʿādiyyāt*. Lastly, the term Lawgiver is problematic as it is associated with a person or a prophet, and it is largely suitable for the Hebrew religious culture.

Fiqh, Uṣūl, and the Legal

Fiqh is the corpus of writings about the precepts and principles of Shariʿah, as stated in the Qur'an and Sunnah, and its prescriptions as deduced in a specific time and space. Different jurisprudential schools of fiqh have naturally formed as scholars differed in their estimation of the context of the texts and the intent behind them. They reconciled different hadiths by considering how the Qur'an judges the issue or this class of issues, and how any resultant understanding fits within the *kulliyāt* of Shariʿah (i.e., its universal and undisputable general principles). Fiqh is a human production that pays specific attention to the understandings of the Companions of Prophet Muhammad, which have a referential weight; nevertheless, fiqh also stands for understandings that are tied to time and space.

Typically, fiqh rulings (*aḥkām*) are expressed at five levels: required (*farḍ*), recommended (*mandūb/mustaḥab*), disliked or recommended against (*makrūh*), prohibited (*ḥarām*), and permissible (*ḥalāl* or *mubāḥ*). The permissible category is the middle point in which there is no specific Shariʿah Text but, nevertheless, fits well within the universals of Shariʿah, thus being permissible. It is a category of *ʿādiyyāt*, the ordinary matters in life including the most rudimentary to the most crucial. This is quite relevant to the subject of *maqāṣid*, since its approach attends for the original goal of *aḥkām* (rulings), therefore, avoiding proceduralism. The approach of *maqāṣid* helps in prioritization should conflict between *aḥkām* arises, and could serve in the very derivation of *aḥkām* (according to some scholars).

It is imperative to note that fiqh is not interchangeable with law (commonly understood as procedural law), even though there is something shared between them—both being attempts at understanding and organizing life within the

Islamic framework. Fiqh navigates political, economic, and social matters, but the worship aspect is so present in it, and it would be egregious to imagine that law can enter personal this realm.

Furthermore, what makes differentiating fiqh from law imperative is that law in modern societies is associated with the state. Shariʿah and fiqh are personal and communal, despite their interconnection with polity, economics, and other aspects of life. For example, personal hygiene is a fiqh recommendation based on Shariʿah Texts; we cannot imagine the state has anything to do with it. Zakat is a required charity in which the state might get involved in its collection, partially or fully. Yet, the obligatory aspect of zakat flows from the community to the state, and not the other way around. Furthermore, zakat is a *farḍ* (religious obligation) and the individual has to spend specified amounts to specified classes of need, regardless whether it was collected by authorities or not. Moreover, law is unitary while fiqh is multiple, and such multiplicity may occur within the same country, and at times within the same community or even within a single family.

As for fatwa, it is not a religious edict in the legal sense. Different ulama (scholars of Shariʿah who analyzes the texts of Qurʾan and Hadith, trying to reach generalized rules in the different aspect of life) can reach different fatwas regarding the same matter, and a fatwa (within the Sunni sphere) is not binding on individuals as it is merely a scholarly opinion (and within the Shiʾite sphere, a person can opt for a different *mujtahid*). Moreover, a fatwa could be debated and countered. And most notably, fatwa stands as a moral declaration more than a direct order for action. It is only the Muslim judge's edict that is binding, because political authority appoints judges. Yet, the decision of the qadi is not arbitrary, as he or she is bound by a cumulative fiqh literature and the rules of *uṣūl al-fiqh*.

Uṣūl-al-fiqh is the discipline that elaborates on the proper way of dealing with texts and their different statuses, the place of logical tools (e.g., deduction and induction), and the role of language critical in this discipline. For example, *uṣūl* offers rules for reconciling two hadiths on a matter when the indication of one hadith is specific and that of the other is general. Another example is the proper way of resorting to *qiyās* (analogical reasoning).

And it should be noted that sometimes the term Shariʿah is used interchangeably with the names of its sciences, such as *fiqh* or *uṣūl al-fiqh*. But this loose use is only a shorthand meant to stress that the product of such disciplines is not something arbitrary or a mere personal opinion.

The most problematic aspect in referring to law when invoking Shariʿah and fiqh is the issue of violence. Invoking law in our modern system is tightly connected to the state and its means of normalized violence. A state can act on behalf of the Muslim community to administer and enforce few fiqh sanctioned penal prescriptions, yet their legitimacy is anchored in fiqh views accepted by the community of believers, not the state. Naturally, the state does mobilize means of enforcement as a mere political act, but supposedly it should not violate a general principle of Shariʿah.

Maṣlaḥah

The term *maṣlaḥah* and its plural, *maṣāliḥ*, appear frequently in the book because it is the center of the *maqāṣidī* approach—the aims of Shariʿah approach. In fact, *maṣlaḥah* and *maqṣid* are sometimes used interchangeably.

Maṣāliḥ is sometimes translated as interests, but it is not interest in the utilitarian sense. *Uṣūl al-fiqh* usually speaks of three kinds of *maṣāliḥ*. There are the Allah-recognized *maṣāliḥ* (*maṣāliḥ muʿtabarah*), the annulled *maṣāliḥ* (*maṣāliḥ mulghāt*), and the unrestricted *maṣāliḥ* (*maṣāliḥ mursalah*). An example for the first kind of *maṣlaḥah* is working hard to care for the family. The example of the second *maṣlaḥah* is taking usury or intoxicants. The judgment on such actions is established by a direct text of Shariʿah, referred to as *dalīl* (evidence). But the judgment might not be supported by a singularly spelled-out *dalīl*, rather, based on whether it fits or clashes with Islam's general principles and orientation. The examples on this third kind of *maṣāliḥ* are infinite as they are of which Shariʿah is silent; they can include matters like forming a committee to discuss a communal issue, estimating the fair tax on importing luxuries, or opening a new road in a town.

Therefore, *maṣlaḥah* is not sheer utility nor is it selfishness even if it confers rewards and is beneficial. Furthermore, invariably the term *maṣlaḥah* assumes a balance between the individual and collective outcome. Speaking of the uniqueness of Islam as a religion, the term *maṣlaḥah* ruptures the reductionist views on religion, as *maṣlaḥah* is welfare that relates to both the temporal world and the hereafter. In this book, we tried to minimize the use of the term interest, and we invoked the terms welfare, well-being, benefit, interest, and public interest as appropriate.

Religion

While there is no one agreed-upon definition of the term religion in modern writing, the case of Islam adds to the perplexity. The secular understanding of religion restricts it to the realm of myth and the opposite of reason. In sociology, the Durkheimian functionalist framework considered religion as a good myth as it confers cohesion to the community. Weber had a specific view of Protestantism as compatible with capitalism, while he had a specific problem with eastern religions; in general, he associated religion with magic.

Interestingly and surprisingly, for long the field of the sociology of religion understood religion within the confines of rational choice theory—believers in religions simply seek self-satisfying intangible rewards. On the other hand, phenomenology has a deep appreciation of religion and its place in the psycho-social realm of individuals and society. Yet, its regard of religion is too esoteric.

Despite that the term religion is largely mishandled by secular academic writings, this book uses it (and does not use the term *dīn*), assuming that the reader is aware enough about the uniqueness of Islam, its encompassing nature, and its simultaneous attention to the temporal world and the hereafter.

Widely-Used Terms

Lastly, we briefly note some widely used terms in the Muslim literature that nevertheless are not unproblematic. We start by the choice of saying, Allah or God, as they are not actually equivalent. In the Arabic language there is no plural form of the word Allah, nor could it be made to indicate femininity as other Arabic words could. Related to that is the pronoun "he", as it does not signify masculinity in Arabic linguistics when used with non-person entities.

Equally troubling is the dual expression pleasing/fearing Allah; the first could carry the implication of the need to receive pleasure, and the second could imply vengefulness. In the Qur'anic narrative, the constellation of meanings such as in the words *shukr* and *ḥamd* (pleasing and thankful) to Allah, as well as *khawf* and *khashyah* (fearing and watchfulness) are associated with the Qur'anic term *ʿabd*. The proper understanding of the term *ʿabd* (usually expressed as servant) is the key for understanding the former terms as both expressions are usually used in reference to the person, the *ʿabd* of Allah.

The Qur'anic term *ʿabd* is a noun (plural *ʿibād*), and *ʿabada* is the verb form, while *ʿibādah* is the infinitive which is usually translated as worship, and the *ʿābid* is the person who preforms *ʿibādah*. This term, *ʿabd*, and its derivations are largely misrepresented, thus misunderstood, and neither the word servant nor slave captures the meaning of *ʿabd*. The other term that we need to introduce is *ṭāʿah*, which is customarily translated as obedience. However, *ṭāʿah* denotes going along with willingness and agreeableness. The essential relationship between the Creator and the created, as expressed by the Qur'an, revolves around those two root words: *ʿibādah* and *ṭāʿah*. Those terms together denote, at once, deference and love as well as following guidance with full cognitive persuasion and the contentment of the conscience.

No wonder that in the Qur'an Allah endearingly calls on His people using the expression "O my *ʿabds*." Indeed, love is a component of *ʿibādah*, and Ibn Taymiyyah asserts that "*ʿibādah* subsumes humbleness and love together... and that who submits to another person with aversion is not an *ʿābid* to him, and if a person loves something and does not submit to it he is not an *ʿābid* to it."[7] Interestingly, the 5th Hijri century language scholar, al-Thaʿālibī, in his book *Fiqh al-Lughah wa Asrār al-ʿArabiyyah* (The Fiqh of Language and the Hidden Gems of the Arabic Language), lists eleven levels of love (*ḥub*), eight of them are healthy and three are detrimental, noting that the expression "*ʿabd* to Allah" (Abdullah) is connected to *taym*, which is the eighth highest level of healthy love.[8] Obviously, there are no equivalent English terms that capture such nuance.

We hope that the reader notices the meticulous balance in the above-mentioned Qur'anic expressions, as they are void from: (1) the acrimonious relationship between God and people found in some scriptures; (2) the subjugating expressions and implications found in some religious literature; and (3) the arrogant rebellious expressions encountered in philosophy literature. And by this point, the reader should appreciate how crucial it is to rejuvenate Islamic terms and their ecology of meaning.

ʿUmrān

ʿUmrān is rather a challenging term as Ibn Khaldūn used it his own way. The term ʿumrān appears in the Qurʾan, and it is associated with *istikhlāf* and the responsibility of humankind to carry on and actualize the call of the Qurʾan. Furthermore, Ibn Khaldūn used the term *ḥaḍārah* in connection to ʿumrān, and at times as one of its aspects even though his own concept of ʿumrān is more comprehensive.

Ibn Khaldūn contrasted three structural settings, the natural, the Bedouin,[9] and the urbanist (the *ḥaḍar*). However, such mention is not simply for their substantive qualities, rather, to discern societal laws as they relate to the overall historical development of societies. Nomadism (*al-badāwah*) does not carry negative connotations in Ibn Khaldūn's thought; to the contrary, it is superior in five dimensions: (1) existential, where it represents a pure state; (2) psychological, where it represents independence and chivalry; (3) social, where it is associated with solidarity and strong bonds; (4) economic, where it is associated with self-sufficiency; (5) political, where it is associated with the readiness to defense and the rejection of arbitrary dominance. On the other hand, the urbanist lifestyle (*ḥaḍar*) is associated with laxity, docility, and moral corruption. Ibn Khaldūn discussed in detail the *ḥaḍārī* setting where there is a great deal of complexity and integration of tasks. And in such setting the organic solidarity of the nomadic setting gets lost, replaced by a solidarity (*aṣabiyyah*) among a ruling class (almost monopolized by them) to which the common people have to submit.

Yet, *ḥaḍārah* is not all negative in the perspective of Ibn Khaldūn. And while *ḥaḍārah* involves refined sensibilities, it is also the complex mode of living that Ibn Khaldūn admirably notes; it is the setting where the branches of knowledge grow, and where elaborate developments, vigorous economy, specialization, and large cities flourish. Ibn Khaldūn dedicates his effort to delineate the *ʿumrānī* nature of *ḥaḍārah* (i.e., its structural and cultural features and its place in historical development) in light of what Allah wants from humankind on earth. In some instances, Ibn Khaldūn does state that the *ḥaḍārah* is a high state of ʿumrān, but this is only a generic use of the term. Otherwise, ʿumrān stands for the qualities of the setting; for example, Ibn Khaldūn speaks of the nomadic *'umrān*. Furthermore, the dynamics of *'umrān* underly the cycle of historical developments.

To add to the challenge of reading the terms *'umran* and *ḥaḍārah*, I note that many contemporary Arabic writings, interacting with the English literature, equated the term *ḥaḍārah* with civilization. But the term civilization stands on its own in Western language; it gained currency during the colonial project of western European countries, considering that uncivilized nations could be subjugated and their resources could be appropriated as part of the White Man's burden to civilize the backward barbarians. Not all of the use of the term civilization is as much terrible, but it remains problematic. Furthermore, the term civilization is connected to the concept of citizenship with its specific modern context; such layer of meaning is totally incongruent with the term *ḥaḍārah*.

The contemporary use of the term *ḥaḍārah* in Arabic literature falls within three camps. For modernist writers, the use of the term *ḥaḍārah* reflects the idea of progress and an agreeable reaction to Western cultural imperialism, and many casual writers connect it to development (*tanmiyah*). The second group uses the term in reference to the totality of the historical development of a cultural bloc, including language, religio-cultural aspects, philosophy, science, inventions, economic activities, etc. This choice is close to the expanded use of the term civilization in the English language.

The third camp invokes the term *ḥaḍārah* with a special reference to the Islamic experience. Malek Bennabi, tracing the footsteps of Iqbal, made the term *ḥaḍārah* the pivot of his discourse, but he only offered a by-the-way definition that does not fit well with his own theme. Yet, Bennabi made a creative opening for the term *ḥaḍārah* in connecting it to *ḥuḍūr* (authentic cultural manifestation).[10] Ismail al-Farūqi, and later Mona Abul-Fadl, gave life and depth to the term *ḥaḍārah*, connecting it to the overall quest of the Islamic phenomenon for shaping reality along the lines of the precepts of Islam, emphasizing Islam's unique *tawḥīd* worldview that is reflected in every corner of Muslim reality; so did Abdelwahab Elmessiri but without frequently invoking the term.[11] The Islamic intellectual circles in Egypt, spearheaded by the efforts of Saif AbdelFattah and his colleagues, including Nadia Mahmoud Mostafa and Omar al-Sayyid, made the term "*ḥaḍāri* perspective" a title for their quest to illuminate key Qur'anic concepts that are rich in their philosophical implications, Islam's epistemological purview, and the proper Islamically-minded approaches in social sciences.[12] Meanwhile, in the Turkish intellectual circles, Ahmet Davutoğlu worked on rehabilitating the term civilization and defined six parameters that speak of the Islamic, or the Western, civilizational worldview, and it was Ibrahim Kalın that gave civilization a clear definition as a worldview manifested and objectified in time and space.[13] Thus, in the Islamic intellectual circles *ḥaḍārah* equals civilization or civilizational worldview, and almost equals *'umrān*. Indeed, this third school frequently uses the term *ḥaḍārah* and *'umrān* interchangeably. In general, such a use subsumes meanings associated with the term Islamicate and shares the focus of the sociology of Islam line of research.

In this book on *maqāṣid*, the use of the concept *'umrān* is akin to the third school with one decisive conceptual notation: *'umrān* does not simply denote substantive matters, rather, it primarily points to the internal logic of the Muslim system as it marched throughout history and the dynamics of its various institutions guided by Islam and Sharī'ah universals. At its core, *'umrān* signifies the architecture of social reality and its genetic map. As such, it addresses the social system, both at the structural and cultural levels. Therefore, religion and language, social, economic, and political dynamics, as well as history and geography, all are present and considered basic *'umrāni* dimensions. *'Umrān* is not *ḥaḍārah*, yet at the end it points to what we refer to as civilizational aspects and patterns. While there were several attempts to coin an English equivalent to the term *'umrān*, two of them are worthy of mention: "meta-history" by Abu Yaareb al-Marzouki, and "the sociology of civilization" by Receb Şenturk. This book will use the original term *'umrān*, not its approximations.[14]

At this point, the reader should appreciate the reason why this work has used the term *'umrān* along with *maqāṣid*. It is because such an approach allows for mobilizing the concept of Sharī'ah to address the breadth of human reality and the societal system where historical laws operate; keeping in mind the ecology of the terminology noted above is crucial for understanding the subject. That is especially true since the prose in the original Arabic version utilized expressions woven from root words in the Qur'an and hadith, something that necessarily cannot be captured by translation. We have tried our best to make this English version both readable and at the same time free from modernist sensibilities that could unconsciously infiltrate the understanding of such a subject.

With respect to the book's structure, it is composed of three main parts. Part One begins with a brief review of the early pioneering contributions of *maqāṣid*, followed by due attention to the later modern contribution to *maqāṣid* by Ibn ʿAshūr, and then reviews some of the more important contemporary contributions to *maqāṣid*. Part Two discusses technical subjects and concepts within the field of *maqāṣid* that are crucial to expanding and refining *maqāṣid* theory. Lastly, Part Three offers a special contribution to the development of *maqāṣid* through incorporating insights from the social sciences along the *ʿumrānī* approach of Ibn Khaldūn. This special contribution, prompted by Taha Jabir al-Alwani's call to further develop the higher aims of the Shariʿah, requires a different approach to reading Shariʿah texts.

The study of *maqāṣid* is certainly a lofty discipline, and this work hopes to charter a novel approach to engaging with and understanding this discipline that proves invaluable to furthering its development and its potential for addressing today's needs. Needless to say, any academic contribution to *maqāṣid* thought, such as that being made with this work, is inevitably an ijtihad, and the nature of human production is that it is prone to shortcomings and in need of revision and further insight. As such, I seek forgiveness from Allah for any flaws or shortcomings associated with this work.

PART I

LITERATURE REVIEW

1

Stages in the Development of the Discourse on *Maqāṣid al-Sharīʿah*

The notion of *maqāṣid al-Sharīʿah* (aims of Shariʿah) is soundly rooted in the Shariʿah itself; a Shariʿah that is universal and which has an ample capacity for reflection and reason. The Qurʾanic discourse, in fact, criticizes ignoring higher aims and myopically approaching religion such that it leads to deleterious outcomes. We find that even the rituals of Islam serve higher goals beyond their mere outward form. This is attested to in a hadith wherein the Prophet Muhammad had observed a man performing ritual prayer in an ostensibly hasty and therefore deficient manner, and tactfully advised him to "Pray again, for you have not prayed," reminding him of the higher objective in upholding the prayer's spiritual dimension.

There are, in fact, several instances within early Islamic tradition demonstrating that the concept of *maqāṣid* was operable in minds and actions. One of these was during the caliphate of ʿUmar, when Muslims were confronted with unprecedented developments as a result of encountering neighboring civilizations. It was ʿUmar's wisdom and keen perception that propelled him to examine matters within the framework of *maqāṣid al-Sharīʿah*, as was the case in his decision—after consulting the other Companions—to not apportion captured land in Iraq. Or as in the case of imposing zakat on horses after they were no longer used exclusively for jihad.[1]

Another example of *maqāṣid* application in early Islamic tradition was when the Muslim community hastened to compile the Qurʾan out of necessity to preserve the religion after those who had memorized it had dispersed from Madinah and many of them had died. Yet, another example was in the development of the discipline of hadith; a development essential to ensure the soundness of the hadith, especially after the fact that Muslim generations following the life of the Prophet Muhammad were no longer able to hear directly from him. Similarly, in response to changes in Muslims' circumstances and the expansion of Muslim territory, the fiqh schools developed, followed by the emergence of the discipline of *uṣūl al-fiqh* (principles of Islamic jurisprudence), the latter of which offered jurists a framework and guidelines for the derivation of fiqh rulings.

The *maqāṣid al-Sharīʿah* were therefore a main driving force in approaching issues and circumstances confronting Muslims since early Islamic tradition, and the notion of *maqāṣid* can be found rooted in the Islamic primary sources. Muslim jurists undoubtedly paid attention to consequences, and the main pillar of the principles of *uṣūl al-fiqh* was based on the *maqāṣid* at a very early stage. The branch of knowledge encapsulating *maqāṣid* itself came about at the right time, having emerged within a framework of intellectual and practical development, and shaped in a manner befitting to the needs of that time.

1.1   Three Pivotal Periods in the Development of *Maqāṣid*

Literature on the subject of *maqāṣid al-Sharīʿah* points to five prominent scholars in this field: Abū al-Maʿālī al-Juwaynī (d. 478/1085), Abū Ḥāmid al-Ghazālī (d. 505/1111), al-ʿIzz Ibn ʿAbd al-Salām (d. 660/1262), Shihāb al-Dīn al-Qarāfī (d. 684/1285), and Abū Isḥāq Ibrāhīm al-Shāṭibī (d. 790/1388)—all of whom played a significant role in establishing a framework for the study of *maqāṣid*. Three pivotal periods in the development of *maqāṣid* can be identified. The first of these was shaped by al-Juwaynī and his student al-Ghazālī. The contribution of al-Juwaynī was set out in his book *al-Burhān fī Uṣūl al-Fiqh*, wherein he proposed five levels of aims: necessities (*ḍarūriyyāt*), general needs (*ḥājah ʿāmah*), complementary matters (*mukaramāt*), preferable matters (*mandūbāt*), and matters that cannot be subjected to reasoning (*mā lā yumkin irjāʿahu ila al-ʿaql*). This was followed by his work *Ghiyāth al-Umam fī Iltiyāth al-Ẓulam*, in which he discussed political matters. Al-Juwaynī was followed by al-Ghazālī, who introduced the notion of the "preservation" of necessities and collocated the necessities of which al-Juwaynī had spoken, namely: religion (*dīn*), life (*nafs*), intellect (*ʿaql*), lineage (*nasl*), and property (*māl*).

The second pivotal period in the development of *maqāṣid* corresponds to the works of al-ʿIzz ibn ʿAbd al-Salām and his student al-Qarāfī. Al-ʿIzz further developed *maqāṣid* thought in two of his treatises, *Maqāṣid al-Ṣalāh* and *Maqāṣid al-Ṣawm*, and in his book *Qawāʿid al-Aḥkām fī Maṣāliḥ al-Anām*, in which he discussed in detail the intricate relationship between benefit and harm. In characterizing al-ʿIzz's contributions, Ahmad al-Raysuni comments:

Whatever the case, since the time of ʿIzz al-Dīn up until now, all discussion regarding benefit and harm, including their definitions, types, classification and order, and how to determine which outweighs the other, and everything else that has been contributed to this subject matter, is owed to him. There may have been additional minor contributions, but hardly any discussion after him goes beyond the framework that was set out by him and his student al-Qarāfī.[2]

We then have al-Qarāfī, in his book *al-Furūʿ*, who continued the work begun by his teacher on *maqāṣid*. Among his contributions to the field was the differentiation between the various actions of the Messenger on the basis of whether they were done in the capacity of a Messenger (conveying the revelation), a judge, or a leader. Consequentially, rulings derived from the Prophet's actions, as well as the principle of *sadd al-dharāʾiʿ* (blocking the means that may lead to harm) are informed by this differentiation.

Al-Qarāfī affirms in his book *al-Iḥkām* that the *maqāṣid* approach is widely known and accepted, without there being any scholarly difference concerning it.[3] The reason for this is because scholars deemed the notion of taking a ruling derived from a previous context and applying it to a different context (thus ignoring the *maqāṣid* and therefore the rationale for that ruling) to be detrimental. It is contrary to scholarly consensus and reflects ignorance of Islamic teaching. It should be understood that aspects of the Sharīʿah are contextually informed and, therefore, that rulings may change depending on context. This, however, is not a promotion of lax alternative methodological approaches to deriving law for those not qualified to engage in ijtihad. Rather, being qualified to engage in ijtihad is, in fact, a condition for applying the *maqāṣid* approach; an approach that serves to guide the ijtihad process and that itself was arrived at through the mechanisms of ijtihad and supported by the consensus of scholars.

The third pivotal period in the development of *maqāṣid al-Shariʿah* coincides with al-Shāṭibī and his work *al-Muwāfaqāt*, whereby an entire comprehensive methodology was crystallized. His method was distinguished by the fact that he combined *uṣūl al-fiqh* with *maqāṣid al-Shariʿah*. Al-Shāṭibī states: "Paying attention to the *maqāṣid* was known in the past, and people of reason based their decisions on that, thus attaining what was in their best interests. They looked at these *maqāṣid* and acted within that framework consistently, whether they were people of wisdom and philosophy or otherwise."[4] He further states:

> The teachings that came in Makkah, which formed the initial teachings of Islam, were mostly general rulings and were not specific. They were in accordance with what wise people regarded as good and in accordance with the dictates of ethics and morals of adhering to everything that is customarily regarded as good manners and avoiding everything that is customarily regarded as bad manners, apart from the issues where reason has nothing to do with determining the rulings, such as the rulings on prayers and the like.[5]

1.2 The Historical Context behind the Development of *Maqāṣid* Thought

It is worthwhile here to briefly reflect on the situation of the caliphate and political stability at the time when these scholars were young and in the earlier stages of their lives, as historical events may have an indelible impact on the memory and on the formation of one's emotions and thoughts. Iraq, Syria, Egypt and the Maghreb were under the control of the Fatimids, and al-Juwaynī's adult years came after the emergence of the Qaramitah (Qarmatians, Carmathians) in the Arabian Peninsula (277-470 AH). As for Persia and Khorasan, they were under the rule of the Buyids (Buwayhids – 334-447 AH) and Ghaznavids (366-579 AH). Al-Juwaynī, from Khorasan, was an Ashʿarī who was forced to flee to the Hijaz because of Buyid enmity towards him due to this affiliation. He would move to Makkah, where he earned the title *Imām al-Ḥaramayn* (Imam of the Two Sanctuaries). Al-Ghazālī emerged at the time of Yūsuf ibn Tāshfīn, and we know that al-Ghazālī thought of visiting him after the fall of Toledo and after the Battle of al-Zallaqah (Sagrajas, 476 AH). The contribution of al-ʿIzz, a Damascene who lived most of his life in Egypt, would come approximately one and a half century after the contributions of al-Juwaynī and al-Ghazālī.

In Egypt, al-Qarāfī came some forty-odd years after al-ʿIzz (so his life experience was somewhat similar), at the end of the Ayyubid era, when they had entered a state of decline after their dazzling achievements at Ayn Jalut and the defeat of the Mongols. Ibn al-Qayyim lived in Damascus after al-Qarāfī, and al-Shāṭibī the Andalusian came after Ibn al-Qayyim. We find that this succession of scholars focused on renewing the methodology of actualizing Shariʿah in life in an unprecedented manner. And the geographic stretch of those scholars cannot be missed, signifying that shedding of *taqlīd* and cultural decadence was a common concern among the learned. In the wake of the Crusader and Mongol invasions and the ensuing chaos, these scholars focused their efforts on highlighting the fundamentals of Islam and connecting all minor issues to those fundamentals, with the aim of creating an intellectual anchor for Muslims in the way in which they dealt with real-life events.

As for the era of Ibn Taymiyyah, it was dominated by political and social strife, which impacted the contributions he and his student Ibn al-Qayyim would make to the Hanbali School. And though these contributions reflected *maqāṣid* thought, they were not categorically identified under the field of *maqāṣid*. Nonetheless, the fatwas of Ibn Taymiyyah are distinguished by the fact that they thoroughly gave attention to the context of each case and bore in mind the probable outcomes and consequences of applying the rulings. With respect to Ibn al-Qayyim, his understanding of *maqāṣid al-Sharīʿah* compelled him to reject *fiqhī* literalism and rigidity. This is attested to in his famous statement in *Iʿlām al-Muwaqqiʿīn*:

The Shariʿah is based and founded on wisdom and on what is in people's best interests in this world and the hereafter. It is all justice, all compassion, all benefit and all wisdom. Therefore, any issue that drifts away from justice towards injustice, from compassion towards its opposite, from benefit to mischief, and from wisdom to foolishness, cannot be part of the Shariʿah, even if it is inserted into the Shariʿah by way of misunderstanding. The Shariʿah is God's justice among His servants, His mercy towards His creation, His shadow upon His earth, and His wisdom that points to Him and to the truthfulness of His Messenger (ṢAAS).[6]

Regarding al-Shāṭibī's *maqāṣid* theory, we may note three particular features to his methodology. First, certain statements of his pertaining to the role of reason in religion appear conflicting. Second, he is adamant in linking *maqāṣid* theory to *uṣūl al-fiqh* as a way of legitimizing the former's place within the Shariʿah and dispelling any notion of it being a deleterious innovation. Lastly, he affirms the practical value of the *maqāṣid* and their role in renovation for an era that fell below the ideal lofty standard dictated by religion.

1.3 The Role of Reason and its Place in al-Shāṭibī's Thought

Perhaps nothing better illustrates the delicate matter of reason in al-Shāṭibī's thought than does the introduction to his work. The introductions of books have special significance as they portray what the author wishes to contribute and his awareness of the possibility of erring. Writing in a time when conventional thinking was in place, we see that al-Shāṭibī's introduction carefully crafted his words, emphasizing that he is not introducing a deviant innovation in religion. Indeed, his time was marked by the controversy over the revelation-reason duality, along with the differentiation between worthy and unworthy knowledge.[7]

With respect to the relationship between revelation and reason, al-Shāṭibī appears to come close to adopting the notion of duality, though he limits the role of reason with respect to revelation. He says, "Rational evidence, if it is to be used in this field of knowledge [*uṣūl*], is only to be used on the basis of textual evidence, or as a help to understand what this textual evidence indicates, or in support of what this textual evidence points to, and the like. It cannot be used independently in determination, because this is a matter of Shariʿah and reason is not a *Shāriʿ*."[8] However, elsewhere, he affirms, "The *Shāriʿ* went to great lengths in explaining the reasons and wisdom behind the prescription of rules and regulations that are connected to customs and traditions."[9] Even though the context of the first quote was *uṣūl* and the context of the second was *'ādiyyāt* (general life affairs), the role of reason is operative in both.

The way in which reason is deployed to understand a scriptural text is informed by the extent to which the text is universally applicable as well as the degree it is connected to the prevailing circumstances at the moment of revelation. In this regard, al-Shāṭibī and his followers adopted an essential and decisive precept in dealing with a text, which is that what matters is the general meaning of the text and not simply the direct meaning. And restricting oneself to merely looking at the prevailing circumstances pertaining to the text confines the text to a historical setting and time. The message of Islam cannot be the final message unless the general meaning of the text is not bound by space and time. Therefore, we suggested the term *tazāmun* (concurrence) as an alternative to the term *asbāb al-nuzūl* (reasons for revelation) in referring to the relationship between the text and the past circumstance.[10]

Although al-Shāṭibī affirmed the role of reason, when he elaborates on its details he delves into unnecessary precautions, such as when he says, "When scripture and rational thinking are in harmony with regard to some issues of Sharī'ah, that is all well and good, provided that precedence is given to scripture and it is followed by reason, and that reason is subordinate to the text. Therefore, the framework of rational thinking when examining an issue is to be allowed only as much as scripture allows (and it is not be given free rein)."[11] If that which is permissible may become an act of worship, depending on one's intention (as al-Shāṭibī asserts), and everything is permissible in principle, then what need is there to introduce this artificial contrast between scripture and reason?

The desire to put an end to *fiqhī* disputes and to establish an understanding of the holistic aims of Sharī'ah may explain why al-Shāṭibī adopted this approach, which is prevalent in *al-Muwāfaqāt*. His approach, moreover, is based on substantiated evidence derived on the basis of thorough research on the one hand, and on basic principles of logic on the other. Furthermore, it is achieved by identifying evidence that will lead to definitive conclusions concerning the aims of Sharī'ah and their holistic principles. By way of induction (*istiqrā'*; which involves a holistic reading of the primary sources and the extrapolation of particular references from within them), a number of consistent principles and aims are arrived at and certainty may be achieved. Thus, through the process of induction, one can ascertain specific or general *maqāṣid*.

1.4 The Intellectual Context behind al-Shāṭibī's Work

We should consider al-Shāṭibī's work from the vantage of the intellectual setting of his time, a period marked by the challenge of unchecked reason of philosophers. The discipline of *uṣūl al-fiqh* provided a platform for the reconciliation of reason and revelation, to the extent of forming a symbiotic relationship between them. It is as such that he began to highlight the distinctions between his work and what was prevalent at his time when he coined phrases and terminology that reflected opposites or dualities, such as: giving a specific meaning to a text that is general in meaning (*takhṣīṣ al-ʿumūm*); restricting the meaning of a text that is broad in meaning (*taqīd al-muṭlaq*); giving precedence (*taqdīm*); making secondary (*taʾkhīr*); fundamental issues (*uṣūl*); minor issues (*furūʿ*); fundamental and holistic (*aṣlī kulī*); fundamental but specific (*aṣl muʿayyan*); fundamental and wider in application (*aṣl aʿam*); minor and more specific in application (*faraʿ akhaṣ*); and "speculative" (*ẓannī*); and "definitive" (*qaṭʿī*).[12]

With regard to terminology dealing with *sharʿī* evidence, he coined phrases and terminology such as: "scholarly consensus constitutes proof" (*al-ijmāʿ ḥujjah*); "a report narrated by one or a few narrators at each stage of the chain of transmission" (*khabr wāḥid*); "analogy constitutes proof" (*al-qiyās ḥujjah*); "reaching a conclusion that is not based on a text, analogy, or scholarly consensus because there is no text and no precedents" (*istidlāl mursal*); and "juristic preference" (*istiḥsān*).

He also coined phrases referring to the levels and strength of evidence, such as: "indication that a thing is definitive" (*ifādat al-qaṭʿi*); "within the context of speaking in general terms" (*majra al-ʿumūm*); "opposing on the basis of rational thinking" (*al-muʿāriḍ al-ʿaqlī*); "the foundations of fundamentals" (*qawāʿid al-uṣūl*); "the five indispensables" (*al-ḍarūriyyāt al-khams*); "the foundations of Shariʿah" (*qawāʿid al-Sharīʿah*); "lack of abrogating text" (*ʿadam al-nāsikh*); "induction" (*istiqrāʾ*); and "many reports with different wording pointing to the same meaning" (*al-tawātur al-maʿnawī*). As a result of abiding to these dualities, the *maqāṣid* approach of al-Shāṭibī remained restricted to the dictates of *uṣūl al-fiqh*, which bestows accuracy on *fiqhī* matters but prevents *maqāṣid* from becoming a completely independent branch of knowledge with its own tools and terminology.

1.5 The Ultimate Aim of Shariʿah

Al-Shāṭibī asserted that the ultimate aim of Shariʿah is to rectify the condition of the Muslims. He says in *al-Muwāfaqāt*, "Discussing any issue that has no practical application is discussing something for which there is no evidence that it is to be approved. What I mean by practical application is the deeds of the heart [beliefs and emotions] and physical deeds, as this is something that is required by Islamic teaching."[13] Al-Shāṭibī rejects pure theoretical philosophy, but not philosophy that has some practical, real benefits. He states, "The spirit of knowledge is action; otherwise knowledge on its own is useless and of no benefit."[14] And he affirms that knowledge should be the standard for measuring the validity or otherwise of deeds and customs, stating,

> What is meant by the knowledge that is required is obligatory knowledge, so that deeds and actions may be done in accordance with it and without drifting away from it, whether those deeds have to do with the heart (beliefs and emotions), the tongue (speech), or physical actions. If these deeds are done in accordance with that knowledge, without drifting from it, then this is the essence of knowledge. Otherwise, it cannot be knowledge because of the deeds failing to comply with it, for that is a kind of knowledge turning into ignorance.[15]

Ibrahim Zain affirms the importance of the connection between knowledge and action in al-Shāṭibī's thought, stating:

> The conclusion reached by al-Shāṭibī's analysis of the concept of knowledge and action, when discussing the fundamentals of Shariʿah, played a great role in resolving the intellectual issues associated with *istiqrāʾ* (induction). It was an analysis which elucidated: the meaning of knowledge and action, various levels and types of knowledge, the different levels of scholars in their discussion of knowledge and action, the meaning of knowledge and how to translate it into action, ways of examining and confirming academic principles, and the role of actions in that approach.[16]

Zain goes on to say, "Undoubtedly, the issues of *istiqrā'*, definitiveness, certainty, consistency and holism, all come under the heading of what al-Shāṭibī did of re-examining the connection between knowledge and action."[17]

What we have noted above was a brief survey of worthy efforts in the journey of *maqāṣid*, emphasizing that it was an *ummatic* project and not simply an accidental and individual ijtihad. And we cannot miss that such *maqāṣidī* work was multi-*madhhab*, as al-Juwāynī, al-Ghazālī, and al-'Izz were Shāfi'īs, al-Qarāfī and al-Shāṭibī were Mālikīs, and Ibn al-Qayyim was a Ḥanbalī. Prior to that the Ḥanafī *madhhab* frequently used *istiḥsān*, and the Mālikī *madhhab* emphasized *maṣlaḥah* (welfare, well-being, benefits, and interests including public interests).

We move now from premodern eras to that after the rise of European modernity. We encounter noted ulama (scholars of Shari'ah) feeling the urgency to revive the *maqāṣid* approach in order to address the needs of the Ummah in a time of change. Such contemporary work is not separate from the general effort to face the challenges globally pressed by secular modernity. And this is the subject of the following chapter.

2

The *Maqāṣid al-Sharīʿah* and Modernity

The modern age has given rise to many challenges that may be summed up on two levels: changes at the practical level, in the way people live their lives, and changes at the intellectual level, in concepts and ideas. These practical and intellectual challenges have undoubtedly infringed upon the system of traditional societies; a system in which family and religion play a major role. It is as such that in reviewing literature pertaining to modern *maqāṣid* thinkers in this section, we do so within the purview of how these thinkers approach the impact these practical and intellectual challenges of modernity have on an Islamic worldview for life. More concretely, we focus on the literature of three important modern-day *maqāṣid* thinkers who have treated the challenges of modernity in their *maqāṣid* thought: Shah Walīullah al-Dehlawī (d. 1176 / 1762), as well as Ibn ʿAshur (d. 1973) and ʿAllal al-Fasi (d. 1974) in the mid-twentieth century.

2.1 An Early Contribution

In the introduction to his book *Ḥujjat Allah al-Bālighah*, Shah Walīullah al-Dehlawī says, "…the most essential branch of Islamic knowledge, as far as I am concerned, and the highest in status and greatest in value, is knowledge of the wisdom behind and implications of rulings and certain actions."[1] Al-Dehlawī then devotes a chapter to the Qur'anic notion of *Sunnat Allah* (the general laws of material and socio-historical existence) that is referred to in the verse, "[This is] the established way of Allah with those who passed on before; and you will not find in the way of Allah any change" (Qur'an 33:62). For al-Dehlawī, *Sunnat Allah* refers to "forces that are embedded in this universe."[2] Put differently, *Sunnat Allah* are the fundamental laws related to creation and regulations related to moral life, which are not subject to alteration, as such that they prevailed over previous generations and will continue to do so over the present and future generations. Al-Dehlawī's approach led him to steer clear of duality and opposites in trying to understand the reason and wisdom in the creation and in the commands of religion, and instead focus on understanding harmony between reason and revelation. This in turn led him to the notion of *irtifāqāt*, a term he coined that conveys the notion of "human universals."[3] Al-Dehlawī was very keen to avoid modern, materialistic interpretations of causality, and held that humans ascertain beneficial universals, noting that "Allah (SWT) would not be pleased neglecting the latter two, and none of the prophets ever enjoined neglecting them."[4]

Al-Dehlawī's concept of human universals is aimed at understanding the relationship between the nature of humankind and the universe. It is in this regard that the wisdom of the Shariʿah becomes apparent and an ultimate proof that it is from God, for it is suited to the nature of people. For al-Dehlawī, human universals can be classified according to two types of lived experience. One type pertains to those in rural or small communities, such as desert dwellers. A second type pertains to those in urban or heavily populated regions, wherein there is a great deal of interaction among people and needs to be met, and, as an outgrowth, the development of civilized manners and wisdom. In such urban regions, important guidelines are worked out to organize and regulate all needs and interactions to the extent that they become adopted and officially established by society. [5]

Al-Dehlawī goes on to discuss a third type of human universal, which pertains to "establishing a ruler to judge between people on the basis of justice, deterring the disobedient among them, standing up to transgressors, collecting taxes from them, and spending taxes as they should be spent."[6] The details of this third human universal focus on regulating life with regard to customs, traditions, and proper personal conduct that a person would absorb by growing up in that society, and on social issues that are widely accepted among city dwellers. In many ways, al-Dehlawī's discourse resembles Ibn Khaldūn's when discussing *siyāsat al-madīnah*, "the governance of urban society." He says, "As cities contain large numbers of people, it is not possible for them to all agree on adhering to the path of what is fair and just, or keeping one another in check, unless there is someone who is in a position of authority, without which there would be a great deal of fighting. Order, therefore, cannot be maintained in the city except through a man whom the majority of decision-makers all agree to obey, and who should have helpers and have power."[7] He further tells us that,

> All of the above is supported by reason. And there is consensus among all nations of humanity, regardless of the distances between their lands and the differences in their religions, that the intended objective behind appointing a king could not be achieved except through him. But if he shows some shortcomings or negligence, they will see that this is contrary to what is proper and will resent it. And even if they keep quiet about it, they will be keeping quiet whilst feeling rage in their hearts.[8]

He goes on to tell us (referring to his chapter entitled "Mankind's Consensus on Human Universals") that "It should be understood that human universals exist in every single city and in every population without exception, and no nation of moderate temperament and sublime character is devoid of that, from the time of Adam until the Day of Resurrection."[9]

In his chapter "*Adāb al-Maʿāsh*," al-Dehlawī provides several examples of the application of this third human universal in real life. Regarding this, he says:

> Generally speaking, there are accepted social guidelines in every field and among people of any land, no matter how far apart they are; although after that, people may have different approaches, depending on the field in question. As such, physicians base these guidelines on what is regarded as good in terms of medicine; astronomers base them on the features of the stars; religious leaders base them on kindness as detailed in their scriptures. Each community has its own mores and manners by which they are distinguished, according to differences in temperament, traditions, and the like.[10]

He then discusses issues having to do with household management, ending the chapter in question with the words, "You will never find any community but that they believe in these guidelines with regard to different fields and strive to implement them despite their differences in religion and the distances between their lands. And God knows best."[11]

Al-Dehlawī then discusses issues having to do with political administration and the duties and responsibilities of rulers and people, and issues having to do with organization of economic life, taxes, and earning a living;[12] all of which, he asserts, require the role of reason. He tells us, however, that "People inevitably need capable, well-qualified scholars who do not limit knowledge to what may be gained through reason alone, but also through intuition."[13] It is as such that al-Dehlawī emphasizes there being various approaches in religion, despite the shared concerns of religion. He says, "It should be understood that the reasons why an approach may develop and take a particular shape are many, but they may be summarized under two categories: that which concerns normal occurrences in daily life and that which concerns unexpected matters that arise."[14]

In the context of discussing modesty between the two sexes, al-Dehlawī attempts to establish the attention of *fiqhī* regulations to people's cultural attitudes, the desirability to each other, status, and practicality. He asserts that such considerations are taken into account in Shariʿah:

All of these factors are taken into consideration among *maḥrams* [persons among which sexual relationship is prohibited]. That is because prohibited sexual relations among the very close kin is thought of as associated with low desirability [thus, rules regarding their interrelationships were relaxed]. And discouragement is one reason in blocking yearning. Lengthy companionship results in the decease [of desire] and in inattention, in addition to that covering among close kin is troublesome. Therefore, the sunnah required covering among *maḥrams* that is less stringent than covering among other non-*maḥram* relationships.[15]

Al-Dehlawī's keen insight into the nature of mankind, largely informed by the natural sciences of his time, is illustrated elsewhere in his work:

With all that humankind possesses of God-given faculties—mobility, receptivity to inspiration, the ability to understand natural sciences, to reason, and to develop different branches of knowledge—human beings are able to cultivate, plant, engage in trade, and interact with others. And God has allowed there to be different roles among people—roles that are either by nature or attained by circumstance. He has allowed some to be leaders and others followers; some to attain wisdom, whether in a spiritual or worldly sense, while others who merely follow in these areas. We find all this reflected in both rural and urban communities.[16]

Al-Dehlawī's remarks here clearly reflect a *maqāṣidic* approach, an approach that adopts the ideas of Ibn Khaldūn and the notion that societies are subject to laws. His approach, in fact, is deeply influenced by *maqāṣid* thought, for he states that the field of *maqāṣid* dictates specifying what is obligatory, what is essential, and what comes under the heading of manners and etiquette. Moreover, he speaks of two branches of knowledge that are distinctly different in their nature and what they deal with: knowledge of benefit (*maṣāliḥ*) and harm (*mafāsid*), and knowledge of legislation, criminal codes, and the laws of inheritance. He affirms that the Prophet Muhammad used to engage in ijtihad, and that his ijtihad was based on examining benefit and harm, and that Allah protected him from developing a view that was wrong.[17]

2.2 Ibn ʿAshur's Methodological Overhaul

Ibn ʿAshur (d. 1973) benefitted from and arguably surpassed al-Shāṭibī's contribution to *maqāṣid* theory in a new era that faced unfamiliar challenges. His contribution is regarded as the first in this field since the demise of the caliphate and ever since Muslims were confronted with epistemological uncertainties, wherein they developed a desire to choose selectively from their Islamic heritage in light of modernity and its secularism. In what follows, we discuss the methodological reform achieved and promoted by Ibn ʿAshur; a reform that was unprecedented for the modern era and which led to the further development and expansion of *maqāṣid* theory. In addition to treating Ibn ʿAshur's contributions, we will visit the work of ʿAllal al-Fasi (d. 1974), a contemporary of Ibn Ibn ʿAshur who also contributed to the development of *maqāṣid* theory.

Though Ibn ʿAshur praises pre-modern figures such as al-ʿIzz and al-Qarāfī for their contributions to the field of *maqāṣid*, it was al-Shāṭibī's contributions that inevitably became the focus for him in approaching the field, treating al-Shāṭibī's thought in a way that would inform his own thinking but while not allowing it to impinge on his effort to further develop the field. And whereas al-Shāṭibī's approach treated both universal and particular *maṣāliḥ* (well-being and Shariʿah-recognized benefits) and the relationship between them, Ibn ʿAshur's approach to *maqāṣid* is more abstract. For Ibn ʿAshur, the general aims of *tashrīʿ* (Islamic guidance to people's life) consist of the deeper meanings (*maʿānī*) and inner aspects of wisdom (*ḥikam*) considered by the *Shāriʿ* in all or most of the areas and circumstances of *tashrīʿ*. They are not confined to a particular type of Shariʿah commands. They include the general characteristics of Shariʿah, its general purpose, and whatever notions contemplated by *tashrīʿ*. They also include certain meanings and notions that are present in many though not all of the Shariʿah commands.[18]

In similar fashion to Ibn ʿAshur's characterization of the *maqāṣid* and their relation to Shariʿah, al-Fasi says, "Shariʿah is but rulings based on *maqāṣid* and *maqāṣid* that give rise to rulings."[19] He adds, "The aims of Shariʿah form the eternal reference point for Islamic jurisprudence, whether it has to do with working out rules and regulations or with judicial matters. It is not an alien element; rather it is at the heart of Shariʿah."[20] However, it should be noted that al-Fasi's ideas remained general descriptions of how Shariʿah should be approached, and he did not develop a full theory of *maqāṣid*. Nevertheless, the contribution of al-Fasi bolstered such an approach of which Ibn ʿAshur became the master. In characterizing the unprecedent contributions Ibn ʿAshur made in Islamic thought, Ahmad al-Raysuni says, "The foremost contribution that distinguished Ibn ʿAshur was his contrasting for the first time between *uṣūl al-fiqh* and *maqāṣid al-Sharīʿah*. His innovative contribution included both developing a framework and delineating the central elements for *maqāṣid* theory."[21]

Ibn ʿAshur's theory on *maqāṣid* contrasts with al-Shāṭibī's theory in that the former is not based on distinguishing between the aims of the *Shāriʿ* and the objectives of the *mukallaf* (competent and responsible person in the sight of Allah) as in the case of the latter. Rather, Ibn ʿAshur's theory is based on distinguishing between the general and particular aims of the Shariʿah.[22] The principal aspect of his theory concerns the *maṣāliḥ* (welfare, benefits, and public interests) in human transactions and conduct. This is in contrast to the approach of early scholars whose primary focus is on interests in the realm of individual conduct, interests that relate to a person's life, and to following the exemplary way of Shariʿah.

A. Juxtaposing Fiqh and *Uṣūl al-Fiqh*

Ibn ʿAshur's innovative theory departs from the traditional approach established in *uṣūl al-fiqh*. The contribution of al-Shāṭibī was so weighty and reconciled generational contributions to the approach of *maqāṣid*. Yet, the strength of al-Shāṭibī's formulation with its tight *uṣūlī* scaffold constituted its limited-ness—it is too crystalized of an approach incapable of accounting for new class of circumstances. The moment was ready for a paradigm-shifting work, and it was born through Ibn ʿAshur's contribution.

Ibrahim Zain tells us, "Ibn ʿAshur understood the methodological problems of examining texts according to the inductive method of the rational sciences. He was not content with al-Shāṭibī's approach of deducing certainty through induction. Nor did he agree with al-Shāṭibī's position that *uṣūl al-fiqh* and its outcomes were definitive and not subject to further inquiry."[23] Zain holds that Ibn ʿAshur was determined to improve upon the outdated methodologies associated with previous Islamic sciences; methodologies that he believed were informed by particular circumstances surrounding the development of these sciences at their time. He further explains that,

> Ibn ʿAshur distinguished between *uṣūl al-fiqh* and *maqāṣid al-Sharīʿah* in that the former was mainly concerned with deriving rulings from the primary sources on the basis of technical linguistic analysis, while the latter was concerned with understanding the wisdoms or objectives behind these rulings. As *uṣūl al-fiqh* was not able to render such wis-doms or objectives, it became necessary to fulfill this void through the development of a new discipline, which inevitably became the science of *maqāṣid*.[24]

By advancing the science of *maqāṣid*, Ibn ʿAshur thus sought to rise above historical differences and disputes within and between the juristic schools in the field of *uṣūl al-fiqh*. This new discipline of *maqāṣid* essentially had the makeup to transcend partisan identity.

Offering perspective on the feat that Ibn 'Ashur achieved in his contribution to the development of the approach of *maqāṣid* against the backdrop of established tradition, Zain states:

> Some may hold that going beyond established tradition and reconstructing it in a new framework, thus going beyond the juristic school (*madhhabī*) paradigm, as Ibn 'Ashur had done, would be inconceivable. And perhaps it was easier for Ibn 'Ashur to establish the *maqāṣid* discipline directly upon the foundation of the Qur'an and Sunnah, transcending that *madhhabī* paradigm along with the drawbacks associated with *uṣūl al-fiqh* in its development approximately two centuries after the establishment of the science of *fiqh*.[25]

We should add, however, that Ibn 'Ashur well-recognized the value that traditional works in *uṣūl al-fiqh* brought to the development of this science. Yet, he undoubtedly recognized the paramount need to renovate the science. It is as such that he says:

> Likewise, if we want to lay down definitive and categorical principles for the understanding of the Shari'ah, we need to return to the traditionally accepted propositions of *uṣūl al-fiqh* and reformulate them. We should critically evaluate them, rid them of the alien elements that crept into them, and supplement them with the results of thorough comprehension and careful thought. Then, we need to reformulate the whole and classify it as an independent discipline called "science of the higher aims of the Shari'ah" (*'ilm Maqāṣid al-Sharī'ah*).[26]

B. Real Ideas and Universal Conventional Ideas

One of the distinctive contributions of Ibn 'Ashur is his differentiation between *ma'ānī ḥaqīqiyyah* (real ideas) and *ma'ānī 'urfiyyah 'āmmah* (universal conventional ideas); that is, there are issues that are absolute in nature and issues that are related to custom and convention. Concerning the latter, he says, "The universal conventional ideas consist of time-tested notions that are familiar to the general public and acceptable to them, owing to their conformity with the public good."[27] His approach is similar to that of Ibn Khaldūn's, which is based on the recognition of human society and on the accumulation of knowledge, and that the scholars' understanding or focus should not be limited to knowledge of texts only. He affirms this idea indirectly with his four conditions for something to be regarded as an aim of Shariʿah, namely: certainty (*thubūt*), evidence (*ẓuhūr*), consistency (*inḍibāṭ*), and regularity (*iṭṭirād*).[28]

C. The Collective Dimension and Expanding the Concept of *Maqāṣid*

Ibn ʿAshur's innovative *maqāṣid* theory sought to disentangle *uṣūl al-fiqh* from some of its tethered methods, methods which had negatively impacted its development. It is in light of this that he tells us, "From an inductive examination (*istiqrāʾ*) of numerous indicants in the Qurʾan and the authentic Prophetic traditions, we can with certainty draw the compelling conclusion that the rules of the Islamic Shariʿah are based on inner reasons (*ḥikam*) and causes (*asbāb*) that devolve upon the universal goodness and benefit of both society and individuals."[29] In a similar fashion, al-Fasi says, "The main aim of the Islamic Shariʿah is to populate and develop the earth and to safeguard a system of coexistence therein, so that life on earth may continue to be sound by means of the righteousness of the people dwelling on it, by means of them doing what they are enjoined to do of upholding justice, observing righteousness and being sound in mind and deed, and to continue making good use of the earth and to bring forth the benefits of the land to serve the interests of all."[30]

Ibn ʿAshur divides *maṣāliḥ* (welfare, benefits, and interests including public interests) into those that are universal (*kulliyyah*) and those that are particular (*juzʾiyyah*). He explains, "In juristic terminology, *maṣlaḥah kulliyyah* means that which equally concerns the whole community, very large numbers of its individuals or one whole country. By *maṣlaḥah juzʾiyyah* is meant anything other than that."[31] Regarding universal and particular *maṣāliḥ*, al-Fasi puts forward the principle that a harm which is narrow in scope is allowed for the purpose of warding off a harm broad in scope. In other words, the *maṣāliḥ* of society or community are to be given precedence over the *maṣāliḥ* of the individual, and the individual should sacrifice his own interests for the sake of the interests of the society or community.

Though the methods of *uṣūl al-fiqh*, with their heavy reliance on linguistic and comparative analytical tools, did well to ascertain the universal and particular in the primary source texts, these methods do not suffice in ascertaining the universal and particular in people's lives. And it appears to be the case that even today's Muslim scholars are rather not clear about the distinction between methods which apply to understanding the primary source texts and those which apply to understanding practical real-world matters. Ibn ʿAshur was certainly cognizant of the tenuous relationship between *uṣūl al-fiqh* and ascertaining the *maqāṣid al-sharīʿah*. With regard to the universality of the Shariʿah's aims and their benefit, he says:

> Therefore, it follows from this that the meaning of the suitability of the Islamic Shariʿah for every time and place must be understood in a different manner as follows. Its commands and injunctions (*aḥkām*) consist of universal principles and meanings comprising wisdom and benefits (*maṣāliḥ*), which can be projected into various rulings that are diverse in form but unified in purpose. That is why the fundamental sources of *tasharīʿ* avoided detailing and determination [at the time of Revelation].[32]

Ibn ʿAshur further points out that there has been an over-emphasis on giving a devotional dimension to many rulings that pertain to human dealings and transactions (*muʿāmalāt*), to the point that any reflection on or re-examination of such rulings is regarded as something prohibited. He states:

> In fact, the scholars of fiqh should not have tried to locate devotional commands in the *tasharīʿ* of *muʿāmalāt*. Instead, they should have insured that what was asserted to be devotional rather consists of rules that had subtle and hidden reasons. Many of the rules concerning *muʿāmalāt* that some jurists treated as merely devotional have been the cause of numerous difficulties for Muslims in their dealings.[33]

Ibn ʿAshur also tried to emphasize the collective dimension of Islamic rulings stating, "Accordingly, we should realize that the righteousness intended and praised by the *Shāriʿ* is not confined to righteousness of belief and acts of ritual worship, as some people might wrongly believe. Rather, what is meant by righteousness is setting things to rights in people's worldly condition and social affairs."[34]

Ibn ʿAshur criticizes those jurists who, at times of necessity, only offer lenient dispensations to individual matters and not to collective matters. He points out that just as it is necessary at times to offer such dispensations to individuals, necessity at times also calls for offering lenient dispensations to the public as a whole for the sake of collective interest (*maṣlaḥah ʿāmmah*).[35] Investing in this notion of public interest can lead to new considerations for the field of *maqāṣid* that might prove to be indispensable in dealing with the constantly-changing realities of people's lives. Ignoring such considerations might otherwise lead to harmful consequences. The distinct characteristic of Islamic Shariʿah is its concern not only for the interests of the individual but also for society as a whole. When serving the interests of a few procures harm for the greater society, then priority must be given to the best interests of society. This is to preserve the balance in society; the balance between individual and public interests, between means and ends, and between particular and universal principles.

D. Understanding and Researching *Maqāṣid* should be a Continuous Pursuit

Ibn ʿAshur maintains that understanding and researching *maqāṣid* should be ongoing. This is because *some maqāṣid* may be not apparent in certain eras but become so later on. He tells us:

> In sum, we can say that we are certain that all the Shariʿah commands embody the *Shāriʿ's* purposes, which consist of wisdom, *maṣāliḥ*, and benefits. It is, therefore, the duty of the scholars of the Shariʿah to search for the reasons and objectives of *tashrīʿ*, both the overt and the covert. Some underlying reasons might be hidden, and the minds of scholars are at variance in detecting them. Now, if some or all the scholars of a given period fail to discover some of these aims, this does not necessarily mean that the scholars who come after them will also fail.[36]

Al-Fasi arrives at a similar position (i.e., that the *maqāṣid* are not only discoverable in certain eras but rather may become apparent in any era) in his discussion of effective cause (*'illah*), saying:

> The effective cause (*'illah*) for a ruling may not be the wisdom or objective behind it. The difference between the two is that the effective cause for the ruling is what appears to be the cause on which the *Shāri'* based the ruling, and the wisdom is the *Shāri''s* intended aim behind this ruling, which is to serve the best interests that God has embodied in this ruling of achieving some benefit or warding off some harm or hardship. Basing the ruling on this effective cause is for the purpose of achieving the intended aim behind the ruling.[37]

Ibn 'Ashur goes on to affirm the importance of reason in understanding the aims of Islam. He says, "The description of Islam as the *fiṭrah* means that it is a cognitive natural disposition, since Islam consists of beliefs (*'aqā'id*) and divine guidance (*tashrī'āt*) that are all rational matters or matters that accord with what is perceived and confirmed by reason."[38] He then discusses the importance of understanding *maṣlaḥah*, telling us: "Undoubtedly, the purpose of the *Shāri'* cannot counter *maṣlaḥah*, although it is not necessary that all kinds of *maṣlaḥah* are meant. Therefore, scholars of *tashrī'* must know well the varieties and manifestations of *maṣāliḥ* in themselves and in relation to the contingencies and circumstances affecting them."[39] Ibn 'Ashur's approach here parallels in many ways Ibn Khaldūn's thought, which is informed by the notion that natural laws govern people and societies. His approach, furthermore, to develop principles and guidelines for the science of *maqāṣid al-Sharī'ah*, allows for checks and balances on certain theoretical concepts such as "blocking the means" (*sadd al-dharā'i'*). In this regard, Ibn 'Ashur states, "If the term *sadd al-dharā'i'* had not been used specifically to designate blocking the means of evil as shown earlier, we would have liked to say (and as correctly stated by al-Qarāfī in his *Tanqīḥ al-Fuṣūl*) just as the Shari'ah has blocked certain means [that could lead to evil], it has also allowed others [that could lead to good]."[40]

2.3 Substantive Contributions

The contributions noted above were methodological contributions, and they opened the door to substantive contributions in several pivotal concepts and dimensions, including the natural disposition of human beings, the family system, and issues related to economics and politics.

A. The Concept of *Fiṭrah* (Natural Disposition)

Among prominent later writers on *maqāṣid al-Sharīʿah* who focused on the concept of *fiṭrah* were al-Dehlawī, al-Fasi, and Ibn ʿAshur. Al-Dehlawī emphasized the important impact that *fiṭrah* has and how it consistently manifests itself in human life. Al-Fasi stated, in his discussion of the modern notion of natural laws, "If there is such a thing as natural law, it can most adequately be manifested in the law of Islam."[41] And Ibn ʿAshur established a comprehensive relationship between *maqāṣid al-Sharīʿah* and *fiṭrah* through several *maqāṣid*, including: generality (*ʿumūm*), equality (*musāwāh*), freedom (*ḥurriyyah*), tolerance *(samāḥah)*; and he held that the Shariʿah was not aimed at causing hardship. Ibn ʿAshur thus states, "When we say that Islam is the religion of *fiṭrah*, it means that humankind's natural disposition will accept and be at ease with the fundamentals of Islam and will be in harmony with its regulations and *tasharīʿ*."[42]

Ibn ʿAshur held that the needs of the *fiṭrah* may be attained through humankind's innate inclinations or through the guidance of divine revelation. As such, it is generally appropriate for mankind to respond to their natural inclinations, and to regard divine revelation as guiding and protecting such natural inclinations, given that they are innate (Ibn ʿAshur has elaborated on this understanding of *fiṭrah* elsewhere). Since this notion of *fiṭrah* aligns with prophetic teachings, it undoubtedly proves wrong the illusion which suggests that deviation is innate in humankind. This holds true regardless of how strongly deviation from *fiṭrah* has been entrenched among some people (even to the extent that they no longer see what they do as bad). God says, "This is the natural disposition God instilled in mankind" (Q, 30:30).

In his book *Naẓariyyat al-Maqāṣid ʿinda al-Imām Ibn ʿĀshūr*, Ismail Hassani discusses the concept of *fiṭrah* and different scholarly views concerning its understanding, explaining that what it means is humankind's potential for good and evil, or the potential to be upright in particular. Ibn ʿAshur based his understanding of *fiṭrah* on the idea that it is "the make-up or system on which God based every creature. So, the *fiṭrah* of humankind is the way in which people are created both outwardly and inwardly, that is, physically and mentally. It is a person's aptitude, potentials, abilities, and practices."[43]

Hassani tells us that Ibn ʿAshur regards this concept of *fiṭrah* as something basic and fundamental, that "forms a strong foundation on which many other Shariʿah aims, whether of a general or specific nature, are based."[44] Accordingly, in his research, Hassani found nine levels of rights of varying degrees of importance, including: an individual's right over their body, senses, and emotions (e.g., thinking, eating, sleeping, seeing, and hearing); rights over offspring, such as the right of a woman over the child that she bears (so long as the child has not attained the ability to grasp their rights or Shariʿah rulings); and rights with regard to anything produced by what one owns (e.g., the offspring of livestock, harvest, and minerals or treasure from the earth).

Ibn ʿAshur's notion of *fiṭrah* allows for the *maqāṣid al-Sharīʿah* to be understood in a manner that is in harmony with the spirit of Shariʿah. Ibn ʿAshur says, "It is plain and simple that Islam is the religion of *fiṭrah*."[45] He then comments on the failure of scholars of *uṣūl al-fiqh* to pay sufficient attention to the concept of *fiṭrah*, attributing it to their inclination towards clear and well-defined facts. Preserving and protecting the *fiṭrah* is undoubtedly important; however, over-generalizing its meaning can make the concept arbitrary and abstruse. Therefore, the view we take in this study is that the *fiṭrah* relates to the self or soul (*nafs*), as broadly understood, because it is of the same nature.[46]

In summarizing Ibn ʿAshur's methodology for ascertaining the *maqāṣid al-Sharīʿah*, Hassani notes that Ibn ʿAshur neglects to discuss al-Shāṭibī's view with regard to cases in which the *Shāriʿ* does not point out an underlying reason for a ruling. Ibn ʿAshur's neglect to do so is not because he was unfamiliar with such cases; rather, it was due to the fact that these rulings pertained to the *maqāṣid* of acts of worship (*ʿibādāt*), which Ibn ʿAshur took a different approach to. However, if we reflect holistically on Ibn ʿAshur's *maqāṣid* theory, we see how his methodology can actually lead to the discovery of new ways to ascertain such *maqāṣid*. Ibn ʿAshur's innovative *maqāṣid* theory would, in fact, open the door to discovering hidden *maqāṣid* or *maqāṣid* that weren't discernable up to and in his time.[47]

B. The Concept of Family

Ibn ʿAshur wrote a chapter entitled "The Aims of Rulings on the Family" (*al-maqāṣid min aḥkām al-ʿāʾilah*), in which he discusses matters concerning the stability of society as a whole. He says in the opening:

> The consolidation and proper functioning of the family constitute the foundation of human civilization and the integrating factor of society's order. Therefore, it has been one of the objectives of all regulations of humanity to take special care of the family system. In fact, establishing the family was one of the earliest concerns of civilized human beings in the process of laying down the underpinnings of civilization. Its purpose was to protect descendants (*ansāb*) from doubt about their lineal identity (*intisāb*), that is, that a man confirms the attribution of his children to himself…. Thus, it has always been the aim of the different systems of law to take care of the founding principle of the family unit, namely the association between the human male and female expressed by the term marriage (*zawāj, nikāḥ*).[48]

Ibn ʿAshur believed that the role of the family was to ensure the sound formation and shaping of society, a tradition that exists in all civilizations. In highlighting the honourable nature of the coming together of man and woman in accordance with Shariʿah rulings, he points out that a marriage contract is not to be understood literally as if it were a mere business transaction. Moreover, the dowry in Islam should not be thought of as an exchange for benefits (as some Muslim jurists may imply). If that were the case, then the dowry payment would be ongoing, corresponding to the fulfilment of benefits throughout the marriage, as analogous to paying rent; or it would be a onetime payment for the value of the woman as if she were a commodity, and whereupon it would be returned to the man in the event of a divorce, none of which of course applies.[49]

C. Issues Pertaining to Economic Wealth

Among the important and new contributions that Ibn ʿAshur makes is a detailed treatment of the *maqāṣid* of financial transactions. He says, "To gain deeper insight into this important topic, which only a few scholars of the Shariʿah have covered in some detail, I regard it my duty to treat it thoroughly with special emphasis on its basis."[50] Ibn ʿAshur emphasizes the idea of collective wealth and the importance of giving consideration to the concept of Ummah when addressing wealth and resources. He regarded the generation of wealth to depend on three primary factors, namely: land, labor, and financial capital. These factors are not on equal footing nor are they similar in nature, and to regard them as one and the same adversely affects how to understand different economic activities. There have been, in fact, nations who have possessed natural resources but did not realize their value as wealth, and so they lost the opportunity to prosper from these resources. We should note that Ibn ʿAshur's treatment of the notion of resources and wealth is more relevant to the context of preindustrial economy, and thus clearly not as relevant in the context of today's service-based economy. It behooves us, therefore, to come up with a new approach for today's context that will take into account the impact of such things as experience, knowledge, and human capital, as well as creativity, the arts, and highly-skilled services (such as those related to medicine, law, organization, and management).

When Ibn ʿAshur asserted that "the basic principle concerning ownership is specific to an individual," he followed that by saying, "The individual may act in advance to acquire resources that are permissible to all people, such as grass, tree leaves and picking fruit, in order to take their share before others."[51] Although this approach may be sound in the context of issues of jurisprudence having to do with individuals, it does not meet the higher aims of Shariʿah with regard to issues of wealth and economy. Moreover, Ibn ʿAshur's remarks here are not in harmony with what he states elsewhere about the necessity of protecting public and private individual wealth, wherein he says, "Since that wealth of the community consists of an aggregate, it is protected by establishing appropriate rules for its management both at the public and private levels. In fact, the protection of the community's wealth as an aggregate depends on the protection of its particular components consisting of individual property and wealth."[52]

Ibn 'Ashur ultimately advances five aims of the Sharī'ah concerning economic wealth: marketability (*rawāj*), transparency (*wuḍūḥ*), preservation (*ḥifẓ*), durability (*thabāt*), and equity ('*adl*) in handling it.[53] He demonstrates his innovativeness in establishing a correlation between the increased circulation of wealth through the Islamic institution of inheritance and social and political cohesion. As Islamic communities are traditionally structured according to extended families, the institution of inheritance allows the community to maintain possession and control of wealth circulation. And with respect to justice in relation to wealth, Ibn 'Ashur tells us, "An important aspect of justice in relation to wealth consists equally of the protection of the public interests and the prevention of public misfortune. This concerns specifically the categories of wealth bearing on the vital needs of large social groups, such as food and defense."[54]

Among the important issues that Ibn 'Ashur discusses regards labor. He tells us:

It has been the purpose of the Sharī'ah in all these types of contracts to protect the workers' rights by stipulating specific conditions so that their work is not wasted or undervalued. Therefore, there is no excuse for the investors to impose strict conditions on them, since there are different ways available for the investors to make use of their money. They have the choice of investing it or simply keeping it and spending it on their needs. In contrast, the workers will remain unemployed if they are deprived of the assistance of the investors.[55]

His discussion here is critical, especially that it is relevant to the contemporary economy. It is essential, moreover, for Muslim nations to learn from the experiences of other nations with respect to addressing labor issues.

Ibn 'Ashur establishes eight objectives with regard to labor, the last of which is "shunning all kinds of conditions and contracts that resemble slave labor, such as requiring employees to work the whole or a very long period of their lives for the same employer, so that they have no way out."[56] This matter, however, clearly needs further examination and discussion, as nowadays, equity and benefit for laborers is more likely to be achieved with long-term contracts.

Ibn ʿAshur's valuable contribution to the subject of wealth and labor high-lights a general challenge in the relationship between the Islamic sciences and the social sciences and humanities. Though Muslim scholars may agree on the importance of benefiting from modern contemporary sciences, how to benefit from these sciences has yet to be realized. Unfortunately, most attempts at tapping into these sciences are made at an individual level (rather than at an institutional level) and are often insubstantial.

D. Political Issues

Those writing about the aims of Shariʿah at the time of European dominance pointed out the importance of politics in Islam and discussed the matter in a manner appropriate to developments that were taking place in modern societies. ʿAllal al-Fasi stated:

> After this discussion of the views of Muslim theorists from the time of al-Rāzī until the time of Rashīd Riḍā, we would like to point out two matters: (1) the fact that ultimate referentiality belongs to Allah alone, and this idea is central to all affairs of life. This is something that is well-established and is nonnegotiable for Muslims; (2) authority is for the Ummah, as it is the Ummah that is in charge of appointing decision-makers from among its members in a manner dictated by social and economic developments. That is to be done in accordance with the guidelines set out by Islamic teachings.[57]

He goes on to say, "But the political authority of the Ummah should be exercised within the general guidelines of Islamic Shariʿah and in harmony with its fundamentals. This is the basic difference between the theory concerning political sovereignty according to Islamic teaching and other theories."[58]

Ibn ʿAshur set out guidelines regarding political issues, and what people in authority should try to do and seek to achieve, and how they should go about running affairs in such a way as to achieve the public interest. This includes the issue of how to achieve principles of equality and freedom, defining rights and duties, establishing justice, running the financial system of the Muslim community, defense of the Muslim community, setting up government, establishing policies on a basis of moderation, establishing tolerance, devising ways of disseminating education and awareness among the Muslim community for both male and female, protecting the new generation from all that is detrimental to their well-being, establishing policies with regard to dealing with other nations (foreign policy) based on tolerance and fulfilment of treaties, and disseminating the beauty of Islam and truths about the faith to humanity. One of the main impacts of the concept of brotherhood and the truest testimony thereof goes back to the teaching that Muslims are equal on the basis that they all belong to the faith of Islam.

According to Ibn ʿAshur, there are two aspects to equality, one of which pertains to creed where there is complete equality, and the other pertains to *tasharīʿ* where there is variance. Al-Fasi points out that some cases concerning equality are undoubtedly just and fair, whilst others are undoubtedly unjust. Regarding as equal one who is deserving and one who is not is the essence of injustice; and making everything absolutely equal can also lead to injustice. For Ibn ʿAshur, the issue of equality is nuanced. He says, "In between the two categories [of cases, as mentioned by al-Fasi,] is a third, more nuanced area where laws and regulations, and their objectives, come into play. But some of these laws and regulations may go to extremes. Undoubtedly, the ideal is for the laws and regulations of Shariʿah to take a middle course that is just with regard to equality."[59]

With regard to the notion of freedom, Ibn ʿAshur discusses it in some detail. He tells us:

> Freedom is something for which humankind has an inherent love and inclination towards because it allows for growth of human potential when the person is able to think freely, speak freely, and act freely. And in an environment that is free, talented people are able to compete in areas of innovation and research. Therefore, it would not be right to restrict freedom unless it was for some pressing reason such as to ward off a proven harm or to procure a significant benefit, in which case the consent of those who would be opposed to this would be of lesser consideration.[60]

Ibn ʿAshur, moreover, believes that freedom and equality are fundamentally interconnected. He says, "It has already been established that equality is one of the aims of the Shariʿah. It necessarily follows that equality of the community's members in freely conducting their personal affairs constitutes one of the primary goals of the Shariʿah. This is what is meant by 'freedom'."[61]

When discussing the development of slavery and the mistreatment of servants, and how Islam addressed slavery, Ibn ʿAshur notes the prevalent situation [of dependence on slavery] among different nations [at the advent of Islam,] and how Islam as such took a gradual approach [in abolishing slavery,] given that it was so intertwined in the entire ancient system of life. Ibn ʿAshur goes on to provide two primary definitions of freedom, the first of which denotes the opposite of slavery, and the second is one's ability to act freely and handle one's affairs. This latter definition refers to the right of all humans in general, for Allah has created in people reason and freewill, has instilled in them the ability to take action, and has given them the right to use their freedom as something that is inherent and natural in creation.[62]

Freedom, furthermore, may be divided into freedom of belief, freedom of thought, freedom of speech, and freedom of action.[63] These freedoms should be properly understood from within an Islamic ethos. Ibn ʿAshur says, "With regard to defining freedom and its appropriate limits, that is something very difficult, critical, and unclear for a lawmaker who is not infallible. Therefore, people in authority should deliberate on this issue and should not be hasty in making decisions [regarding restrictions on freedoms,] because imposing restrictions more than what is called for to ward off harm and achieve exigency interests (*maṣāliḥ ḥājjiyyah*) in limiting freedoms would be an injustice."[64]

The concept of *maṣāliḥ* (welfare, well-being, benefits, and Shariʿah-recognized interests including public interest) in Islamic guidance also dictates that it would not allow for absolute freedoms to be divorced from responsibilities; also, assuming that freedoms automatically balance each other is not warranted. To the contrary, when such an approach is taken, it would lead to chaos, nihilism to the detriment of society's interests. However, the basis for having certain necessary restraints on freedom should be guided by ethical considerations. In this regard, Ibn ʿAshur points out how religion could be coopted for political control, telling us, "Freedom is most resented by oppressors, tyrants, and deceptive leaders. They have never ceased, from the earliest times, to use deceitful tactics in order to impose restrictions on freedom and even to suppress and stifle it. And they have done so through heathen customs of divine lineage to gods that allow them to supress people."[65]

3

Contemporary Trends in Writings on *Maqāṣid*

The Qur'an and Sunnah are the sources of Shariʿah, and our contemporary time has witnessed the continuous effort in researching and advancing the science of *maqāṣid* through focusing on the general frameworks established by these two sources. Contemporary writings on *maqāṣid* generally focus on three main areas: (1) educating the general public about the aims of Shariʿah; (2) revisiting previous work on *maqāṣid* for the purpose of improving and expanding upon it; and (3) examining issues relevant to *maqāṣid* and working towards their resolution. In what follows of this section, I attempt to summarize seven contemporary approaches to *maqāṣid*. The first of these is the approach of the scholar Abdallah Bin Bayyah, whose *maqāṣid* thought we find to be in many ways similar to al-Shāṭibi's. The second of these is the approach taken by the prominent *maqāṣid* thinker Ahmad al-Raysuni and his prolific work in disseminating *maqāṣid* thought in the contemporary era. I follow this by looking at the contributions of Ismail Hassani, namely his work in applying the study of *maqāṣid* to other disciplines. I then discuss the writings of Hasan Jabir and his work in defining universals. This is followed by a discussion of Jasser Auda's innovative integration of modern methodologies from other disciplines into *maqāṣid* thinking. Lastly, I introduce two *maqāṣid* writers whose works have sought to expand the study of *maqāṣid*: Gamal Eldin Attia and his comprehensive approach to extend the *maqāṣid* to various aspects of life, and Abd al-Majid al-Najjar and his more specialized approach to adding new dimensions to the study of *maqāṣid*. All of these contributions are distinguished by the fact that they do not merely summarize or repackage the works of earlier scholars; rather, they are genuinely new contributions in that they attempt to expand the discipline of *maqāṣid* by connecting it to real-life contemporary situations. Their approaches, therefore, are not lacking in innovativeness, and, moreover, have revived *maqāṣid* discourse.

3.1 In the Footsteps of al-Shāṭibī (Abdallah Bin Bayyah)

Al-Shāṭibī's contribution to *maqāṣid* thought is widely regarded as distinct and foundational to the field and is acknowledged for its virtue by Muslim scholars. The contemporary scholar Abdallah Bin Bayyah upholds what he characterizes as al-Shāṭibī's judicious approach to *maqāṣid*, as compared to those who have gone to extremes in their approach. In describing one extreme, he says: "There are those who, [in identifying or deducing a *maqṣid* from Qur'an or Hadith], go beyond the normative meaning of that text and believe the meaning to be comprehensive and applicable in all situations without limits, thus neglecting that the text's meaning [and the *maqṣid* being identified or deduced from it] may be subject to certain boundaries."[1] He then goes on to describe the other extreme, telling us, "There are those who are unable to decipher the objectives because they myopically cling to the specific meaning of texts such that they ignore greater meanings, objectives, and wisdoms typically found in them; thus, limiting the application of the text to the specific circumstances associated with it. In other words, this extreme essentially narrows a text's scope to the extent that a *maṣlaḥah* can no longer be deduced from it."[2] As for the balanced approach, Bin Bayyah says, "The correct approach is somewhere in between these two extremes, giving what is comprehensive its rightful position and giving what is specific its due."[3]

Al-Shāṭibī was aware of the danger of inclining towards one extreme or the other, and he warned against overlooking what is specific when focusing on what is comprehensive, and against turning away from what is comprehensive when dealing with what is specific. Bin Bayyah thus concludes that al-Shāṭibī took a middle course, and adds, "Based on this discussion, we refute the notion that the *maqāṣid* are independent of *uṣūl al-fiqh*; rather, they are indeed interconnected, like body and soul."[4] In addition to the universal aims of Shariʿah, there are also particular objectives that are applicable to individual cases, and specific objectives having to do with certain areas of fiqh.

We can see from Bin Bayyah's approach that he provides substantial treatment of real-world issues concerning Muslims cognizant that circumstances and situations can change. But we can see also an embrace of al-Shāṭibī's nomenclature and the essential role given to *uṣūl al-fiqh* in understanding the aims of Shariʿah. Even though Bin Bayyah's definition of *maqāṣid* is broad in scope, his methodology is more confined.

For Bin Bayyah, "The *maqāṣid* are the spirit of the Shariʿah, its ultimate aims and goals."[5] He further holds that "The *maqāṣid* form major principles not captured by the science of *uṣūl al-fiqh*. They also form general principles that are interconnected with aspects of *uṣūl al-fiqh*, and other principles that are more specific, serving to explain those general principles or complementing them. It is as such that the Shariʿah is considered comprehensive, with none of its rulings or expressions being without wisdom."[6] In summing up the concept of *maqāṣid al-Sharīʿah*, he says, "They essentially serve as a tool to derive the five *fiqhī aḥkam*. To serve as such, they need to be practical and applicable for real-world matters, rather than merely theoretical and abstract."[7] Critics of Bin Bayyah's approach to *maqāṣid* will undoubtedly view it as restrictive and daunting, and that it does not allow benefit from other various sciences; making it virtually impossible for anyone to apply.

3.2 Reintroducing the *Maqāṣid* for a New Era (Ahmad al-Raysuni)

The contributions to *maqāṣid* thought of Ahmad al-Raysuni represents a beacon in contemporary discourse on *maqāṣid al-Sharīʿah* and provides an intelligible reintroduction of al-Shāṭibī's *maqāṣid* theory. Al-Raysuni's work on *maqāṣid* also offers a serious treatment of the concept of *maṣlahah* (welfare) and follows in the rigor and comprehensive approach found in Ibn ʿAshur's *maqāṣid* work. Al-Raysuni's work, moreover, is invaluable for bringing the subject of *maqāṣid* into the academic fold and discourse on Shariʿah. Among the distinguishing features of his work is not allowing *uṣūl al-fiqh* to adversely confine the study of *maqāṣid*; rather, al-Raysuni contributes to advancing the study of *maqāṣid* into a formal contemporary discourse of Islamic thought, wherein scholars and researchers of various disciplines might benefit from.

One of the main ideas that distinguishes al-Raysuni's contribution is his emphasis on the rationality of the Shariʿah. He tells us, "The *maqāṣid* may be known through rational thinking and sound logic which realize that the Shariʿah cannot but be based on wisdom and mercy, justice and fairness, and a balanced approach and a proper evaluation of things; because this is the normative way of God with regard to all of His creation, and because this is what is dictated by His perfect attributes."[8] Al-Raysuni goes on to define the innovative aspects of al-Shāṭibī's theory as being four: (1) the great expansion of the study of *maqāṣid*; (2) connecting between the objectives of the *Shāriʿ* and the objectives of the *mukallaf* (competent and responsible person in view of Shariʿah), and highlighting the way in which they are interconnected; (3) developing a sound methodology to ascertain the objectives of the *Shāriʿ*; and (4) the compilation and precise formulation of comprehensive principles, within the framework of which particulars are ordered and theories are developed.

Al-Raysuni praises al-Shāṭibī for understanding that the reason for a ruling is to achieve benefit and ward off harm. In regard to understanding this inter-relationship between rulings and their ultimate aims, he says, "The rulings of the Shariʿah and the evidence thereof produce and provide *uṣūlī* issues, *tashrīʿ* theories, and *fiqhī* principles. The *maqāṣid* then brings all of this together and systematically organizes them such that they become as one functioning body, serving one another."[9] Al-Raysuni then provides us with the following summary of guidelines for ascertaining the aims: (1) to deduce the objectives in accordance with the dictates of the Arabic language; (2) to consider underlying causes (*ʿilal*) and clear benefits (*maṣāliḥ*) of a text's ruling without neglecting the apparent meaning of the text; (3) to distinguish between primary objectives and secondary objectives; and (4) to take into account silence on the part of the *Shāriʿ* in situations which call for *tashrīʿ*, this being an indication to adhere to the limits set by the text without adding or subtracting anything – especially being pertinent to acts of worship.[10]

3.3 Delineating Guidelines for Applying *Maqāṣid* to other Sciences (Ismail Hassani)

In his work *Naẓariyyat al-Maqāṣid ʿinda al-Imām Muḥammad ibn ʿĀshūr*, Ismail Hassani treats the subject of *maqāṣid* within the purview of addressing contemporary issues. Just as al-Raysuni had captured and made more accessible to the modern generation al-Shāṭibī's significant contributions to *maqāṣid* theory, Hassani attempts to capture and introduce us to Ibn ʿAshur's *maqāṣid* theory. Among the important features in Ibn ʿAshur's thought which he highlights is the consideration given to harmonizing Shariʿah (whether pertaining to beliefs or actions) with *fiṭrah* (innate human nature). And among his points of emphasis is that rights and duties among and between people is ultimately based on procuring good and benefit (*maṣlaḥah*).

Hassani shares Ibn ʿAshur's view with regard to establishing a political framework in order to preserve and protect the five indispensables (*al-ḍarūriyyāt*; that are essential to the well-being of the Muslim community and general society), as well as the needs (*al-ḥājiyyāt*) and enhancements (*al-taḥsīniyyāt*). In adopting these, Hassani calls for them to be defined in such a way that "that which is variable ought not be controlled by that which is invariable."[11] He asserts that the new approach calls to consider that narrowing the scope of indispensables among ancient *uṣūlīs* is a matter of the past.[12] Hassani holds that Ibn ʿAshur's development of a methodology to ascertain the aims of the Shariʿah had thus enabled *maqāṣid* thought to be relevant in addressing issues pertinent to the social system and to the objectives of freedom and equality in particular.

Hassani asserts that "the profoundness of Ibn ʿAshur's *maqāṣid* thought comes through in the serious treatment he gives to ascertaining the *maqāṣid* of the *Shāriʿ* from the discourse [of *nuṣuṣ*]."[13] And this holds true from a linguistic perspective, whether in regards to the syntactical structure of the text, "how the words are structured," or the situational context of the text, "pertaining to the Qur'anic text's context, such as in regards to the events surrounding its revelation or reasons for revelation."[14] Hassani sorts the *maqāṣid* into three categories: some are speculative, some are based on conjecture but are very close to being definitive, and some are definitive. This is an aspect of the inductive approach constructed in Ibn ʿAshur's *maqāṣid* theory; an approach which was relied upon in ascertaining the *maqāṣid al-Sharīʿah*. Finally, Hassani importantly provides us with three critical matters of methodological import: (1) defending the role of reason in shaping the theory of *maqāṣid*; (2) emphasizing the role of academic specialties in law, sociology, political science, and applied as well as empirical sciences not only in *taḥqīq al-manāṭ* (ascertaining the applicability of the reason of a ruling), but also in *takhrīj al-manāṭ* (extracting the reason), all of which is central to *maqāṣid* theorizing; and lastly (3) noting that Islam's primary source texts are subject to interpretation from two angles, linguistic and legislative, which need mutual consideration in order to work out all possible meanings.[15]

3.4 Attempting to Define the Universals (Hasan Jabir)

Hasan Jabir's thesis, *al-Maqāsid al-Kulliyyah fī Daw' al-Qirā'ah al-Manzumi-yyah li al-Qur'ān al-Karīm*, attempts to ascertain the universal *maqāsid* directly from the Qur'an through a systematic methodology. Jabir notes the difficulty in ascertaining the *maqāsid* through *usūl al-fiqh* alone or through fiqh rulings, the latter of which jurists arrived at to address particular matters pertaining to the context of their time, and as such, are limited in their capacity to be relevant to new developments or for universal application. Moreover, the specialized nature of the science of fiqh makes it rather inadequate to grasping general Qur'anic values, these being key to the process of ascertaining *maqāsid*. Jabir asserts that his methodology to derive universals from the primary source texts differs from those methodologies having to do with linguistic analysis, such as are applied by linguists, sociologists, and psychologists. He holds their methodologies to be limited, despite their efforts to derive universals from the texts; whereas his systematic methodology is distinguished by its ability to address new developments. He qualifies all this by adding that though there is no dispute concerning the Qur'an being "immutable and not subject to change," understanding its meanings may vary from one reader to another, depending on such factors as the generation, level of awareness, or outlook of the reader. After explaining the characteristics of his systematic reading of the Qur'an, Jabir goes on to emphasize the pivotal importance of *fitrah* (innate human nature) [to *maqāsid* thought]. He says, "After delineating the main themes of the Qur'an, attempting to discover the relationships between them while searching for an overarching theme, I arrived at *fitrah* as being the overarching theme to anchor a systematic approach to *maqāsid* thought."[16]

Jabir's work offers an outline of his research into *maqāsid* under the heading "The Universal Objectives and their Hierarchical Structure." The conceptualization is comprised of two dimensions, that pertaining to human nature and that pertaining to the role of *tashrīʿ* (the precepts and implications of Shariʿah). The part on legislation is comprised of three complementary and intersecting areas: worship, human nature, and charity. With respect to the fundamental aim of worship, al-Jabir tells us that it is for the purification of people. For Jabir, purification of people, otherwise elevating them to a higher standard, is also the purpose being served in the application of laws and regulations (which he treats in discussing the notion of *fiṭrah* under the first part pertaining to human nature). What is perplexing, however, is his designation of human nature as "absolute truth," wherein it "is synonymous with justice and the basis for values (after *tawḥīd*), and from which many other values stem."[17] We understand from this that Jabir's discussion of the notion of truth comes in the context of legal rights and not in the context of its meaning vis a vis falsehood.

It is apparent that what the Qur'an means by "honoring the sons of Adam" [Qur'an 17:70] is far broader than the understanding of it that Jabir adopts in his discourse (i.e., modern opportunistic). If we want to sum up Jabir's understanding of the *maqāṣid al-Sharīʿah* within a framework of viceregency (*istikhlāf*), we will find that it is, according to him, justice, excellence, and worship, with the objective of worship serving to reinforce the objectives of justice and excellence. Jabir regards the Qur'an as being the only source for the basis of rulings, and he maintains that *uṣūl al-fiqh* alone is not sufficient in deducing the *maqāṣid*. He holds, moreover, that the science of *maqāṣid* can be applied to other disciplines and methodologies in reinforcing and supporting *uṣūl al-fiqh* such that it achieves what was intended by those who pioneered the field, which is identifying universals.

With respect to the category pertaining to human nature, Jabir holds that jurists can derive most of the evidence for rulings in this area from the Qur'an, relevant aspects of the Sunnah, and universal objectives (*maqāṣid kulliyyah*). As for *istiḥsān* (juristic preference), *maṣāliḥ mursalah* (unrestricted interests), and *sadd al-dharāʾiʿ* (blocking the means that may lead to harm), they are among the principles and methodologies that could be used for deriving rulings in correspondence with the *maqāṣid al-Sharīʿah*.[18] He goes on to say that "Most of what the scholars of *uṣūl al-fiqh* regard as evidence is not really evidence, apart from that which is directly from the Qur'an and Sunnah…for such principles as *qiyās* (analogical reasoning), *istiḥsān*, and *maṣāliḥ mursalah* cannot be applied to the area of worship, as was affirmed by al-Shāṭibī and others."[19]

With regard to what could be used as evidence, Jabir explains that the Qur'an and Sunnah serve different roles with respect to matters of worship and matters pertaining to human nature. He believes that the Sunnah should not have the same authoritative legislative role in matters having to do with human nature as it does with regard to matters of worship. He goes on to say:

> It is possible to regard the Qur'an as the only source for the basis of rulings having to do with human nature. As for the Sunnah, some of its rulings may be sound for our time, on the basis that they explain the rulings of the Qur'an in a manner that was suited to the era in which the Messenger (ṢAAS) lived, but some others may not be suitable for our era in light of the developments in human society over the centuries.[20]

Among the commendable and distinguishing features of Jabir's work is its innovativeness and the depth of its discourse. However, his treatment of the subject matter presents itself as incohesive and unmethodical. Moreover, his outline of the hierarchical structure of the universals is rather ambiguous. Thus, the strength of Jabir's work lies in its comprehensiveness, while its weakness is in its abstruseness.

3.5 Deploying Ideas from Beyond Tradition (Jasser Auda)

Jasser Auda's work, *Maqāsid al-Shariah as Philosophy of Islamic Law: A Systems Approach,* is a pathbreaking contribution that uses System Theory to establish a framework for the concept of *maqāṣid.* Auda sees *uṣūl al-fiqh* as a system that is comprised of the following six features: cognition, wholeness, openness, interrelated hierarchy, multidimensionality, and purposefulness. These six features ultimately serve the Shari'ah, which he defines as "a purposeful system guided by its objectives." [21] With respect to the feature of cognition, he holds that *fiqh* is human cognition (*idrāk*) of revealed knowledge (i.e., God's commands). The feature of wholeness dictates giving precedence to universal fundamentals over partial rulings. As for the feature of openness, it is highlighted by the notion that Islamic law takes into consideration contextual factors. Regarding the feature of interrelated hierarchy, it is that the elements of the system are connected. The feature of multi-dimensionality calls for a more nuanced consideration of matters as opposed to a simplistic binary approach, as is found in such constructs as obligatory/prohibited, abrogating/abrogated, good/bad, and certain/uncertain; constructs which can fail to capture realities that often fall somewhere in between. As for purposefulness, it is perhaps the most important of the features. It dictates that the Islamic legal system should take all appropriate measures to fulfill its ultimate goals or objectives.[22]

Auda proposes a new concept-based classification of the theories of what he called Islamic law. He presents this in a chart depicting a two-dimensional illustration of the current various sources of Islamic law versus the current various levels of authority given to them. From this, he identified three major "tendencies" in various contemporary theories of Islamic law, namely, traditionalism, modernism, and postmodernism. On the horizontal axis of the chart are the six current various sources of Islamic law, namely: Qur'anic verses, Prophetic traditions, Higher *Maqāṣid*, Rulings of traditional *madhahib*, Rationality, and Modern values/rights. On the vertical axis of the chart, he presents seven current various levels of authority given to these sources, these being: Proof (*ḥujjah*), Apologetic interpretation, Re-interpreted, Supportive evidence, Minorly criticized, Radically re-interpreted, and Radically criticized.[23]

Based on the intersection between the horizontal sources and vertical levels of authority given to these sources, Auda was able to identify the three broad trends of Traditionalism, Modernism, and Postmodernism. I found Auda's findings to be quite perplexing, especially in regards to the eclectic group of Muslim figures he associates with Islamic Modernism, and within it, Reformist Re-interpretation. He includes among the early contributors to Reformist Re-interpretation, Muhammad ʿAbduh, Muhammad al-Tabtaba'i, Muhammad Ibn ʿAshur, and Ayatollah al-Sadir. Among later contributors include Muhammad al-Ghazali, Hasan al-Turabi, Abdullah Darraz, Sayyid Qutb, Fathi Osman, and al-Tijani Hamed. And among the more recent contributors are Taha Jabir al-Alwani, Abdul-Karim Soroush, Fazlur Rahman, Salim al-ʿAwa, and Ali Abdel Raziq.[24] Auda holds that among the common links between the aforementioned figures is their contextual and thematic approach to the Qur'an.

Auda reaches five core conclusions concerning the role of *maqāṣid*: (1) that they be regarded as evidence; (2) that they form the basis of interpreting texts and in determining whether a text is specific in meaning; (3) that they be used in clarifying apparent conflicting texts; (4) that they form the reference point with regard to what is specific or general in meaning, and what is open-ended and what is restrictive; and (5) that achieving the objective becomes the ultimate deciding factor when there is a dispute about what is open-ended or restrictive (not simply relying on the analytical tools of language or logic to settle the dispute).[25] Auda concludes his work with a fifteen point summary proposal for supporting the feature of "purposefulness" in the system of Islamic law. These include: achieving the objectives constitutes evidence; moral values should have the status of ratio legis for related rulings; coherence and harmony between different parts of Shari‘ah may be used to expand or add to the idea that the text should not be odd in nature; and, a *maqāṣid* approach could fill the gap of missing contexts in hadith.

The question here is the legitimacy of applying a theory from outside Islamic tradition to the discourse on *maqāṣid*, especially given that the theory which Auda deploys is not minor but rather quite significant in its scope to treat the subject. We should keep in mind that material theories such as this are not always adequate for treating subject matters that depart from an Islamic worldview. It would perhaps have been more judicious on the part of Auda to have offered some qualification for the application of such a theory, lest it be thought that any random theory can simply or uncompromisingly be applied to Islamic tradition. One needs thus to proceed cautiously in applying any material theory to Islam, doing so only when it clearly supports and does not undermine the fundamental values and integrity of the religion.

Jasser Auda's systems approach to Islamic law and *maqāṣid* thought is certainly a unique contribution. However, he does not produce any new solutions that did not already exist in the Islamic intellectual heritage. His work can partly be summed up as emphasizing the notion of avoiding restrictions and deploying broad universal principles that are to be found in *uṣūl al-fiqh*. Despite some of its flaws, the innovative theory he introduces to us has great potential for further development.

3.6 Expanding the *Maqāṣid* and Applying them to all Aspects of Life (Gamal Eldin Attia)

Gamal Eldin Attia's work *Naḥwah Taf‘īl Maqāṣid al-Sharī‘ah* is distinguished by its expansion of the *maqāṣid*. Attia asserts that leading Muslim scholars of the past rejected the notion that the aims of the Shari‘ah are confined to the longstanding five essential *maqāṣid*. His comprehensive approach to the *maqāṣid* parallels that of Ibn ʿAshur's, though their methodologies also differ in many aspects. Central to Attia's theory is the idea that the aims of the Shariʿah are realized on four levels: individual, family, community, and humanity. He thus expands the *maqāṣid* to twenty-four. His additions incorporate the thought of other scholars who have called for expanding the *maqāṣid*, and he deemed it essential to add the objectives of justice, freedom, equality, and human rights.[26]

Attia's work is distinguished, moreover, by its depth of engagement with the historical discourse on *maqāṣid al-Sharīʿah* as well as its critical approach to making *uṣūl al-fiqh* the sole foundation of the science of *maqāṣid*, while also devoting serious treatment of the contemporary context. His work does not therefore simply rehash previous contributions in the field of *maqāṣid*; rather, it re-examines these contributions and highlights their differences in ascertaining and applying the *maqāṣid*. Attia's approach to the *maqāṣid* introduces us to important topics that further our understanding of the subject. These topics include: the role of reason; establishing the order of the *maqāṣid* in relation to each other; establishing the order of the means (*wasāʾil*) associated with each of the *maqāṣid* according to the categories of essentials (*ḍarūriyyāt*), exigencies (*ḥājiyyāt*), and enhancements (*taḥsīniyyāt*); and the criterion on the basis of which a given ruling or means is to be placed in the category of essentials, exigencies, or enhancements.

Attia notes that al-Shāṭibī's view falls short in the consideration of reason as compared to earlier scholars such as al-ʿIzz, Ibn Taymiyyah, and Ibn al-Qayyim. He states:

In my view, al-Shāṭibī's position to put certain restraints on the role of reason in ascertaining the *maqāṣid* does not account for the cases meant by al-ʿIzz ibn ʿAbd al-Salām, which pertain to what the *Shāriʿ* did not have a say in it, otherwise a legislative void, in treating given matters. It is for this reason that Ibn ʿAshur's view to expand the *maqāṣid* is of great value, especially in modern times, wherein the area of legislative void is expanding exponentially as a result of astonishing developments across various aspects of life. As such, there does not appear to be a conflict between adhering to the guidelines set out by al-Shāṭibī for ascertaining the *maqāṣid al-Sharīʿah* and adding new guidelines when it is called for.[27]

Attia, thus, puts into perspective those who had taken a more conservative approach to the use of reason, *fiṭrah*, and human experience in ascertaining the *maqāṣid*. His view is that reason, *fiṭrah*, and experience are in fact essential to ascertaining the *maqāṣid*, a view that is shared by al-Raysuni, Hassani, and Ibn ʿAshur.

With regard to the common hierarchical ordering of the *maqāṣid*, Attia tells us that it is not definitive and can be altered. For Attia, the ordering of the *maqāṣid* should be akin to concentric circles, wherein some indispensable *maqāṣid* fall within broader indispensable *maqāṣid*, with the *maqṣid* of preserving religion being the broadest circle. It is important to note here that there is a lack of agreement on his ordering, an ordering which includes the higher objectives of the law (*maqāṣid al-ʿāliyah*) and is not limited to the universal objectives (*maqāṣid kulliyyah*). Attia holds that the ordering of indispensables (*ḍarūriyyāt*), exigencies (*ḥājiyyāt*), and enhancements (*taḥsīniyyāt*) does not cover all aspects of life to which the *maqāṣid* should apply. Moreover, he objects to making the exigencies (*ḥājiyyāt*) and enhancements (*taḥsīniyyāt*) merely subordinate to the indispensables (*ḍarūriyyāt*); rather, he believes that the exigencies (*ḥājiyyāt*) and enhancements (*taḥsīniyyāt*) should play a foundational and comprehensive role similar to that of the indispensables (*ḍarūriyyāt*).[28]

Attia is therefore of the view that, (1) The *maqāṣid al-Sharīʿah* should not be confined to the indispensables only, but rather should include the exigencies (*ḥājiyyāt*) and enhancements (*taḥsīniyyāt*) as important objectives to be realized along with the indispensables (with the indispensables being the absolute fundamental objectives to be realized, but with the aim of also fulfilling—to the extent possible—the exigencies and enhancements); and (2) The categories of indispensables, exigencies, and enhancements are not only concerned with achieving the objective itself, but rather they are also concerned with the means that will lead to the objective. Moreover, the availability of the means determines the appropriate category within which the objective will fall, whether of the indispensables, exigencies, or enhancements.[29]

Attia's work represents a critical examination of the traditional approach to *maqāṣid*, and it addresses the differences and various conflicting issues within the discipline that have restricted it from becoming more comprehensive and practical in application. There are three particular guidelines of nine that he offers in regards to ascertaining the *maqāṣid* which are worth noting here: (1) ignoring that which is not relevant to the *maqāṣid*, even though it might appear to be; (2)

identifying the *maṣāliḥ* of the Shariʿah and not just interests in general; and (3) giving due consideration to both religious and worldly *maṣāliḥ* (welfare, benefits, and public interests) as if they are one interactive entity.[30]

We can see from these, as well as other aspects of his work, that Attia essentially lays the foundation for a new conceptualization of the *maqāṣid*. This new conceptualization is especially demonstrated in his designation of various *maqāṣid* across four broad categories (Individual, Family, Ummah, and Humanity), within which the five universal *maqāṣid* along with other *maqāṣid* become noticeably clear. In further expounding on his theoretical approach to the *maqāṣid*, Attia briefly refers to Ibn ʿAshur's theory, telling us that Ibn ʿAshur had "examined particular rulings and attempted to derive universal principles from them, but ended up focusing on the details of these particular rulings and the wisdom behind each of them. Whereas, my theoretical approach is distinguished by its systematic approach to ascertain universals from particular rulings without allowing the particularity of them to diverge me from arriving at the universals behind them."[31]

To better capture Attia's theory, it is worthwhile to summarize it in the following chart:

Individual	Family	Ummah	Humanity
1 Preservation of human life	1 Regulation of relations between the sexes	1 Institutional organization of the Ummah's affairs	1 Mutual understanding, cooperation, and integration
2 Preservation of the intellect	2 Preservation of progeny (or the species)	2 Preserving the security of the Ummah	2 Fulfilling the role of human vicegerency on earth
3 Preservation of personal piety	3 Achieving harmony affection, and compassion	3 Establishing justice	3 Achieving global peace based on justice
4 Preservation of honor	4 Preservation of family lineage	4 Preservation of religion and morals	4 International protection of human rights
5 Preservation of material wealth	5 Preservation of personal piety within the family	5 Cooperation, solidarity, and shared responsibility	5 Dissemination of the Islamic message

Individual	Family	Ummah	Humanity
--	6 Regulating the institution of the family	6 Dissemination of knowledge and preservation of reason in the Ummah	--
--	7 Regulating the financial aspect of the family	7 Populating and developing the earth and preserving the Ummah's resources	--

The aforementioned summary illustrates a positive expansion of the *maqāṣid* that moves beyond the constraints imposed within traditional *uṣūl al-fiqh*. Moreover, it is an attempt to systematically organize Ibn ʿĀshur's contributions. Ibn ʿĀshur, as well as those who would follow him, had extended the discourse on *maqāṣid* to include their application in relation to the collective, a shift from the prevailing discourse which had primarily focused on the *maqāṣid* as they pertain to the individual. It would in fact be a deficiency if the *maqāṣid* were not more general in application such that they apply broadly across various disciplines. Attia's expansion of the *maqāṣid* is thus a significant contribution, and it is the hope that it will curb disputation concerning how to approach them.

Attia's contribution reflects a legalistic and organizational approach. It also reflects a real desire to connect the *maqāṣid* to contemporary sciences. It is as such that he discusses the application of *maqāṣid* to the fields of education, economics, sociology, and the natural sciences. Perhaps the greatest challenge for Attia was trying to tackle the rather complex issues in these fields that related to various philosophical and methodological matters.

It is interesting and important to note that Attia uses the rendering *ḥifẓ al-tadayyun*, "preservation of personal piety," rather than the more common rendering of *ḥifẓ al-dīn*, "preservation of religion." I would contend that *maqāṣid* theory needs to convey both notions, that of preserving religion and that of preserving personal piety, such that they are understood to be central for all aspects of the *maqāṣid* (see my chapter on methodology for further discussion of this matter). Attia states that his *maqāṣid* theory is deeply rooted in the notions of divine oneness (*tawḥīd*) and justice (*ʿadl*).[32] This is reflected in his diagram illustrating the relationship between juristic theories and the Sharīʿah sciences. He places doctrine at the center of his diagram, since it constitutes the foundation and wellspring of all Islamic sciences, with moral values arising from it.

Attia's theoretical formulation is not entirely in accordance with traditional *uṣūl al-fiqh* (though the innovative aspects of his theory are not arrived at in a vacuum, as he constructs it with reference to the opinions of scholars, Qurʾanic verses, and contemporary Islamic thought). There appears to be a conflict, however, between the clear diversion of Attia's *maqāṣid* theory from traditional *uṣūl al-fiqh* and his remarks that "it is important to connect the *maqāṣid al-Sharīʿah* to *uṣūl al-fiqh*, and that they be developed within a unified framework."[33] This is clearly demonstrated in his innovative designation of various *maqāṣid* across four broad categories (Individual, Family, Ummah, and Humanity), all of which markedly divert from the mechanisms of traditional *uṣūl al-fiqh*.

The primary role of *uṣūl al-fiqh* for Attia is serving as a determinant to justify the adoption of less conspicuous rulings. And he calls to treat *ūṣūl* and *maqāṣid* in a single framework. However, as I frequently noted, *uṣūl al-fiqh* alone tend to impose limitations on the discipline and application of *maqāṣid*.

In addition to Attia's new contribution of expanding and categorizing the *maqāṣid*, he also introduces two broad divisions of *maqāṣid*, the *maqāṣid* of creation (*maqāṣid al-khalq*) and the *maqāṣid* of Islamic overall regulations (*maqāṣid al-sharʿ*). It is important to distinguish between them. The former refers to the purposes behind having been created by God—that is the purposes behind creation (*maqāṣid al-ʾamr al-takwīnī*), whereas the latter refers to the intents behind the obligations on human beings in their role of stewardship (*maqāṣid al-ʾamr al-taklīfī*). The purposes or aims behind creation (*maqāṣid al-khalq*) include three subcategories: primary objectives, secondary objectives, and objectives that have to do with those who are addressed with responsibility (*maqāṣid al-mukallifīn*). With regard to the objectives of the Islamic system (*maqāṣid al-sharʿ*) and the higher objectives (*maqāṣid ʿāliyah*), or the general objectives (*maqāṣid ʿāmmah*), they may be divided into universal objectives (*maqāṣid kulliyyah*), specific objectives (*maqāṣid khāṣṣah*) (which are categories that have to do with various aspects of the Shariʿah and different sciences), and particular objectives (*maqāṣid juzʾiyyah*) (which concern the reasons (*ʿilal*) and wisdom (*ḥikam*) behind secondary (*farʿiyyah*) rulings).[34]

The higher aims of the Shariʿah (*maqāṣid al-Sharīʿah al-ʿāliyah*) may be summarized as,

> …surrendering to Allah, acting as His vicegerent, developing and populating the earth through faith and what it requires of righteous deeds that may lead to happiness in this world and the hereafter and that cover all material and spiritual aspects of life, striking the right balance between the *maṣāliḥ* of the individual and those of society, taking into consideration both national interests and the interests of humanity as a whole, and striking the right balance between the *maṣāliḥ* of the present generation and the *maṣāliḥ* of future generations. All of that is for the benefit of the individual, the family, the Ummah, and humanity.[35]

What distinguishes Attia's work in particular is its inclination to connect theory to application, or at least to think of the possibility of applying theory to real-life situations. Thus, when Attia discusses the notion of *maqāṣid*-based ijtihad (an idea which al-Raysuni emphasizes), he considers its practical realization, and as such, calls for not allowing the *maqāṣid* to be treated or viewed separately from *uṣūl al-fiqh*; rather, he calls for making the *maqāṣid* an advanced branch of Islamic jurisprudence which serves to support and assist it in developing its remaining branches.

Attia's work is undoubtedly pioneering and distinguished for its introduction of an innovative and comprehensive theory of *maqāṣid*, a theory which critically engaged with other *maqāṣid* theories to develop the field further. Moreover, Attia's theory should be noted for its attempt to establish the *maqāṣid al-Sharīʿah* as a practical discipline relevant to the lives of contemporary Muslims.

3.7 Qualitative Expansion of the *Maqāṣid* (Abd al-Majid al-Najjar)

Among the distinguishing features of Abd al-Majid al-Najjar's work *Maqāṣid al-Sharīʿah bi Abʿād Jadīdah* is its balanced approach, wherein it might reference *uṣūl al-fiqh* as a general support for the argument, brings examples of fiqh rulings, and expand *maqāṣid* and reinterpret them; and overall, it attempts to not stray from the dominant views in the field. His study underscores the imperative to increase understanding of the *maqāṣid*, treating and systematically capturing the pertinent issues within the field, and bridging the gap between theory and practice such that the *maqāṣid* play a more effective role in addressing real-life matters and rapid changes confronting Muslims.

In calling for broadening the scope of the *maqāṣid,* al-Najjar says, "The ultimate aim of the Shariʿah is to enable one to attain that which is in their best interests by fulfilling the purpose of their existence, which is represented in the notion of viceregency on earth. This can only be achieved by reforming oneself and reforming society so that it leads to both happiness in this world and the hereafter."[36] Al-Najjar points out that Muslim culture tends to understand the notion of "Shariʿah" as referring only to obligations and admonitions pertaining to individual conduct, and that a reductive understanding has been also attributed to *maqāṣid al-Sharīʿah.* However, the notion of "*maqāṣid al-Sharīʿah*" should be understood to encompass more, namely matters of faith. Thus, the discipline of *maqāṣid* should be understood to serve two primary roles, supporting the derivation of the Islamic regulations in accordance with a particular objective, and astutely applying them to real-life matters.

Al-Najjar holds that the notion of having the *maqāṣid* address real-life matters is "not a task limited only to the fiqh scholars who engage in ijtihad; rather it is the task of all Muslims, each according to their ability."[37] As with Attia, al-Najjar's aim is for everyone to have a proper understanding of the aims of Shariʿah such that they better understand rulings and their proper application, whether with regard to themselves or others. His study sets forth four broad aims of the Shariʿah: preserving the value of human life, preserving human essence, preserving society, and preserving the surrounding physical environment. Al-Najjar's approach, however, does not stop at these four broad goals; rather, it goes into detail concerning them, including two objectives within each of them (eight in all). He discusses certain issues associated with each of these that the Shariʿah gives due attention to in order to achieve these objectives.

The Universal Goal	The Objectives	Aspects of the Objectives
I. Preserving the value of human life	1. Preservation of religion	A. By availing its modalities
		B. By removing constraints
	2. Preserving the humanity of humans	A. Innate disposition
		B. Human dignity
		C. Purpose of life
		D. Human freedom

The Universal Goal	The Objectives	Aspects of the Objectives
II. Preserving the essence of humanity	1. Preserving the human sole	A. Physical maintenance
		B. Moral preservation
	2. Preserving intellect	A. Physical maintenance
		B. Moral preservation
III. Preserving the society	1. Preserving offspring	A. By reproduction
		B. By maintaining lineal descent
	2. Preserving social structure	A. Maintenance of social institutionalism
		B. Maintaining social relations
IV. Preserving the Physical Surrounding	1. Preserving wealth	A. Through earning and economic development
		B. Protection from spoilage
		C. Protecting property rights
		D. Protecting its value
		E. Exchange and circulation
	2. Preserving the environment	A. From spoilage
		B. From pollution
		C. From over-consumption
		D. Through development

In discussing the aim of preserving religion (*ḥifẓ al-dīn*), al-Najjar rejects the common narrow understanding of it. According to al-Najjar, preservation of religion "is not limited to preserving individual religious piety (*ḥifẓ al-ta-dayyun*), as some imagine;"[38] rather it is more comprehensive than that and includes beliefs and obligations, whether they have to do with belief in the unseen, such as belief in the hereafter, or they have to do with the seen world of faith, such as prayer, seeking knowledge and other matters that are enjoined or admonished with regard to individual conduct. On the basis of this comprehensive understanding of religion, the preservation thereof may be achieved by making available means to support it and removing obstacles that hinder it. Making available means that support religion includes the facilitation of ease and forbidding going to extremes, "because when religious practice takes the form of extremes and exaggeration, the religious person soon wearies," which deters anyone who wants to become religious and has not yet started.[39]

One of the means of preserving religion is through ijtihad, which is a collective obligation upon Muslims. Ijtihad is essential because "if Muslims do not strive to attain the best answer of an inconclusive textural reference (*dalīl*), then they may fall into acting according to an unlikely possibility [of meaning] or even something delusional, inevitably they would miss the correct [intent] of religion."[40] For al-Najjar, the means of preserving religion also includes the dissemination of its teachings such that it be properly understood, and warding off negative influences on religion, such as interpretation based on false whims and desires, intransigence, distortion, confusion, and the like.

As for the objective of preserving a person's humanity (*ḥifẓ insāniyyat al-insān*), al-Najjar opines that it deserves to be treated in a separate discussion. The reason for this, he points out, is due to the overwhelming issues surrounding this matter today; issues pertaining to blatant transgression against human dignity, whether on a philosophical and cultural level or on a practical, real-life level. Humanity today is confronted by all kinds of deviant ideas, from purposeless, nihilist philosophies that dismiss the purpose of humankind's existence altogether, to existentialism that dismisses any idea of anything in human nature being immutable, to claims that everything is constantly changing, to laws and regulations that dismiss the unique nature of each sex.[41]

Al-Najjar holds that there are four aspects to the objective of preserving a person's humanity. One of these is preserving the *fiṭrah* (innate human nature) by maintaining its balance and fulfilling its requirements, which includes preserving human dignity and the sense of humanity's stewardship of their surrounding environment. Another of these is preserving the understanding that life serves a purpose; an understanding that is unique to humans and distinguishes them from animals. Yet another of these is preserving human freedom; for all that exists in creation is driven to its destination in a way that is unavoidable, except humans, for they were created with a free will to choose.[42]

Al-Najjar notes the vastness of the concept of human essence (*al-dhāt al-insāniyyah*). It fundamentally consists of a physical body and a soul, with the soul being a set of elements and forces. The human essence includes senses, physical desires, feelings, memory, imagination, and a thinking mind.[43] This broad understanding of the human essence, which includes both its physical and spiritual dimensions, is very important to approaching the *maqāṣid*, especially that the traditional approach to the *maqāṣid* reduces the scope of human essence in such a way that it becomes rather difficult to relate it to the context of preserving a person's humanity.[44]

Just as it is critical to preserve the physical aspect of humans, which may be achieved by making available means of survival and well-being and warding off anything that may cause physical harm, it is no less critical to preserve the intangible humanity of a person. Not doing so would otherwise lead the human soul to become overwhelmed with grief and fear, thus hindering its purpose of developing and populating the earth. The preservation of a person's humanity may be achieved through constant purification of the soul and through achieving a sense of security.[45]

With regard to the preservation of intellect, it is achieved by the well-known material approach (of avoiding such harmful things as intoxicants), as well as by an intangible approach through the liberation of thought and education. The notion of thought relates to the mind trying to understand reality, which Shariʿah rulings support by liberating the mind from that which hinders it internally and externally and which thus restricts the individual. As for preserving the intellect through education, al-Najjar offers a valuable and detailed discussion of this. He tells us that there are three aspects to attaining education. One of these is understanding what is around us in order to gain knowledge of facts in an objective manner, so that one will be able to fulfil their role in life. Another of these is learning through mindful thought, which goes beyond merely understanding facts and is more similar to contemplation. Yet another of these is through methodological learning, wherein the thinking process becomes organized and systematic, and thus avoids falling into error.

For al-Najjar, one of the fundamental methodological principles pertaining to the intellect in its search for truth is understanding reality. This includes understanding reality as it is witnessed in the signs of the universe, or as it is learned from historical events or from real-life situations. Humans may thus reflect on all this such that they discover the true nature of things, at which point they may continue to facts and realities beyond this.

Al-Najjar then discusses the universal aim of preservation of society (*ḥifẓ al-mujtamiʿ*), which includes the preservation of offspring (*ḥifẓ al-nasl*) and the preservation of the social structure (*ḥifẓ al-kiyān al-ijtimāʿī*). The former may be achieved through reproduction and maintaining lineal descent, while the latter may be achieved through the preservation of social relations by means of strengthening communal bonds, preserving justice, and reinforcing solidarity. Another aspect to preserving the social structure is the preservation of social institutions. What al-Najjar means here is that society should be formed on the basis of social entities that are governed by a system within them, and that system further governs their relationships with the broader social structure.

The preservation of society may be achieved, moreover, by preserving the institution of the family, including family values, and thus protecting it against selfish individuality. As such, every individual is deemed to have a role within the broader social order or system. The preservation of society may also be realized through the institution of the state. In this regard, al-Najjar asserts that society is the source of authority, in the sense that the Ummah, viz-a-viz the institution of the state, has authority over itself. As such, any system that is to be adopted to run, organize, or develop the affairs of a nation, should be in accordance with the will of the nation and with its consent. Consultation (*shūrā*) is the mechanism which helps to identify and implement the decision making of the Ummah and should be adhered to, whether it concerns the exchange of views among individuals and different segments of society in order to reach a majority decision, or whether it concerns shaping the relationship between society and its representative political leadership.[46]

The fourth universal aim al-Najjar discusses is the preservation of the physical surroundings, which in turn is achieved by preserving wealth and the environment. According to al-Najjar, the preservation of wealth is realized through five means, namely: earning a living, economic grown and development, preservation of property rights (which is deeply entrenched in human nature), circulation of wealth, and business activities. As for the preservation of the environment, it may be realized by protecting it from destruction, pollution, excessive consumption that is far removed from sensitivity towards the cycle of the environment, and exhaustion of its resources; all of this leads to an imbalance in the environment. Preserving the environment also includes protecting—through development and growth—that which is at risk of diminishing.[47]

Al-Najjar maintains the importance of defining the ways to ascertaining the aims of the Shariʿah. He deems that the jurist's role should not only be concerned with ascertaining the objectives, but also the methodology deployed to ascertain them. He moreover believes that researchers on *maqāṣid* did not give due attention to how the *maqāṣid* should be ascertained, neither in classical nor modern writings. After noting that the two primary sources of *maqāṣid al-Sharīʿah* are the Qurʾan and Sunnah, al-Najjar references al-Shāṭibī and Ibn ʿAshur in providing us with four ways through which the *maqāṣid* may be ascertained. These include: (1) explicit divine commands; (2) textual evidence from the Qurʾan and Sunnah; (3) inductive analysis of the Qurʾan and Sunnah; and (4) the actions of the Prophet.[48]

Al-Najjar believes that scholars of *maqāṣid* today should go beyond the existing classification of the *maqāṣid*, especially given that the study of *maqāṣid* continues to develop and that what already exists in the categorization and ordering of the *maqāṣid* is a subjective product of previous scholars' efforts. As such, he holds that scholars of later generations should be allowed the opportunity, through sound research and ijtihad, to revisit and further advance the field. The caveat of course is that their efforts to do so be well-grounded and familiar with what has already been contributed in the field.[49]

Al-Najjar goes on to offer five categories of *maqāṣid*. These are according to: (1) whether they are definitive, speculative, or imagined; (2) whether they are universal, qualitative, or particular; (3) whether they are broad or narrow in scope; (4) whether they are fundamental, ultimate objectives, or merely means of attaining the ultimate objectives; and (5) the benefit (*maṣlaḥah*) being sought and whether that benefit is of the indispensables (*ḍarūriyyāt*), exigencies (*ḥājiyyāt*), or enhancements (*taḥsīniyyāt*). He believes that the categories of indispensables, exigencies, and enhancements should function collaboratively in preserving the universals.[50] He says, "The aims of the Shariʿah are those which preserve the general universals (*kulliyāt*). This preservation may be achieved through that which is indispensable, that which is exigent, and that which is enhancing, and the examples that are [usually] brought for those categories aim, upon verification, to preserve the universals, despite that they do so to a lesser degree than that of the indispensables. Similarly, the enhancements preserve the universals to a lesser degree than that of the exigencies."[51] Al-Najjar further notes that these three categories are not necessarily mutually exclusive but rather may overlap and interact with one another and may even vary in their value to a given area. Moreover, he rejects what he deems to be a limited understanding of some of the universals, including the notion of preserving religion (*ḥifẓ al-dīn*) and preserving human life (*ḥifẓ al-nafs*).

Al-Najjar's approach may be summed up as having two dimensions: that of examining the *maqāṣid* in theory, which includes defining how they theoretically prioritize among one another; and that of examining the *maqāṣid* in application, which includes knowing what could affect their order of prioritization. His approach is informed by what is generally recognized in the study of *maqāṣid* in regards to their order of prioritization and in regards to what is definitive or speculative, what is indispensable or exigent, and all other categories pertinent to the *maqāṣid*. It is thus important to note that the order of prioritization of the *maqāṣid* is not absolute, as some would have it, and the jurist must therefore actively and judiciously determine this order when engaging in *maqāṣid*-based ijtihad. Concerning this, al-Najjar says, "Even after the *maqāṣid* have been ascertained by whatever method, the jurist must still distinguish and prioritize between them, including determining whether they are indispensable, exigent, or enhancing; whether they are primary (*uṣliyyah*) or secondary (*farʿiyyah*); and whether they are universal (*kulliyyah*) or particular (*juzʾiyyah*)."[52] For determining the appropriate level of *maqāṣid*, al-Najjar uses criteria that take into consideration: (1) the strength of evidence, (2) the strength of the impact, and (3) the extent of the impact. And these go along the warnings and encouragements found in Shariʿah.

Al-Najjar's study is regarded as pioneering. It follows a balanced approach, incorporating previous contributions in the field of *maqāṣid*, while avoiding delving into controversial matters or weighing between various views. His primary focus was to broaden the scope of *maqāṣid* and to develop a new approach that was not confined to any singular or methodological issue. It is as such that his approach treats different areas including belief, social life, and finance. His approach, moreover, delves into fiqh matters in order to further explicate his thought. Al-Najjar composed his work for a broad audience and not only for specialists of *maqāṣid*. For al-Najjar, knowledge of *maqāṣid al-Sharīʿah* should be of concern to every Muslim, regardless of their academic specialty or background, such that on the basis of understanding the *maqāṣid*, one will be able to apply them to any area of specialization.[53]

PART II

METHODOLOGY

4

Ascertaining the *Maqāṣid al-Sharīʿah*

The fundamental question pertaining to the *maqāṣid al-Sharīʿah* regards how to ascertain them? It is concerning this question wherein lies different interpretations and approaches, which in turn lead to various outcomes. The dominant approach to ascertaining an aim (*maqṣid*) of the Shariʿah is through identifying it directly from a text (i.e., Qurʾanic verse or hadith) or deducing it from an aggregate of texts. Modern *maqasid* thinkers such as Ibn ʿAshur and ʿAllal al-Fasi went beyond this approach in further developing the methodology to ascertaining the *maqāṣid*. Al-Fasi provides the following concise statement regarding deriving *maqāṣid*, "The Shariʿah is rulings embodying *maqāṣid* and *maqāṣid* embodying rulings."[1] Al-Raysuni says, in attempting to clarify al-Fasi's statement, "The meaning here is that the aims of the Shariʿah are taken from the rulings of the Shariʿah, and the rulings of the Shariʿah are arrived at by knowing the aims of the Shariʿah. In essence, this statement best characterizes the relationship between *maqāṣid* and ijtihad and the derivation of rulings."[2]

The premodern approach to ascertaining *maqāṣid* perhaps sufficed for a context wherein Muslim political power was prevalent and Islam was central to the state and informed its political system; and wherein the judiciary was based on fiqh and *uṣūl al-fiqh*. This, however, is not the case today. Rather, Muslim communities globally find themselves confronted with all sorts of new challenges that impinge on Islamic tradition. It is as such that there is a critical need to further develop and advance the role of *maqāṣid* for Muslims today. In what follows, we examine two key matters central to the development of the *maqāṣid*: the role of induction (*istiqrāʾ*) in ascertaining *maqāṣid*, and how the *maqāṣid* engage with matters of fiqh.

4.1 The Boundaries of Induction (*Istiqrāʾ*) and its Efficacy

Al-Shāṭibī's *al-Muwāfaqāt* established a methodology to approaching the texts (Qur'an and Sunnah) wherein induction (*istiqrāʾ*) was used to derive universals, going beyond the mere gathering of dispersed particulars. Offering a Qur'anic basis for this approach, he tells us, "What is meant by "guard" in the verse, 'We have, without doubt, sent down the Message; and We will assuredly guard it (from corruption)' (15:9),[3] is the preservation of the universal or holistic principles in the Qur'an. And that is also what is meant in the verse, 'This day have I perfected your religion for you' (5:3).[4] In other words, these Qur'anic verses do not refer to merely preserving particulars, but rather universals."[5] Induction in and of itself is no more than giving proper consideration to the particulars of the Shariʿah in relation to the universals that encompass them. We should note, as al-Raysuni reminds us, that in addition to induction, al-Shāṭibī defined the following four other ways in which the objectives of the *Shāriʿ* may be determined: (1) consideration of primary, explicit commands and admonitions; (2) consideration of general commands and admonitions; (3) consideration of secondary objectives; and (4) the *Shāriʿ's* silence concerning an issue despite that the context calls for clarification and *tashrīʿ*. With respect to induction, we can ascertain that it is the most important and the strongest method to discover and confirm a *maqṣid*.

In describing the relationship between the *maqāṣid*, ijtihad, and Qur'an, al-Shāṭibī goes on to tell us:

> If ijtihad is employed in order to derive rulings from Texts [ie., Qur'an verses of hadiths], knowledge of the Arabic language will be required. If, on the other hand, it is for the purpose of discerning the concepts of benefit and harm regardless of what particular texts have to say, this does not require knowledge of the Arabic language. Rather, all it requires is a holistic and detailed knowledge of the higher objectives of the Shariʿah.[6]

Al-Shāṭibī's statement nevertheless begs the question of whether it is sound and avoids conflict or contradiction? Let us reconsider it with the following understanding. If a matter of ijtihad pertains to the consideration of benefit and harm that is not directly dependent on textual linguistic analysis to determine the benefit and harm, and if we employ the *maqāṣid al-Sharīʿah* to decipher the benefit and harm, and if these *maqāṣid* are based on an inductive approach to the Sharīʿah Texts—an approach which requires knowledge of Arabic according to al-Shāṭibī—then this essentially means that we are in fact referring this matter of ijtihad to the *nuṣūṣ* (Sharīʿah Texts) by the indirect means of the *maqāṣid* (which, as we have mentioned, are arrived at through an inductive approach to the *nuṣūṣ* that requires knowledge of Arabic). Thus, it is appropriate to question the adequacy or clarity of al-Shāṭibī's differentiation of what requires the mastery of Arabic language and what does not.

Mustapha Tajdin points to this problematic statement of al-Shāṭibī and notes that Taha Abd al-Rahman tries to solve this apparent contradiction by saying that, as a term, *maqṣid* embodies three aspects: the signification of the text, its content as intent and sentiment, and the attainment of a goal. The first two require the knowledge of the Arabic language, while the third is rational and does not require Arabic language knowledge.[7]

Al-Shāṭibī and other *uṣūlis* would agree that an inductive approach to the *nuṣūṣ* relies heavily on knowledge of Arabic. The issue for *uṣūlis*, however, regards the validity of arriving at universals through induction. The issue arises due to the fact that an inductive approach to gather universals also necessitates exploring matters beyond the scope of fiqh and *uṣūl al-fiqh*. Nonetheless, it is through an inductive approach to the *nuṣūṣ* and exploring matters beyond the scope of fiqh and *uṣūl al-fiqh* that we may arrive at the *maqāṣid al-Sharīʿah*.

Yunus al-Sawalihi describes al-Shāṭibī's inductive approach as being two-fold, summarizing it as follows: (1) Deducing the predominant characteristics surrounding the text pertaining to a command or admonition such that it enables deciphering the general reason or *ʿillah* (underlying reason) behind that command or admonition; this being done through the modes of *ʿillah* determination that are at the core of the inductive approach (i.e., derivation, verification, and refinement of the basis of the rule); and (2) Deducing these reasons or *ʿillah*s specifically to capture a partial *maqāṣid*.[8] It appears, however, that this specific approach to determining particular *maqāṣid* may result in a contradiction of sorts, or undermine conformity and consistency within the theory. Probing too deeply into *uṣūl al-fiqh*, moreover, inevitably leads to the researcher being impacted by the differences of opinion in that branch of knowledge. Al-Sawalihi goes on to state, "What is perhaps most surprising in al-Shāṭibī's theory is his merging of the inductive processes of historical texts and Islamic texts for the purpose of ascertaining the *maqāṣid al-Sharīʿah*."[9] That is based on al-Shāṭibī's words, "The Ummah is unanimously agreed that the Shariʿah is established to preserve the five indispensables, which are: religion (*dīn*), life (*nafs*), intellect (*ʿaql*), lineage (*nasl*), and property (*māl*)."[10]

In examining al-Shāṭibī's work, one hardly finds any consideration of the experiences of other nations, neither in any of his arguments nor statements. Even where he does mention such experiences, it is not of any substance to have benefit. (On the other hand, we do find a serious study of human experience in Ibn ʿAshur's work.) In critiquing al-Shāṭibī's inductive approach and neglect of human experience, al-Sawalihi opines:

> Al-Shāṭibī's inductive methodology poses certain questions: (1) Why did he insist that the particulars which confirm the *maqāṣid al-Sharīʿah* within the framework of the texts are innumerable, despite that the texts of the Qurʾan and Sunnah are limited and finite?; (2) How credible is his inductive approach to the human experiences in the historical context of which he wrote?; and (3) What is the logical foundation for making a connection between an incomplete inductive approach to historical human experiences and a complete inductive approach in the field of Islamic texts? It is rather difficult to find clear answers to these questions in his *al-Muwāfaqāt*.[11]

Al-Sawalihi's critique is well-founded and important to understanding the methodological impediments that prevented al-Shāṭibī's *maqāṣid* theory from applying an inductive approach to history. This becomes all the clearer when we bear in mind Ibn Khaldūn's sociological approach and theory of history.

The study of social history is predicated on travelling through the earth and examining the experiences of previous nations. Discounting these experiences under the pretext that the Shariʿah is silent on them would be ill-advised, especially given that these experiences have no direct technical bearing on the derivation of Shariʿah rulings. These experiences, however, are invaluable in providing historical lessons that can inform the application of Islamic teachings with the change of time; rightly so, given what we hold to be the finality and universality of Islam. The Qurʾan, in fact, provides teaching lessons—including lessons pertaining to matters of belief—from historical accounts of previous peoples. It is such Qurʾanic accounts and their lessons that also formed the basis of Ibn Khaldūn's approach to history.

At this point it is appropriate to introduce the concept of *majārī al-ʿādāt*, which is a critical concept in al-Shāṭibī's thought and which he repeatedly used. He invoked this term in several related contexts that point to three dimensions: (1) the experiences of societies in different aspects of life; (2) what people of wisdom would judge as moral and right; and (3) social laws in reference to personal responsibility judged according to the principle of causation in the relationship between cause and effect. This concept is crucial because al-Shāṭibī repeatedly asserted that the Shariʿah could never clash with *majārī al-ʿādāt*— the preponderant ways established in the human experience.

Furthermore, al-Shāṭibī used a closely related concept, *maḥāsin al-ʿādāt*, invoked specifically in the context of *ʿurf*, such as marriage norms, norms in adornments, and the level at which ornamentation would not be considered excessive (*isrāf*). He specifically used this concept in weighing Sufi ascetic behaviors and what of their lifestyle would be considered harsh and negligence in the eyes of Shariʿah.

Al-Shāṭibī goes on to discuss the notion and role of empirical generalities in reference to *maqsid* as being of two types, one type corresponds to *ḍarūriyyāt* and *ḥājiyyāt* (indispensables and exigencies), while the other corresponds to *taḥsīniyyāt* (enhancements). Al-Shāṭibī says:

> One type pertains to general ways of conduct that do not differ from one era, nation, or set of circumstances to another, such as eating and drinking, or rejoicing and mourning... The second type pertains to what varies according to time, place, and circumstance, such as styles of dress and dwelling, and particular social habits and mannerisms.[12]

Such division of the preponderant of human behavior mirrors the division of *ahkam* (regulations) in Shariʿah, where they are also of two types:

One that is sanctioned by a *shar'ī* support, whether approving an action or disapproving it... or just allowing it as something permissible to act upon or not. The second type of the established ways is where there is no positive or negative *shar'ī* support toward it [i.e., the Shari'ah is silent about it]. [13]

This is the closest point of convergence between the discourses of al-Shāṭibī and Ibn Khaldūn. Nevertheless, the focus of al-Shāṭibī is how the application of *aḥkam* stays in harmony with empirical generalities, while the focus of Ibn Khaldūn is how empirical generalities form the inner logic of the movement of history including the movement of Islam itself. Yet, both of their works point to the concurrence of reason and revelation.

Al-Shāṭibī's theory was a breakthrough with regard to achieving one type of the *Shāri''s* objectives, which he expresses by saying, "The *Shāri''s* objective with the Shari'ah is to liberate the *mukallaf* (the competent and responsible person in the sight of Allah) from the control of his whims and desires, so that he becomes an *'abd* of Allah by choice, just as he is by necessity." [14] Understanding that there is this type of objective points to the necessity of differentiating between objectives concerning the *mukallaf* and those aims of the Shari'ah which will inevitably be broader and more comprehensive.

A further question is whether an inductive approach to the Shari'ah Texts through the methodology of *uṣūl al-fiqh* is reliable, or whether the science of *kalām* (natural theology) can offer an alternative or supplemental methodology? The science of *uṣūl al-fiqh* is aimed at defining the rulings intended by the *Shāri'* on the basis of the *nuṣuṣ*, so as to direct and shape real-life situations in accordance with those rulings, and then to practically apply them. The science of *kalām*, on the other hand, seeks to achieve the same goal but in a manner using a method that seeks to purify real-life and eliminate false and deviant concepts. The scholar of *kalām*, however, will never be able to achieve this unless he understands the sound rulings according to which he should shape real-life situations. [15]

It should be noted here that it is not that induction is not a powerful tool in exploring *maqāṣid*, rather, *maqāṣid* cannot be adequately formed by induction alone. And whether we agree with the view of Ibn Ḥazm, that precedence should be given to knowledge based on demonstration (*burhān*) over that based on inductive analysis (*istiqrā'*), or the view of al-Rāzī, that experience leads to certainty while inductive analysis leads to knowledge that is based on conjecture, or Ibn Taymiyyah on the uncertainty of logical deduction, or the view of the scholars of *uṣūl al-fiqh*, that precedence should be given to inductive analysis, whichever view we favor, the matter does not go beyond being knowledge that is relative and is thus not absolute. In regard to knowledge based on demonstration, no matter its strength, this knowledge does not go beyond the level of speculative certainty. And it may be undermined by another matter that is also based on speculative certainty, because certainty that is based on experience and demonstration is limited and cannot, under any circumstances, refute all that could undermine the conditions and methods used to reach this certainty. The same applies to knowledge that is based on inductive analysis; even when it is preponderant, it cannot go beyond the level of conjecture. Rather, that which is designated as preponderant comes under the category of prevalent and not under the category of absolute certain facts—in accordance with al-Ghazālī's characterization—regardless of whether it concerns natural sciences, laws that govern the universe, or fiqh issues that are based on corroborative evidence and the way in which universal and *uṣūlī* principles are derived.

As for rulings pertaining to matters which do not come under the categories of faith and the unseen, such as rulings that have to do with organizing everyday life or guidelines pertaining to conduct, such rulings are even further removed from attaining the level of absolute certainty. Regardless of the extent to which scholars strive to identify reasons for and the objectives behind these rulings, their efforts will not procure a level of absolute certainty wherein a majority of scholars will confer (i.e., you will find scholars who, in examining the same issues, will have different outcomes).

There are thus certain subjectivities and biases in the one performing the demonstration or inductive analysis that may inevitably lead to different results. Al-Ṣawalihi goes on to summarize his thorough examination of al-Shāṭibī's work in thirteen points that express his appreciation for al-Shāṭibī's brilliant contribution, while being critical in that he "was unsuccessful in clarifying the problematic issues in inductive analysis."[16] We should note that there are but a few major matters that are of definitive certainty. And these are not arrived at only through rational evidence (whether by means of demonstration or inductive analysis), but rather through faith and universal concepts.

The aforementioned discussion affirms the relative nature of human knowledge; so long as there is a divine text and human reasoning, the interaction between the two will be endless. It is an interaction which enriches and enables Islam to be universal and eternal. Undoubtedly, the current weak state of the Ummah is a by-product, as al-Alwani has suggested, of a fissure between revelation and reason. The notion that human knowledge is relative in nature, however, should not lead us to discredit conclusions based on rational arguments, possibilities, certainties, and empirical proof. Rather, any knowledge that we inherit—including that which has come from the most esteemed scholars whom we believe God has granted deep understanding, and whose writings have for centuries been important sources for Muslims—is knowledge that is subject to the constraints of time and place (a constant feature of human nature). This human knowledge that we have inherited should be revisited. In fact, it should be reassessed and developed further. To do so is perhaps the greatest way of honoring such knowledge, and it is an acknowledgement of the work of pioneering scholars who provided the foundation for it. It is no wonder that the knowledge we have inherited has included differences on particular issues; even on matters wherein there was purported consensus. Claiming consensus can only be invoked if we mean by it the universals of Islam, not the particulars of ijtihad.[17]

4.2 The Relationship between the *Maqāṣid* and Fiqh

Most writings on *maqāṣid* try to link the *maqāṣid al-Sharīʿah* to the rulings of the Shariʿah, even though these various writings differ in the degree of the connection between them and the extent to which they regard the *maqāṣid* as directing and guiding the fiqh process. These writings, moreover, engage with the *maqāṣid* in a manner similar to the way in which *uṣūl al-fiqh* engages with fiqh. Just as *uṣūl al-fiqh* provides guidelines for the process of deriving detailed rulings, the *maqāṣid* are regarded as a means to help consolidate all fiqh issues within a single framework and to understand the wisdom and reasons behind the rulings, while also helping guide the jurist when approaching new issues. If you study and reflect on much of what has been written about the *maqāṣid al-Sharīʿah*, you will find that it has been limited to examining different fiqh views and attempting to resolve which views are more correct on the basis of understanding the *maqāṣid al-Sharīʿah* and to broaden the concept of *al-maṣāliḥ al-mursalah* (public welfare) and their utilization. I shall refer to the juristic differences without going into detail (because the point here does not concern accepting or rejecting these details).

According to al-Shāṭibī, there are three ways to ascertain the aims of Shariʿah: (1) explicit texts from the Qur'an or Sunnah; (2) identifying the basis or reason (*ʿillah*) of Islamic rulings; and (3) an inductive analysis of the Qur'an and Sunnah. In expounding on the relationship between the *maqāṣid* and *uṣūl al-fiqh*, Ibn ʿAshur says:

> If we want to lay down definitive and categorical principles for the understanding of the Shariʿah, we need to return to the traditionally accepted propositions of *uṣūl al-fiqh* and reformulate them. We should critically evaluate them, rid them of the alien elements that crept into them, and supplement them with the results of thorough comprehension and careful thought. Then, we need to reformulate the whole and classify it as an independent discipline called "science of the higher aims of the Shariʿah" (*ʿilm maqāṣid al-Sharīʿah*). In other words, we should leave the discipline of *uṣul al-fiqh* as it is, a source from which the methods of formulating *fiqhi* argumentation could be derived. As for those elements of it which fall within the purview of our purpose of systematizing the study of *maqāṣid al-Sharīʿah*, we should incorporate them as part of the foundational principles of this noble discipline: *ʿilm maqāṣid al-Sharīʿah*.[18]

Ibn ʿAshur, moreover, believed it was imperative for jurists (more so than ordinary people) to know the aims of Shariʿah. In expounding on who should know the *maqāṣid*, he states:

> Not every *mukallaf* is required to know *maqāṣid al-Sharīʿah*, for this is a subtle kind of knowledge. The duty of lay people is to learn the ordinances of Shariʿah and accept them without being required to know their purposes (*maqāṣid*), for they do not possess the capacity and skill to identify and apply them accurately in their proper context. Ordinary people should be introduced to the knowledge of the *maqāṣid* gradually

in tandem with the increase of their studies of the various Islamic disciplines. This is to avoid their incorrect application of the *maqāṣid* that they are taught, with undesirable results, thus defeating the true purpose of this knowledge. It is the duty of the learned to comprehend these *maqāṣid*; as we have already mentioned, scholars vary in this according to their competence and understandings.[19]

We can clearly understand why Ibn ʿAshur places responsibility for knowing the objectives with the jurists (as opposed to including ordinary people as well) when we consider his methodology for ascertaining the *maqāṣid*. Included in this methodology are: (1) two types of inductive analysis (*istiqrāʾ*), with one type being an exhaustive examination of the provisions and commands, whose effective causes are known, and the second type being examining the numerous textual proofs of Shariʿah commands and rules (*aḥkām*) that have a common underlying reason (*ʿillah*); (2) Qurʾanic textual proofs whose connotations are clear such that, according to the Arabic usage, it is very unlikely that their meaning is something other than what is apparent (*ẓāhir*); and (3) through the contiguously transmitted traditions (*sunnah mutawātirah*). It is quite evident that these three methods are fiqh methods used to derive fiqh rulings and are also being used to ascertain the *maqāṣid*, potentially diminishing the *maqāṣid* from the level of objectives to the level of principles and guidelines.

The problem that thus arises in many writings on *maqāṣid* is that they are heavily influenced by the logic and methods applied in the science of fiqh, which in return can impose unnecessary restrictions to the process of ascertaining *maqāṣid*. Put differently, applying the methods of fiqh can result in the tendency to become distracted by the means at the expense of arriving at the aims, and therefore not maximizing the potential of ascertaining comprehensive *maqāṣid* that are widely applicable in scope.

In discussing the role of Arabic under the chapter heading "Insufficiency of the Literal Methodology without Knowledge of Higher Objectives," Ibn ʿAshur says, "Never has speech in any human language, nor any of its genres and styles in a particular language, been sufficient by itself to indicate the intent (*maqṣid*) of the speaker in such a way that would preclude any possibility of doubt about the signification (*dalālah*) of his words."[20] He then goes on to say, "If having deep knowledge of the Arabic language and the miraculous nature of the Qurʾan is of great help in knowing the meaning intended by God (in a particular verse)... then understanding the objectives of the *Shāriʿ* behind Islamic rulings will be of greater help in understanding the meaning intended by the *Shāriʿ*."[21]

We previously referred to the problem of introducing the notion of blocking or unblocking the means that may lead to considerable harm in the context of the *maqāṣid*. Let me add some further notes to this discussion. According to Ibn ʿAshur:

> If we regard blocking the means as being one of the fundamentals of deriving rulings, and blocking those means is appropriate in some circumstances, then the scholars of ijtihad are to be entrusted with examining the circumstances to determine whether means should be blocked or not. They should do this by determining whether unblocking a particular means will still lead to harm. So long as that is the case, then it is to be blocked. But when it will no longer lead to harm the matter will revert to the original ruling.[22]

Ibn ʿAshur discusses this under the heading "The Shariʿah tends to avoid prescribing detailed regulations" and in the context of discussing *muʿāmalāt* (human transactions or interactions), which the *nuṣuṣ* do not discuss in detail, unlike acts of worship. The notion that *muʿāmalāt* are not discussed in detail is something that Muslims must bear in mind at times when they are confronted with new issues. Practically speaking, however, this point has no bearing on the subject of *maqāṣid*; that is, the aim behind the field of *maqāṣid al-Sharīʿah* is to provide general guidelines, and not to help the jurist find precise answers to perplexing issues. Ibn ʿAshur states:

> One more thing must be pointed out here concerning the understanding of the Shariʿah and practice of ijtihad. It is the distinction between excessiveness (*ghuluw*) and the blocking of means. Indeed, this is a subtle distinction, for while the question of the blocking of means arises whenever there is depravity, excessiveness means the indulgence in subjoining a permissible practice to what is obligatory or forbidden. Excessiveness includes also performing some Shariʿah prescriptions

in a more difficult way than what is actually required, on the pretext of fearing to fall short of the *Shāriʿ's* purpose. This attitude has been described in the Sunnah as exaggeration (*taʿammuq*) and hair-splitting (*tanaṭṭuʿ*).

Excessiveness thus exists at different levels. It may be clarified as devoutness (*waraʿ*), whether individually by committing oneself to some difficult practices or by compelling others to accept hardship. Other degrees of excessiveness may belong to blameworthy whispering (*waswasah*). Here, indeed, jurists and jurisconsults are faced with a serious challenge. They ought to avoid the pitfall of excessiveness and be careful what measures they prescribe for the people.[23]

It may be said that the concept of *maṣāliḥ mursalah* (public welfare and unrestricted interests) that are in harmony with the aims of Shariʿah but for which there is no particular textual evidence, is broad enough and can substitute for the concept of *maqāṣid*. However, the concept of *maṣlaḥah* is often limited in application to a specific matter and connected to a particular ruling. The concept of *maqāṣid*, to be theoretically enabling, should be broader and more comprehensive than the concept of *maṣāliḥ* in order for the former to serve as the general guidelines of Shariʿah.

Al-Shāṭibī had expanded the avenues of derivation beyond what was prevalent among *fuqahas* (jurists), as did Ibn ʿAshur to an even greater extent. A hallmark of Ibn ʿAshur's *maqāṣid* theory, in fact, was to go beyond the concept of *ʿillah* (justification for a ruling) and to search for the greater wisdom behind Shariʿah from within the purview of procuring or enhancing benefit and repelling or reducing harm. It behooves us to further develop *maqāṣid* theory such that it can address all aspects of societies' needs. Achieving this requires judiciously building upon the contributions of earlier scholars, while also setting aside aspects of their contributions which may inhibit such development.

4.3 Review of Key Concepts in *Maqāṣid* Thought

This section attempts to offer a further exposition of key concepts critical to understanding and applying *maqāṣid* thought. We begin with a discussion of *maṣlaḥah* as it is prone to being misunderstood and manipulated. We then address the concept of *ḍarūrah* (i.e., the notion of necessity or that which is indispensable), a concept that when misrepresented, unnecessarily constrains the framework of Shariʿah. We follow this by expounding on the concept of *ḥifẓ* (preservation), which is also prone to misunderstanding that can result in the misapplication of Shariʿah. Lastly, we provide discussion regarding whether the *maqāṣid* should be limited to the traditional five or expanded.

A. *Maṣlaḥah*

The term *maṣlaḥah* has been frequently used, and we remind again that it cannot be reduced to interest in the narrow sense, and it subsumes the meanings of welfare well-being, benefits, and Shariʿah-recognized interests including public interests. Ahmad al-Raysuni holds that there has been renewed discourse on the issue of reconciling between *nuṣuṣ* (Shariʿah Texts) and the principle of *maṣlaḥah*, projecting that it will become a central issue of discourse in our time, much like those discourses pertaining to the reconciliation between the *naṣ* and reason, *aḥād* hadiths (transmitted by a singular chain of narrators), captious theological questions regarding whether the Qurʾan is created, the Divine attributes, and other well-known issues throughout Islamic intellectual history that have been debated. The discourse pertaining to reconciling between *nuṣuṣ* and *maṣlaḥah* overlaps in many ways with the discourse surrounding the reconciliation between the Shariʿah Texts and reason, especially given that the latter discourse is part and parcel to informing the former. This latter discourse, as al-Raysuni notes, re-emerges in the early twentieth century through the thought of Jamal al-Din al-Qasimi and Rashid Rida, and is then revived in the mid-twentieth century by Mustafa Zayd and Abd al-Wahab Khallaf.[24]

Ibn ʿAshur, like al-Shāṭibī, designated three categories of *maṣlaḥah*, namely *al-ḍarūriyyāt* (indispensables), *al-ḥājiyyāt* (needs), and *al-taḥsīni-yyāt* (enhancements). He further added two broader categories, universal *maṣlaḥah* (concerning the Ummah as a whole) and particular *maṣlaḥah* (concerning a certain segment of the Ummah or certain individuals—i.e., having particular circumstances). With respect to particular *maṣlaḥah*, he designated three types: definitive, speculative, and illusionary. Ibn ʿAshur's taxonomy of *maṣlaḥah* certainly offers a great deal of benefit, especially in that it captures and accommodates the role of reason and experiential knowledge in the process of ascertaining and applying the *maqāṣid*.

Al-Raysuni's theory of *maṣlaḥah* offers further categorization and important detail. His taxonomy includes associating *maṣlaḥah* with each of the traditional five *ḍarūriyyāt* (indispensables). He also adds two broad categories of *maṣlaḥah*, that which is tangible and that which is intangible. Al-Raysuni, moreover, gives great consideration to the context of time when thinking about *maṣlaḥah*; meaning that with the passage of time, a *maṣlaḥah* may seize being a *maṣlaḥah* and may even become a *mafsadah* (harm), or vice versa. This indicates the importance of not basing *maqāṣid* on time sensitive matters such that the *maqāṣid* become susceptible to change in the same way that *maṣāliḥ* change according to time.[25]

Al-Raysuni disagrees with al-Ṭūfī's view that there could be a conflict between the principle of *maṣlaḥah* and Shariʿah Texts in the area of *muʿāmalāt* (human transactions and temporal affairs) and *ʿādāt* (customs), and that *maṣlaḥah* should be given precedence over the *nuṣuṣ*. He asserts that al-Ṭūfī failed to provide any evidence for his view and that it is but a theoretical assumption. Indeed, *maṣlaḥah* should never wield control over Shariʿah texts, and if ever there is a conflict between a perceived *maṣlaḥah* and soundly interpreted text, the latter should be given precedence. But even before arriving at such a conclusion, there of course should be a holistic and exhaustive treatment of the texts in an attempt to evaluate the *maṣlaḥah* before dismissing it; neither the empirical validity of *maṣlaḥah* is easily determined nor the implications of the text are static. Al-Raysuni's judicious engagement with *maṣlaḥah* must be understood in light of what he holds to be its distortion and misapplication by modernist thinkers, which he goes on to illustrate. For al-Raysuni, ijtihad must play a critical role in properly evaluating *maṣlaḥah*. He writes:

> I am not of the view that the texts will always provide detailed or specific answers concerning all types of benefit and harm and their different categorizations. However, I do maintain that the texts offer foundational support in the process of ascertaining benefit and harm. Nonetheless, the field of *maqāṣid* remains broad in scope and is ever-expanding, and scholars should continue to examine new issues and

circumstances, and weigh between various needs in light of Shariʿah texts and the sound standards they set.[26]

In my view, expressions used in reference to *maṣlaḥah* and *maṣāliḥ mursalah* are not sufficiently defined, and that is especially true when the means to achieve a *maṣlaḥah* is included in it. The problem that arises is when the means itself is given a status similar to a universal benefit (*maṣlaḥah kulliyyah*). This is problematic for two reasons: (1) There can be constant changes in the means to achieving a particular *maṣlaḥah*; and (2) The means may also be accompanied by or mixed with some partial harm. These reasons therefore may disqualify the means from being given such a universal status. What further exacerbates the difficulty in engaging with the means is that it is generally beyond the scope of the Islamic sciences to delve into a level of analytical examination of them such that their consequences, whether direct or indirect, can be adequately determined. This matter is especially pertinent today where we find the means are varied and abundant, and wherein jurists can generally identify some benefit in a given means even if consideration of it is not warranted, especially when operating in a global system that is not in tune with the Islamic perspective.

Another issue with respect to the subject of *maṣlaḥah* is that some of the well-known statements in reference to *maṣlaḥah* are so general and open-ended that they undermine the true meaning of *maṣlaḥah*. For example, the well-known statement, "Wherever there is a *maṣlaḥah*, there too is the Shariʿah of Allah" is undoubtedly too open-ended and may lead to misapplication. This statement can hold true only with a valid (i.e., scholarly vetted) *maṣlaḥah*. As such, and because this statement may lead to the misapplication of *maṣlaḥah*, it must be qualified by certain parameters, such as adding the caveat that it does not undermine the *maṣāliḥ* prescribed in Shariʿah, and that it does not contradict what is established, either explicitly or implicitly, by the Shariʿah texts. Yet, the addition of such conditions introduces tautology to the statement.

Scholars such as Ibn ʿAshur are of the view that it is more beneficial to focus on greater *maṣāliḥ* that are well-established, as doing so would make it more inclusive of many types of *maṣāliḥ* that the Shariʿah would promote. This is important given the vast number of developments in modern life, any one of which may inevitably have some interest it could serve. Such developments include those in the areas of health and disease control, agriculture, transportation, communication, and other developments in science and technology.

In concluding this section on *maṣlaḥah*, it is worth noting that usage of the term *maṣlaḥah* and the emphasis thereon in classical works may have been a scholarly reaction aimed at correcting the view held by many lay Muslims that the Shariʿah was something restrictive and burdensome. Emphasis on the concept of *maṣlaḥah*, therefore, came by way of responding to real-life issues. However, emphasizing that all of Shariʿah is aimed at fulfilling *maṣāliḥ* should not detract from the comprehensive nature of Shariʿah, and the fact that it is a path of guidance towards a good way of life in all affairs, including matters concerning which there is no specific textual reference.

Lastly, it is also worth noting here some general methodological observations with respect to *maṣlaḥah*:

1   Consideration should be given to both *maṣlaḥah* and *fiṭrah* (innate human nature), which thus allows for universal regularities to be given their due weight (much in the same way as the approach advanced by Ibn Khaldūn).

2   Limiting the references of *maṣlaḥah* to fiqh issues only may make us miss the broader political and socio-economic welfare of society.

3   *Maṣlaḥah* must be defined in a clear manner, and within an Islamic framework.

4   There is a specific need of expressing *maṣlaḥah* in a manner that stands clear from utilitarian thinking that is prevalent in our days.

5   Invoking *maṣāliḥ* in a manner which allows for exceptions is appropriate in applied fiqh issues, but it is not appropriate when discussing general issues of *maqāṣid*, because making exceptions may lead to undermining the original issue of *maqāṣid* under discussion and may restrict the broad scope of *maqāṣid*.

B. The Concepts of *Ḥifẓ* and *Ḍarūrah*

The term *ḥifẓ* (preservation) appeared early in the literature of *maqāṣid* and was considered self-explanatory. The term *ḍarūrah* (indispensability) is encountered in fiqh and in *uṣūl al-fiqh*, especially in regard to circumstances that make a

Muslim not able to do what is obligatory and required. However, *maqāṣid* used the concept of *ḍarūrah* in an abstract and broader sense.

Ḥifẓ (Preservation)

Al-Shāṭibī provided a general, twofold definition for the notion of *ḥifẓ al-maqāṣid* (preservation of the objectives). The first part of his definition is that *ḥifẓ al-maqāṣid* connotes setting up the pillars of the *maqāṣid* and reinforcing their foundation. This meaning thus concerns bringing the *maqāṣid* into existence. The second part is that *ḥifẓ al-maqāṣid* connotes protecting the *maqāṣid* from what could undermine it, including those things which exist at present or are expected to arise in the future. This meaning namely concerns protecting the existence of the *maqāṣid*.[27]

Regardless whether one agrees or disagrees with al-Shāṭibī's two-fold definition, it is relatively substantive and goes beyond a mere simplistic or literal rendering of *ḥifẓ al-maqāṣid*. What is not clear, however, is whether this notion of *ḥifẓ* refers only to *maqāṣid* that already exist and are to be preserved, or whether it also refers to preserving new *maqāṣid* that have come about as a result of Islam's passage through history? As we can see here, especially in the former case, the notion of *ḥifẓ* may be approached by some in a manner wherein it leads to stagnation, the idea being that things of the past are complete and perfect and in no need of further development through human intervention.

Hamid is of the view that use of the term *ḥifẓ* inhibited the *maqāṣid* from going beyond the individual and applying to society. Those who studied the *maqāṣid* understood the limitations implied by the term *ḥifẓ*, so they began to distinguish between *ḥifẓ* in the context of preserving *maqāṣid* that were already established and *ḥifẓ* in the context of preserving *maqāṣid* that included those yet to be established. Understanding *ḥifẓ* in the sense of the former context leaves the impression of stagnation and a lack of dynamism. As such, and to avoid such an impression, *ḥifẓ* should also be understood in the sense of the latter context.[28]

Al-Raysuni, however, strongly objects to the claim that we need to express the need to seek the *maṣāliḥ* [i.e., new *maqāṣid*][29] and not merely preserve them, saying, "This is wrong. When we say that the Shariʿah 'preserves' [i.e., preserves certain *maqāṣid*], it means that they already exist. In other words, there are some beneficial goals to attain first, and some harms to ward off."[30] Those who commented on al-Raysuni noted that the term *ḥifẓ* does not convey the notion of seeking (unless in a metaphorical sense), something which would be unacceptable to the majority of scholars, let alone common folk. It is therefore critical to identify a term that will genuinely capture both meanings [that al-Shāṭibī provided], or to use another term alongside *ḥifẓ*, such as in the expression "the realization and preservation of religion" (*taḥṣīl wa ḥifẓ al-dīn*). Al-Juwaynī had in fact offered a similar expression. In this regard, perhaps the phrase "the realization of the five indispensables" (*iqāmat al-ḍarūriyyāt al-khams*) is more appropriate since it is derived from the Qurʾanic expression, "Establish the religion" (*aqīmū al-dīn*) (42:13), and because it may be used with the other indispensables in such a way as to reflect both meanings, "realization" and "preservation."[31]

It is essential to bear in mind and add to our understanding of *ḥifẓ* the idea that we should continually examine matters. Preserving an objective—in the sense of establishing or protecting it—can only be achieved in accordance with procedures in which factors of time, place, and practicality interact with scholarly efforts to determine how to achieve preservation and protection. Perhaps the word *tazkiyyah* (purification), in the Qurʾanic sense, captures this; and it includes other shades of meaning such as revision, refining, cleansing, and to increase in efforts of following the right path.[32]

An understanding of the concept of *ḥifẓ al-dīn* (preserving religion) that makes it stagnant may lead to either restricting the concept or including everything associated with it, such as preserving morals and manners (which is a main feature of religion), preserving rational thinking (which is the basis of accountability), and preserving everything that the Shariʿah enjoins in all aspects of life. Thus, striving to preserve intellect, lineage, and wealth, is done in accordance with the teachings of religion. In other words, singling out *ḥifẓ al-dīn* as an isolated category is problematic, because the other objectives referred to in the theory of *maqāṣid* (namely intellect, human life, lineage, and wealth) are only to be preserved through understanding the teachings of religion—that is, it is not appropriate to put religion and the other four *maqāṣid* on the same analytical plane.

Ḍarūrah (Indispensability)

In turning to the notion of *ḍarūrah* [a notion that is part and parcel to *ḥifẓ* and whose practical application can pose issues], al-Shāṭibī defines it as "something that is essential to achieving interests in both religious and worldly terms, in such a way that if the *ḍarūrah* is not attained, then worldly affairs will not be conducted in a proper manner; rather they will be run in such a way that will lead to mischief, fighting, and loss of life, and in the hereafter there will be loss of salvation and of the bliss of paradise, which will result in clear loss."[33] And since the indispensable (*ḍarūrī*) is a very critical concept, let us cite the expanded definition that al-Shāṭibī gives, followed by critical assessment. Al-Shāṭibī says:[34]

The five indispensables, as rooted in the Qurʾan and detailed in the Sunnah, are as follows:

- Preservation of religion (*ḥifẓ al-dīn*). This is realized through three dimensions, namely *islām* (i.e., the normative outward features of Islam), *imān* (i.e., the normative beliefs of Islam), and *iḥsān* (i.e., the combined notion of beauty and excellence).

- Preservation of human life (*ḥifẓ al-nafs*). This is achieved in three ways, namely by: (1) establishing its foundation through the legitimacy of procreation, (2) ensuring its survival after its having come into existence by providing food and drink (thereby ensuring its survival from within), and (3) providing clothing and shelter (thereby ensuring its survival from without). The root of all these things is found in the Qurʾan and is elucidated in the Sunnah. Moreover, it is completed through three things: (1) protecting one's progeny from falling into that which is forbidden, such as sexual misconduct, (2) preserving the means by which one's progeny are nourished, including ensuring that they do not consume anything harmful or lethal.

- Preservation of lineal identity (*ḥifẓ al-nasab*). This falls in the same category, its principles being found in the Qurʾan, and their elucidation in the Sunnah.

- Preservation of wealth (*ḥifẓ al-māl*). This comes under the category of possessions and property, and on causing them to grow lest it not suffice for one's needs. Its complement consists in preventing circumstances or conditions which would interfere with the preservation of wealth—doing so through forcible deterrence, prescribed punishments, and guarantees; all of which are found in the Qurʾan and Sunnah.

- Preservation of intellect, or the faculty of reason (*ḥifẓ al-ʿaql*). This concerns that which will not corrupt it or undermine it (and is found in the

Qurʾan). Its complement consists in the legitimacy of a prescribed punishment or forcible deterrence. At the same time, there is no specific reference to it in the Qurʾan; hence, there is no specific ruling on it in the Sunnah. Rather, this has been left to the independent interpretation of the Muslim community.

We should add to these indispensables the preservation of honor (*ḥifẓ al-ʿarḍ*), for it is a well-founded principle in the Qurʾan and is further clarified in the Sunnah through the provisions pertaining to *liʿān*[35] and *qadhf*[36].[37]

Al-Raysuni defines *ḍarūrah* as "*maṣāliḥ* that we cannot do without and there is no way to avoid them."[38] In my view, the aforementioned definitions make *ḍarūrah* too restrictive. *Ḍarūrah* should not only apply to life-threatening, cataclysmic matters; rather, it should be more encompassing, but of course within certain boundaries.

Shariʿah cases involving the *ḍarūrah* to preserve life (*ḥifẓ al-nafs*) generally pertain to dispensations as a result of certain types of hardship that may arise from obligatory acts of worship, such as with the dispensations to break the obligatory fast or to perform *tayammum* (dry ablution) in order to avoid physical harm. Such cases reflect the wisdom and gentleness of the Shariʿah and fall under Shariʿah discourse in *uṣūl* concerning dispensations and avoiding hardship. But the concept should be expanded beyond the direct actions of worship. The *ḍarūrah* to preserve life (in the sense of physical well-being) is a matter of common sense which *maqāṣid* theory should emphasize but without necessarily having to define its parameters; for such parameters concerning the preservation of life may be informed by other areas of knowledge beyond the Islamic sciences, including the applied sciences and experiential knowledge.

As for that which is a *ḍarūrah* (indispensable) to preserving intellect (*ḥifẓ al-ʿaql*), it should include avoiding falsehood and affirming the notion of causality. It should also include meaningful reflection upon the Qurʾan and upon the creation of humans, animals, and other signs in the universe. Defining the boundaries or scope for what is indispensable to preserving the intellect can be challenging. Put differently, what are the fundamental or essential matters related to the intellect that are indispensable for survival? Is it mainly matters of knowledge and information? Or is it the ability to reason? The ability to reason, however, is an ability that is innate, and which also develops through life experience. I therefore believe that what is indispensable to preserving the intellect should be expanded in scope and should be in accordance with the Qurʾanic message for humankind to learn and increase in knowledge (as reflected in the Qurʾanic command to "read" (*iqra*); and in the verse, "Say: My Lord! Increase me in knowledge" (20:114); and in the Qurʾanic expression that God taught Prophet Adam all the names, 2:31). According to the Islamic message, the notion of learning and increasing in knowledge is part and parcel to fostering sound thinking that leads to both worldly and spiritual guidance.

In regard to the preservation of lineal identity (*ḥifẓ al-nasab*), reducing its understanding to its fundamental linguistic meaning (as in the case of the aforementioned *maqāṣid*), whereby it is conceived only in terms of preserving reproduction, will pose certain problems. With respect to the greater objective behind preserving lineal identity, Ibn ʿAshur states:

> By attributing children to their real fathers, the preservation of lineal identity (*ḥifẓ al-nasab*) undoubtedly endows the offspring with a deep sense of filial devotion and obedience to their parents, just as it instills in the parents a profound feeling of affection and compassion for their offspring. This is a real and deeply rooted element of human nature; it is in no way a figment of the imagination. The great concern of the Shariʿah about the protection of lineal identity and its confirmation beyond the slightest doubt stems from a profound consideration of an important psychological aspect of God's mystery in His fashioning of human beings. It's obvious and more immediate objective is to stabilize and enhance the establishment of the family and prevent all causes of disputes resulting from deep-rooted human jealousy or the parents' doubt about their offspring's lineage and vice versa.[39]

Ibn ʿAshur's notion of preserving lineal identity goes beyond the more restricted rendering of "reproduction" and offers comprehensive and broad concepts and ideas that are important to the proper fulfillment of preserving and protecting the family system and social structure. To neglect this conceptualization would undermine the family makeup and inevitably society.

In regard to the preservation of wealth (*ḥifẓ al-māl*), defining its indispensability (wherein which life would not be possible) is rather difficult. In other words, how do we define the bare minimum needed for the preservation of wealth? I ask this in light of the fact that there have been peoples throughout history who were able to adequately live on even the scarcest amount of wealth and provisions.

Similarly, how do we define indispensability as it applies to the preservation of religion (*ḥifẓ al-dīn*)? In other words, what is the bare minimum needed to preserve religion? If what is meant by the bare minimum with regard to religion is that human life would not be possible without belief in the right religion, then there would not have been many nations to have lived (and are still living) with aberrant or purely mythical beliefs. In fact, there are entire civilizations based on religions that we do not consider to be rightly guided. If what is meant by indispensable with regard to religion is the establishment of its fundamental obligations, then there would be no need for the *maqāṣid* to even have to articulate the notion of preserving religion, for establishing the fundamental obligations is already self-evident in the religion.

Finally, it is worth noting here that the concept of *ḍarūrah* (indispensability) in *maqāṣid* writings has generally applied to individuals. However, if we confine *ḍarūrah* to individuals and restrict its application to only matters wherein life becomes impossible, the concept's application to people's lives will not be positively effectuated. An example of what we mean here is in the case wherein a *ḍarūrah* required to save the life of one individual actually leads to the death of others if applied to them. This is an unfortunate consequence of individualism. Paradoxically, prominent proponents of individualism have recently modified their views in recognition that collective cooperation is essential for the survival of all. However, they have not abandoned the underpinnings behind their philosophy; a philosophy which generally conflicts with Islamic ethics as well as those of other religions. The reason the field of *maqāṣid* has historically focused on individuals is because it has been informed by the notion of accountability, a notion which tends to apply to the individual more than the collective. But the notion of establishing religion (i.e., wherein religious culture—teachings, beliefs, values, and practices—manifest within a community) is best realized through the collective (and concern for the collective) rather than individualistically (and concern only for an individual's self-interest).

To restate, confining the meaning of *ḍarūrah* to only matters wherein physical life becomes impossible is unwise and will prove more problematic than beneficial. As such, when considering the *maqāṣid al-Sharīʿah* and defining what is a *ḍarūrah* (i.e., its boundaries), it is essential to keep in mind that the Shariʿah aims to offer guidance for all humankind to a unique form of virtuous life that takes care of its physical aspects without being reduced to it. It is a basic feature of Islam's worldview that there is a solid connection between the destiny of people in the Hereafter and their actions in life, where following the way of the Shariʿah has also blessings on the life on earth.

In that respect, Ibn Taymiyyah remarks that acts of worship ultimately serve *maṣāliḥ* in this world and in the hereafter. This holds true regardless of whether these acts are outward such as the ritual prayer or "inward such as belief in Allah, His angels, His books, and His messengers, and the conditions of the heart and its actions,[40] such as loving Allah, being watchful of Him, sincere devotion to Him, trusting in Him, hoping for His mercy, calling upon Him, and other such matters that come under this category" of *maṣāliḥ*.[41]

We should also note al-Shāṭibī's statement, "Preserving religion (i.e., Islam) essentially entails preserving three dimensions, *islām* (i.e., the normative outward features of Islam), *imān* (i.e., the normative beliefs of Islam), and *iḥsān* (i.e., the combined notion of beauty and excellence)."[42] These three dimensions, however, are very broad and difficult to capture within an *uṣulī* framework. The question then is, how can we apply the three concepts of indispensables (*ḍarūriyyāt*), exigencies (*ḥājiyyāt*), and enhancements (*taḥsīniyyāt*) to the three dimensions of preserving religion, namely *islām*, *imān*, and *iḥsān*? Moreover, how do we reconcile these concepts and dimensions with the four-fold standard developed in Ibn ʿAshur's theory, in which he stipulated the condition that for something to be a *maqṣid* it should be "fixed, apparent, well-defined, and consistent"?[43]

In thus referring to the historical debate regarding knowledge based on Shariʿah texts or rational thinking, the approach that should be taken is to examine both humanity's experiences in light of the substance and purport of Shariʿah texts, in addition to an inductive analysis of the texts themselves. But the issue, from a theoretical point of view, is the conflict between what we are meant to achieve in a broad sense and trying to have the precise definition. It should be noted that some contemporary writings by non-specialists go to extremes in using the term indispensable (*ḍarūrī*) to include every feature of modern life, forgetting that such features are deemed indispensable only if we accept the secular orientation of modern life and consider it an end worthy of being pursued. To the contrary, the concept of indispensable (*ḍarūrī*) should be only mobilized within an Islamic framework and its renewed perspective on modernity. The final chapter of this book will use the concept of indispensable (*ḍarūrī*) in a way close to Ibn ʿAshur's, after making it more abstract to account for the necessary conditions for the functioning of a unique Islamic system, on both the individual and collective levels.

C. Categorizing and Ordering into Indispensables (*Ḍarūriyyāt*), Exigencies (*Ḥājiyyāt*), and Enhancements (*Taḥsīniyyāt*)

Undoubtedly, the three-tier categorization of indispensables (*ḍarūriyyāt*), exigencies (*ḥājiyyāt*), and enhancements (*taḥsīniyyāt*) introduced by al-Juwaynī is among the important features of *maqāṣid* theory. These categories allow the theory to be more effective, comprehensive, and facilitate analysis. They essentially enable the theory to be dynamic and thus steer it away from a narrow understanding that can lead to its misapplication.

We have already discussed the definition of indispensables (*ḍarūriyyāt*). As for the meaning of exigencies (*ḥājiyyāt*), these are matters that are needed in order to alleviate constraints that typically lead to hardship—hardship that can occur in such areas as worship, customary practices, human transactions, and criminal cases. Thus, if exigencies are neglected, people will generally experience hardship. It should be noted, however, that such hardship is not to the extent that it undermines public welfare as the case is with indispensables (*ḍarūriyyāt*). With respect to enhancements (*taḥsīniyyāt*), what is meant is the adoption of that which is of excellence in customs and traditions, and the avoidance of that which is abominable (which people of sound and mature thinking would refrain from). Matters of enhancements generally pertain to the realm of *akhlāq* (virtuous conduct).[44]

Al-Shāṭibī highlights the relationship between these levels in a very clear manner, telling us, "Having established that enhancements are in the service of and complementary to exigencies, and that exigencies are in the service of and complementary to indispensables, it should then be understood that the indispensables are central [and therefore foundational to the exigencies and enhancements]."[45] Al-Shāṭibī goes on to expound on the meaning of this statement in the form of the following five principles:

1   The indispensables are the foundation for exigencies and enhancements.

2   Disorder in relation to the indispensables will lead to complete disorder in the latter two.

3   An imbalance in the realm of the exigencies or enhancements does not necessitate an imbalance in the indispensables.

4   A complete imbalance in the realm of enhancements or exigencies may lead to a partial imbalance in the realm of indispensables.

5   Exigencies and enhancements must be preserved for the sake of the indispensables.[46]

Al-Shāṭibī's hierarchal outline here signifies the complex nature in the relationship and overlap between these three levels. In regard to this, Bin Bayyah confers the importance of observing the interactions between these levels.[47] Al-Raysuni holds that sequencing the indispensables is of little benefit from a practical point of view because they are so interconnected. He thus finds it more appropriate to imagine them as concentric circles. He goes on to add that if what is indispensable is undermined, then other indispensables may also be undermined. Moreover, he holds that conflict between indispensables could not occur, in essence; with the exception being only in minor or tangential matters related to these indispensables.[48]

Al-Raysuni also notes Ibn ʿAshur's rejection of associating indispensable objectives with penal matters only, deeming that this would confine these objectives to very few issues pertaining to individual behavior. This, he tells us, is contrary to Ibn ʿAshur's overall theory, which is distinguished for its expansion of the *maqāṣid al-Sharīʿah* to take into account societal issues on an Ummah-wide level.[49]

Thus, when it comes to societal issues, there should be no set limit in the application of *maqāṣid*. Moreover, it is evident that applying *maqāṣid al-Sharīʿah* (including the three levels of indispensables, exigencies, and enhancements) to societal issues requires the treatment of matters having to do with the civilizational architecture (*ʿumrān*) and, therefore, delving into branches of knowledge and sciences that can assist in evaluating the category of *maqāṣid* which these matters belong (i.e., indispensables, exigencies, or enhancements). Having these three categories of *maqāṣid* signifies the Sharī'ah's embrace of discursive juristic methods and its ability to adapt and address various issues. This especially holds true for the following reasons: (1) the modus operandi for the categories of indispensables, exigencies, and enhancements includes the consideration of time and place; and (2) the *maqāṣidic* approach to the Sharī'ah texts involves a reason-based consideration of practical situations and circumstances.

Some commentators on *maqāṣid* theory, such as philosopher Taha Abd al-Rahman, reject the hierarchal prioritization of these three categories, believing that it detracts from the distinct quality of each of them (*tabayun*).[50] Al-Raysuni holds that, "This three-fold division is based on ijtihad; it is approximate and no more."[51] However, Riyad Adhami resolves the matter in suggesting that each of the five indispensable aims of Sharī'ah occur at one of the three categories of indispensables, exigencies, and enhancements, and therefore producing fifteen levels of priorities. As such, if there is a conflict between two objectives, then any indispensable objective takes precedence over that which is exigent, and any exigent objective takes precedence over that which is an enhancement, regardless of which of the five objectives it is connected to. If two indispensable objectives or two exigent objectives are at the same level, then precedence is given to the one that is connected to the higher aim of Sharī'ah. From this we may understand that there is the following order of prioritization in the event of a conflict: (1) that which is indispensable for the preservation of religion, (2) that which is indispensable for the preservation of human life, (3) that which is indispensable for the preservation of lineal identity, (4) that which is indispensable for the preservation of intellect, and (5) that which is indispensable for the preservation of wealth; then (6) that which is exigent for the preservation of religion, (7) that which is exigent for the preservation of human life, (8) that which is exigent for the preservation of lineal identity, (9) that which is exigent for the preservation of intellect, (10) and that which is exigent for the preservation of wealth; then (11) that which is an enhancement for the preservation of religion, (12) that which is an enhancement for the preservation of human life, (13) that which is an enhancement for the preservation of lineal identity, (14) that which is an enhancement for the preservation of intellect, and (15) that which is an enhancement for the preservation of wealth. Based on the aforementioned, the practical implementation of *maqāṣid al-Sharīʿah* becomes possible for the general public.[52]

D. Are the Indispensable (*Ḍarūriyyāt*) *Maqāṣid* Limited to Five?

Limiting the indispensables of Shariʿah to five or otherwise has nothing to do with identifying *maqāṣid*; rather, it has to do with the art of theorizing. Any academic effort to do so must be focused on whether there is good reason to include another objective as something secondary to a major indispensable objective. Perhaps keeping five indispensable objectives has the advantage of enabling us to easily refer to the writings of earlier scholars and benefitting from what they wrote; otherwise, there is no rational reason not to add to these five objectives if it becomes apparent that limiting the number to five does not suffice. Al-Raysuni asserts that, "Limiting the indispensable [*maqāṣid*] to five, even though there is something approaching consensus regarding them, requires review and examination."[53] Moreover, he holds that what is expected from research on this matter is:

> ...a re-examination of the issue of limiting the known indispensables to five, because these five indispensables are held in high esteem and have great power and authority. Therefore, we should not refrain from adding to these five some other indispensable objectives of which the religious texts spoke highly, and which are no less important and comprehensive than these five indispensables. Moreover, limiting them to five was a matter decided through ijtihad, and adding to the five is something that was discussed by classical scholars, as we have already seen.[54]

Similarly, al-Raysuni calls for further detailed study of complementary indispensables, exigencies (*ḥājiyyāt*), and enhancements (*taḥsīniyyāt*), and for work to be undertaken to set clear guidelines for differentiating between the different categories of all objectives, and determining what is fixed and what is variable in that regard.[55] Hassani calls for a broadening of our understanding of the thought surrounding the topic of *maqāṣid*, believing that by doing so we can better arrive at the aims of Shariʿah, whether related to the embedded meanings of Shariʿah, or related to the objectives that are intended to be achieved through the prescription of certain rulings and beliefs. That is because the science of *maqāṣid* is based on three principles: (1) Understanding what is beneficial (*fāʾidah*) (which is different from the notion of a *maṣlaḥah* to be served); (2) the justification of *maṣlaḥah*; and (3) Understanding the *fiṭrah* (innate human nature), because it cannot be imagined that the Creator Who revealed regulations would allow His law to contradict innate human nature.[56]

In his book *Al-Kulliyyāt al-Asāsiyyah li al-Sharīʿah al-Islāmiyyah*, al-Raysuni reiterates, "It is important to go beyond the five indispensables and their core meanings, and to include some major concepts that have an impact on people's lives at an individual and communal level."[57] He gives several examples of general or universal (*kullī*) concepts to be found in the Qurʾan, such as establishing justice and doing good (*iḥsān*) (cf. 16:90), and he tells us that, "These are the primary foundational principles under which come details, particulars, and applications. Religion as a whole is based on these clear, holistic principles, and all the teachings stem from them."[58] He says, furthermore, that the five indispensables are subject to two considerations: "The first is that they are among the universal or main ideas of Shariʿah; and the second is that they are known in all other religions."[59] Al-Raysuni goes on to emphasize the idea that the universals are comprehensive, and he includes good moral conduct to be among them. He says, "It behooves us not to include good moral conduct as a universal, as those matters related to it are by their very nature universal."[60]

Other scholars who advocate the expansion of *maqāṣid* include the philosopher Taha Abdul Rahman, in addition to al-Najjar and Attia as we have seen. Yet, the expansion could come in the form of identifying additional *maqāṣid* or increasing the scope of existing *maqāṣid*. Allowing the expansion of *maqāṣid* enables the Shari'ah to attain new and global horizons. This and other methodological issues will be discussed in the coming chapter.

5

Notes on Methodology

This chapter discusses certain matters of methodology pertaining to *maqāṣid* theory that are important for understanding the direction of this study and how it should be approached. The first matter concerns theorization; a critical matter especially given that the current approach in theorization in the field of *maqāṣid* may lead to what undermines its value. The second matter pertains to secondary theorization issue, which is aimed at explaining the relationship between Shariʿah, fiqh, and law. The third and fourth matters concern central concepts such as the *nafs* (holistic self),[1] *fiṭrah* (innate human nature), and freedom. It is imperative to discuss these and explain what they are, especially that they are central to *maqāṣid* and are situated differently in this book's *ʿumrānī* perspective in particular. Lastly, the fifth matter addresses the different levels of reading Islamic texts, wherein is offered an introduction to explain the methodology of this research.

5.1 Notes on Theorization

Many are contributing to the topic of *maqāṣid* these days as part of what may be characterized as the revival and overhaul of *maqāṣid* theory—perhaps one of the most important duties and vital priorities of the Ummah today. But what are the conditions that should be stipulated for the process of renewal and overhaul in different fields, including the Islamic sciences? Renewal can come from within the circle of eminent scholarship in a given field, or it can come from without. There is no field that can afford to disallow any contribution but that of its own specialists, especially if it is a field that has to do with religion, which is the concern of the entire Ummah.

What is usually required of one who wants to contribute to a field is to conduct thorough research in order to learn the views of earlier scholars on various major issues, then to add to it by refuting or revising some of them and suggesting more fit alternatives. People from outside the field should be exempted from delving in the minute details of the established field. Indeed, the mission of the contribution of the outsider's attempt at renewal is to forgo certain restrictions and points of contentions that arrest the well established fields. The one who comes from outside does not want to be bound by barriers that were set up in that field, because the advantage of renewal from without and what is hoped for from that contribution is the bypassing of those barriers that kept that field in a state of stagnation. This does not mean that there are no conditions to be stipulated for one who wants to contribute from outside a narrow specialty; rather there are certain conditions, which are as follows:

- One should be aware of different views in the field to which they want to contribute, and the major trends within that specialty.
- One should have a good grasp of the terminology used in this specialty.
- One should have a sound understanding of the basic issues in this specialty and should not frequently err in it, apart from the occasional slip.
- One should have good analytical scheme, so that the contribution goes beyond casual impressions.

Undoubtedly, *uṣūl al-fiqh* is a significant science that has attained a high level of subtlety. Ironically, its full development prevents further creative development. This is not so unusual as it occurs with any science when it reaches a mature stage. It is because a field has reached an advanced level of maturity, its specialists become able to deflect any challenge, even if it was corrective and constructive. By virtue of its maturity, a well-established crystalized field develops answers to critique to the extent that it denies the possibility of further additions. This is a well-known phenomenon discussed in the sociology of knowledge research as well as in the history of sciences. Also, the availability of resources to a field of knowledge and the circumstances that engulfed its disciples largely affects its trajectory of development.

Given the aforementioned manner in which various fields of knowledge unfold and the closure a crystalized field puts on further developments that are not in sync with what became quintessential, Islamic sciences are not immune from this phenomenon. That is especially true in the case of Islamic sciences as they are so central and dear to the faith community that adheres to them. In other words, communal identities of many devout adherents are anchored to the classical corpus of writings. Therefore, new developments in *maqāṣid* would always be challenged by a received view, even if such developments were well theorized. At this point, let us cite Bin Bayyah, who is an icon in defending the classics, and who himself points to some limitedness in the established formulation of *maqāṣid*. Bin Bayyah says, "No one can claim that the major objectives, which some people call the higher objectives, are limited in number. Rather, any [qualified] scholar (through their own intellectual deliberations) can potentially ascertain an objective."[2] Therefore, it is not right for anyone to suggest that the objectives are limited, whether they be universal objectives or particular objectives that pertain to the *mukallaf* (accountable individual). We should understand that the five traditional universal objectives had acquired their authoritative and immutable status not only because of their sound theorization, but also largely due to the fact that they were so widely known and referred to. In light of all this, Bin Bayyah says:

> Therefore, I call for a review of fatwas, which should be measured against a threefold framework. This evaluation should be based on an examination of real-life facts of a case, so as to define the level of hardship and level of need that exist in any given case. We should then evaluate the newly-introduced factors, after which we may look for a ruling on the basis of a specific religious text that is applicable to that case, if possible, provided that the religious text is examined to determine its level of soundness. Then, we may discuss the Shari'ah's objectives, whether universal or general, such as the objective of making things easy. Or, there may be some specific objectives that have to do with a particular case. A fatwa may then be issued on the basis of such a compound and precise process (rather than a process that is oversimplified and susceptible to error).[3]

Bin Bayyah goes on to say:

And there is a fourth element which is not part of the equation, but is essential to the equation, namely the fact that the architect of this process, who will decide its outcome, must be well-versed in Shariʿah, aware of the considerable (in *sharʿī* terms) *maṣlaḥah* that are to be taken into account, and have good knowledge of the balances that the Shariʿah strives to achieve. We prefer to choose the terminology "well-versed" (*irtiyāḍ*) rather than ijtihad, so that we do not find ourselves faced with the conditions that must be met by the *mujtahid*, which are very difficult to attain, and so as to make it easier to issue fatwas in these cases, as long as the fatwas are issued within the appropriate guidelines. This term "well-versed" is one that is used by the Mālikīs when discussing the issue of defining what is a *maṣlaḥah* and the issue of relying on the *maqāṣid* (in order to reach that fatwa), for neglecting any of these elements may lead to economic, social, or political turmoil, which is contrary to what the Shariʿah seeks to achieve and to what is just and right.[4]

Finally, there is nothing more indicative of the limitations of *uṣūl al-fiqh* and its inability to deal directly with major social problems of our time than the fact that when discussing the issue of *shūrā* (consultation) and democracy, Bin Bayyah does not refer to *uṣūl al-fiqh* in any way; rather, he only mentions the concept of justice, which comes under the heading of the major aims of Shariʿah. The reason for this is not that there are few religious texts that speak of political issues; rather, it is the profound changes that have occurred in all aspects of life which compel one to reference the major aims of Shariʿah, as they are more closely attached to the source of Islam and the wellspring of its guidance.

In a similar vein, al-Raysuni states:

It may be said that a theory is broader and more inclusive than a rule, and that a theory is comprised of a number of rules. However, *maqāṣid* theory encompasses both *fiqh* (juristic) theories and *fiqh* principles, as well as particular rulings. Hence, if a *fiqh* theory is, as Gamal Eldin Attia states, "an intellectual conceptualization which has been arrived at through a process of sequential, logical thought or through inductive reasoning based on particular subsidiary rulings,"[5] then *maqāṣid* theory rests on both of these foundations (i.e., logical, sequential thought arising from rational investigation and the doctrinal foundations of Islam, and inductive conclusions).

Maqāṣid theory is generated by sound, rational investigation based on the belief that the Shariʿah of Allah can be nothing other than that of wisdom and mercy, justice and equity, judicious planning and accurate assessment, since it is on the basis of these qualities that God deals with all His creatures, and since they are necessitated by the Divine perfections.

Maqāṣid theory is supported by an inductive analysis of the details of Shariʿah. Thus, whoever examines the rulings of Shariʿah and its texts in their various aspects and fields will perceive many of their objectives and wise purposes. Moreover, whoever pauses to reflect on the outcomes and effects of such rulings will see the benefits which they bring and the harm which they prevent and, as a consequence, will emerge with a comprehensive, integrated conceptualization of the objectives and goals of *maqāṣid al-Sharīʿah*, which, is exactly the *maqāṣid* theory.[6]

Let me note at this point that my motive for writing this book was twofold: to address problematic issues that I believe are undermining the proper understanding of Shariʿah; and to address the lack of harmony in the theorization process, as well as weakness in the connections made between different matters related to the Shariʿah.

5.2 The Relationship between Shariʿah and the Law

There are three basic terms that are often distorted in the context of modern society: Shariʿah, fiqh, and *qānūn*. It is worthwhile here to address this important issue, especially given the relevancy of these terms to increased global interest in *maqāṣid al-Sharīʿah* and the proliferation of works in several languages on *maqāṣid* (including original works and their translations). To begin, the term *sharīʿah* had undoubtedly attained wide-usage and had more than one meaning among different segments of people. Because the term *sharīʿah* encompasses the notion of fiqh, it is often used synonymously with fiqh. However, there are distinct connotations associated with each of these terms that distinguish them apart, and not recognizing this can be problematic in that it can lead to their misrepresentation.

As it has been noted in the discussion of terminology in the English version introduction of this book, the term *sharīʿah* encompasses theological, moral, and practical teachings, all of which stem from the Qur'an and hadith. On the other hand, fiqh connotes scholarly reasoned and interpreted regulations deduced from *sharīʿah*, and the application manner of such regulations in the particular lives and circumstances of people. There does not appear to have been any confusion in the interchangeable usage of these terms historically, as Muslims of previous societies generally understood their intended meaning. This is not the case in our time, however, where there is confusion about such concepts largely due to the influence of foreign ideas on the Muslim culture and the general decline of Islamic learning and identity. It therefore behooves us here to re-examine the etymology and linguistic meaning of the term *sharīʿah*.

Linguistically, the term *sharīʿah* literally means "the path to water," derived from its root meaning "the clear road or path." The root of the term appears in the Qur'an where Allah says, "He has prescribed (*sharaʿa*) for you the religion which He enjoined upon Noah and which We revealed to you (O Muhammad), and which We enjoined upon Abraham and Moses and Jesus" (42:13), indicating that the substance of *sharīʿah* is not specific to the final revelation of Islam but rather is linked to Prophethood and divine teachings. Similarly, the Qur'an addresses the Prophet Muhammad, saying, "Now We have set you [Muhammad] on a clear religious path [*sharīʿah*], so follow it. Do not follow the desires of those who lack [true] knowledge"[7] (45:18). From the aforementioned, what is then meant by the word *sharīʿah* in *Surat al-Ma'idah* perhaps becomes clearer, wherein Allah says, "And do not follow their desires in disregard of the Truth which has come to you. For each of you We have appointed a *shir'ah* and a *minhāj*" (5:48). We find that the main concept of each *shar'* and *manhaj* denotes the general orientation of Islam and its *tawḥīdī* worldview. The aforementioned verses thus demonstrate that *sharīʿah* (which is referred to as *shar'*) is not limited to rulings and regulations, even though rulings are part of *sharīʿah*.

In discussing the meaning of *sharīʿah, minhāj,* and *qānūn,* ʿAllal al-Fasi states that "*shirʿah* is the straight path… and *minhāj* means being guided by the right path."[8] He then elaborates further regarding what he characterizes as the fundamentals of Shariʿah:

> These fundamentals are foundational rules that consist of a comprehensive system of higher fundamentals of truth and law (*qānūn*). They are the primary basis for ijtihad, *tafsīr,* and general fiqh. These fundamentals are in harmony with innate human nature and do not change from one time or place to another… *Minhāj* refers to the intellectual basis on which people live a life of righteousness. There is a *minhāj* or guideline for ruling, which is consultation (*shūrā*), justice, and the like; and there is a *minhāj* for the family, which is love, justice, and compassion.[9]

In discussing the linguistic aspect of the word *sharīʿah,* al-Raysuni states that classical works sometimes restrict its meaning to "rules and regulations," and sometimes broaden its scope "as if it were synonymous with religion, so that *dīn, millah,* and *sharīʿah* – according to this understanding – are all one and the same."[10] He asserts that restricting the meaning of *sharıʿah* to denote rules and regulations has no basis and is contrary to the fundamental guidelines of the Shariʿah, which comprehensively includes such areas as acts of worship, infractions, etiquette, and business interactions, as well as personal matters and other areas.

The proclivity for setting regulations in accessing the Shariʿah's sources is what led to some confusion in understanding what is meant by "Shariʿah sources" and what is meant by "Shariʿah methodology." The often uttered statement that the sources of Shariʿah are four—namely the Qurʾan, the Sunnah, *qiyās* (analogical reasoning), and *ijmāʿ* (scholarly consensus)—became widely circulated, despite the fact that it is erroneous. Such a statement misses to see the difference between the means of reaching fiqh rulings and the sources of Shariʿah. Only the Qurʾan and Sunnah (of which sound hadith is a major part) are the sources of Shariʿah, where the Sunnah stands as elucidation (*bayān*) of the Qurʾan. It is thus important to be continuously cognizant that the concept of Shariʿah is broad, abstract, embodies the general orientation of Islam, and is not limited to fiqh.

Reducing Shari'ah into the legal is even more distortive in understanding the Islamic system, especially in the context of modernity and the secularization of life, which was associated with the erosion of values and replacing morality with legality. As for contrasting fiqh to law, we can briefly observe the following. Fiqh deals with all classes of life issues, including the attainment and refinement of good manners (e.g., greeting each other), virtuous conduct (e.g., visitation of the ill), matters of worship (e.g. rules of proper fasting), economic matters (e.g., what constitutes unlawful usury), etc. Obviously, some of those aspects are not fit for the law, as they are not amenable to precise codification; and if they are turned into rigid rules, they become suffocating. More important is the moral depth in fiqh matters. It is not that the law is void from morality, but that its presence and point of insertion is different. While moral concerns are taken into consideration when enacting laws, the moral content is more visibly present in fiqh as the *mukallaf* (the component and responsible person in the sight of Allah) readily abides by its standards as an act of worship to God and following the example of the beloved Prophet Muhammad, all in the context of actualizing Shari'ah in real life. In other words, if abiding by the law makes a person a good citizen, abiding by fiqh—in the light of *maqāṣid*—makes a person a good human being.

As for matters that are common to both fiqh and *qānūn* (the law), the difference is that matters of fiqh are difficult to codify or make absolute. In this sense, fiqh (along with *uṣūl al-fiqh*) can be linked to legal theory, whereas matters of *qānūn* are fixed and made to be binding. Thus, to turn fiqh into *qānūn* can be problematic. To further explain what we mean here, take for example the fiqh case of someone who has the means to perform the obligatory hajj but fails to do so; or a woman who follows a particular *madhhab* with regard to the length of menses but her *madhhab* is different from the chosen *madhhab* of the state. It would be difficult to render these fiqh issues into *qānūn*.

It is as such that the phrase *al-qānūn al-Islāmī* can be problematic, for it may incorrectly be thought of as referring to the Shari'ah itself, or to fiqh; the meanings of the latter two are broader in scope, more comprehensive, and more noble than the meaning of *qānūn*. In the English language, the term Islamic Law, in capital letters, is often used as a synonym to Shari'ah itself or merely for fiqh. Some suggest that the phrase *qānūn Islāmī* (in the indefinite form) can be used to convey the sense that lawmakers have attempted to base law on Shari'ah teachings and guidelines and therefore can be appropriate to use. Nevertheless, the phrase *al-qānūn al-Islāmī* (in the definite form) is certainly problematic and misleading because Islamic regulations have by their very nature some allowance for organic and fluid development and plurality—within certain limits of course—based on situational and contextual factors, and thus cannot be codified in the absolute sense (i.e., as a permanently fixed code of law). And the jury is still out on the desirability and long-term effect of the late Ottoman effort in codifying fiqh. Furthermore, beliefs, values, and principles are constant, but rulings can possibly change or apply differently depending on circumstances of a case and without contradicting the higher aims of the Shariʿah.

There is a fundamental and important matter that is worth pointing out, which is in regard to the role of law (*qānūn*) in rectifying people's situation. In the context of Islamically spirited governance, it should be understood that laws, constitutions and the like reflect the will and participation of the Muslim community (Ummah) and are not developed in a vacuum. Thus, the rallying call to implement Islamic law (under the banner *ḥukm Islāmī*) as if it was something already established and operational, is overly simplistic, and diverts people from actively addressing the need to reform laws. Doing so is an ongoing process in which Muslims would elaborate the kind of society they aspire to, the extent of the role of ʿurf and other social mechanisms, the degree and aspects in which the state can interfere.

The efforts to develop laws can be undermined (i.e., distorting them) when they are accompanied by such things as extortion and corrupt intents for political expediency. Justice Tariq al-Bushri says in this regard:

When the law (*qānūn*) is issued, it is issued through several state branches on the basis of how these branches evaluate what interests may be served by this law. Therefore, since the modern state has limited authority according to constitutional theories and theories of political science, it is limited in what it can produce of laws. In other words, if one branch of government is limiting another, that is, its executive power is limited by its legislative power, which is in turn limited by its judiciary authority which keeps a watch on the practices of the executive authority in light of the practices of the legislative authority, so as to judge what the executive authority is doing, the state – as it is comprised of these three authoritative branches – is thus limited by its will. [In a secular state] no limitation comes from anything beyond the state, such as a general reference from outside the state which has authority over the state (e.g., Shariʿah), because in that case the state would be subjected to a higher authority from without, that was not produced by the state itself. Thus, we understand that secularism is one of the characteristics of modern states in our societies, and it is one of the prerequisites of such states and one of its main components. In such a manner, the state succeeded in making the society something it owns and of its assets. Consequently, society became a dependent appendage to the state, and not the other way around [as it is the case in the Islamic model].[11]

The aforementioned may prompt us to think of different levels for Shariʿah, from the abstract level to the applied level. These levels can be seen as branches of knowledge and ideas that are separate from the law but have some impact on it. The following table shows the different levels of Shariʿah discourse and their counterparts in law, and how *sharʿī* discourse inform the law (*qānūn*) and legislation.

Correspondence Between the Theorization of *Sharʿī* Knowledge and Legal (*Qānūnī*) Knowledge Through Practical Application

Sharʿī Theorization	Political Administrative Theorization	Legal (*Qānūnī*) Application
Major aims of Shariʿah	Forming a constitutional vision	Constitutional philosophy
Objectives of Ṣhariʿah	Establishing constitutional guidelines and principles	Constitutional frameworks
Principles of uṣūl (al-qawāʿid al-uṣūliyyah)	Establishing legal guidelines and principles	Setting a legal orientation
Uṣūl al-fiqh	Verifying legal guidelines	Legal guarantees
Fiqh (jurisprudence)	Various legal studies	Rules and regulations
Fatwas	Accumulated judicial experience	Cases and precedents

With regard to the aims of Shariʿah as commonly understood, their role in the case of political administrative application corresponds to the role of a basis or reference point on which constitutional principles are to be based. For example, one of the priorities of the constitution would be to preserve intellect and life, and measures that fall under indispensables (*ḍarūriyyāt*) should be given priority over measures that fall under exigencies (*ḥājiyyat*) and enhancements (*taḥsīniyyāt*). This is to be applied throughout the activities of the state. As far as the law is concerned, it should come in the form of constitutional frameworks.

With regard to *uṣūl al-fiqh*, its role in the administration of society and the running of its political affairs is to serve as a reference point according to which legal guidelines and controls are shaped. For example, areas of *uṣūl al-fiqh* such as the universal and particular maxims may provide guidelines when formulating laws and inform the suitability of regulations. Such activities would take place within the context of the state's institutions as well as regulatory and civic institutions, all of which harmonize Islamic cultural mandates with the promulgation of laws.

As for fiqh, its role with regard to administration and running the political affairs of society is that of a resource in which various fiqh views must be examined and selected or combined. For example, when it comes to the rulings on divorce and custody, personal loans and *zakatable* incomes, and the ethical standards expected in administrating public institutions, the different views of the *madhhabs* concerning such matters may be regarded as legal opinions. In the context of the state, and from a legal point of view, this will manifest itself in the form of a set of rulings and regulations.

As for what we have on record of fatwas, its role in the administration of society and the running of its political affairs is that of a material source that could be examined and studied as a supplemental reference, so as to learn from it. For example, we may examine a fatwa that deals with a particular case in particular circumstances and regard it as a judicial precedent. In the context of the state, and from a legal point of view, this will manifest itself in the form of material that may be taken as cases and precedents that are subject to ijtihad as to whether they are binding and to what extent.

The six levels of correspondence between the Shariʿah and the legal realm discussed above may overlap and interact, and each may have an impact on the understanding and application of the other. Each explains and deepens our understanding and helps us to understand problematic issues.

Here, I would like to point to the suggestion of some jurists (*fuqaha'*) that *ʿurf* (custom) be given due consideration as one of the sources of *tashrīʿ*. There are some who interpret the word *ʿurf* in Qur'an 7:199[12] as referring to what is generally known of Shariʿah, and there are others who interpret it as referring to the good traditions or customs of the Ummah and what they are unanimously agreed upon of useful practices that serve its *maṣlaḥah*, because what matters is to be in harmony with what *fiṭrah* dictates of good manners and behavior. In his book *Maqāṣid al-Sharīʿah al-Islāmiyyah wa Makārimuhā*, al-Fasi points out that *ʿurf* in the sense of *ʿādah* (tradition) may be given consideration, but "it should be limited to the original *ʿurf* (i.e., what is right, cf. 7:199) which is one of the noble characteristics of Shariʿah."[13]

But putting this forward without offering clear guidelines in that regard is problematic, as customs might become corrupted with the passage of time. In most cases, the jurists did not differentiate between *ʿādah* (habits or tradition) and *ʿurf* (customs, what people are accustomed to); however, some of them said that *ʿurf* refers specifically to usage of words and *ʿādah* refers to actions. Without guidelines on the way in which we should deal with the *ʿurf* that is prevalent in a given society, we may end up giving some kind of authority to what people are accustomed to doing, and it could go so far as undermining the Shariʿah as the ultimate source of *tashrīʿ*. This is not to undermine the critical role of *ʿurf* in social life. Certainly, the notion of *ʿurf* helps in contextualizing the application of fiqh regulations. What seems lacking in literature is more clarification on the point at which *ʿurf* enters into the equation; for example, *ʿurf* has a larger role in fatwas and in the deliberations of a qadi. And since *ʿurf* could be a remnant of cultural notions not compatible with the Islamic motif, there is a need to develop clear guidelines for its consideration. And God knows best.

5.3 Reconceptualizing the Concepts of *Nafs* and *Fiṭrah*

Writings that refer to the objective of preserving human life (*nafs*) tend to do so on the assumption that the concept of *nafs* is clear and self-evident, not requiring explanation. Discussions on this concept thus considerably restrict its meaning. Al-Najjar notes this and says, "The objective of preserving *nafs* as it is discussed in the various works on the aims of Shariʿah is not able to encompass other meanings or concepts that relate to it, for instance, the concept of human dignity."[14] Another important concept that relates to *nafs* but whose relation to it is rarely discussed is the concept of *fiṭrah*. In Chapter Two, we discussed how Ibn ʿAshur connected the aims of Shariʿah to the notion of *fiṭrah*. And although Ibn ʿAshur reiterated how central the concept of *fiṭrah* is to the aims of Shariʿah, he did not discuss in detail its relation to the concept of *nafs*. Below, I will discuss the concept of *fiṭrah* and expand on the meaning of *nafs*, considering that the former is independent from the latter, though the two concepts are related. The expansion of the concept of *nafs* is central to the *ʿumrānī* perspective of *maqāṣid* that I will present in the final chapter. As the plan for that chapter is to avoid any detailed discussions, I shall discuss the renewed concept of *nafs* here.

To begin, it is important to note that the approach of al-Dehlawī, al-Fasi, and Ibn ʿAshur does not greatly help us in formulating a precise definition of the concept of *fiṭrah*. For example, al-Dehlawī differentiates between three *latāʾif* (faculties) that form the basis of "mankind's behavior and attitude" – namely *ʿaql* (reason or intellect), *qalb* (heart or emotion), and *nafs* (self) – which is proven by "Shariʿah Texts [Qurʾan and Hadith], reason, experience, and the consensus of the scholars."[15] From examining the Shariʿah Texts, it is known "that *ʿaql* is that by means of which humans grasp that which may not be grasped by means of senses. The *qalb* is that by means of which people love, hate, choose, and resolve. And the *nafs* is that by means of which one enjoys food, drink, and intimacy."[16] Al-Dehlawī then discusses in detail the characteristics of each of them:

> The functions of the *qalb* include anger, courage, love, cowardice, contentment, discontent, loyalty to old friends, alternation between love and hate, love of status, generosity, stinginess, and hope and fear. Among the functions of the *ʿaql* are certainty, doubt, delusion, seeking to find causes for every incident, and thinking of how to achieve benefits and ward off harm. The ultimate desire of the *nafs* is to enjoy good food and drink, to love women, and the like.[17]

The problems with these definitions are obvious. The intellect works with the senses in order to understand physical objects, even though the intellect is somewhat independent from the senses when it comes to grasping the abstract. The definition of the heart describes it as the center of emotions, then ascribes to it the function of choosing and deciding, even though the intellect plays a role in choosing and deciding, according to the nature of the matter in question. Obviously, such notions of *nafs* omit the central Qurʾanic concept of its potential for guidance or going astray.[18]

The nature of the *fiṭrah* is a vital matter which requires clarification. Is the *fiṭrah* something which is linked to the *ʿaql* or to the *nafs*? Is it innate or acquired? Ibn ʿAshur discusses this in detail in his book *Uṣūl al-Niẓām al-Ijtimāʿī*, telling us:

It must be the case that what is meant by *fiṭrah* – as in the saying that this religion is described as the religion of innate human nature (*al-fiṭrah al-insāniyyah*) – is the feelings and emotions that people experience when they are not subject to false teachings and bad habits. It is the foundation of the systems on which the earliest human civilizations were built, which was striving to achieve that which serves the *maṣlaḥah* of individuals, ward off harm and mischief from them, and try to attain the truth, whether that was based on the inspiration of innate human nature, or on divine revelation.[19]

This statement, however, poses issues, because if the dictates of the *fiṭrah* stem from innate human nature, then this would mean that all humans are equal in that regard, which in turn would mean that it is part of people's nature. Does Ibn ʿAshur mean that it is possible that the dictates of *fiṭrah* may be attained by means of divine revelation, or that the revelation is only trying to correct what has become distorted of *fiṭrah*, and to clear away what has covered it of whims and desires, traditions and false ideas? What al-Fasi says concerning this topic offers some clarity:

But humankind was created in the best form (cf. Qur'an 95:4), a clear witness against himself or herself (cf. 75:14), with free will. Sometimes a person is overtaken by animalistic instincts, so he is reduced to the lowest of the low (cf. Qur'an 95:5), then he is influenced by his innate nature and his inclination towards religion, so he does good and mends his ways. As he shifts between the two influences, he needs someone to help him; he needs religious teachings and guidelines to rein him in and show him the path; and he needs justice to protect him even from himself.[20]

It seems that al-Fasi's explanatory discussion is much clearer, as he differentiates between good and bad characteristics in the human being. And he states in his book *Maqāṣid al-Sharīʿah al-Islāmiyyah wa Makārimuha*, "Man cannot help being a mixture of animalistic inclinations, which is part of being human, and innate nature (*fiṭrah*) as a spiritual human being."[21]

Elsewhere, al-Fasi says:

> Allah endowed people with reason so that they could distinguish between what is beneficial and what is harmful, and they were granted guidance through religion, which is necessary to their innate nature (*fiṭrah*) in terms of belief and in that it provides humankind with the methodology that leads him to the truth and to the straight path.[22]

Here, al-Fasi affirms the dual nature of humankind (that is, animalistic and spiritual), and he contrasts this with reason, without explaining the limits of reason in distinguishing between what is beneficial and what is harmful, or whether its arena is limited to the tangibles of daily life or also include abstract notions and ideas.

Al-Fasi affirms that humankind has various potentials, as he says, "We have previously explained the meaning of *fiṭrah* and noted that it is innate in humankind."[23] Then he refers to the linguistic differences between nature (*ṭabʿ*), character (*sajiyyah*), attitude (*khuluq*), and habit (*ʿādah*) as he notes:

> We may conclude, from a linguistic point of view, that nature (*ṭabʿ*) and other words with similar meanings refer to something that is innate in everything and which creates in that thing the potential to develop a characteristic, or to acquire it, retain it, or lose it. Some instincts may interact and coexist harmoniously, or some may prevail over others, if they are supported by a precise force. All of that is the decree of the Almighty, All-Knowing (cf. Qur'an 33:38). Thus, the disciplined or refined nature consists of a set of original moral forces and the force that directs or controls it, which is the habit that is controlled by a force of reason or education.[24]

Al-Fasi concludes with an explanation of the *fiṭrah* as he understands it, but it confuses him at the same time. He writes:

> *Fiṭrah* is innate human nature. But the *fiṭrah* with which God has created people is the *fiṭrah* of the human in general terms; the human who

possesses a combination of reason, the ability to acquire knowledge, the potential to attain civility, and the potential to be obedient, in addition to what he has of faculties through which he sees, hears, and imagines, and the curiosity that guides him to acquire some knowledge and develop some behaviors. All of that is so that he will carry out some actions that are unique to him as a human being and distinguish him from other animals, some of which come under the heading of habits and others come under the heading of worship. What is meant by Islam being the religion of *fiṭrah* is that it is the religion which is in harmony with innate human nature, as humankind possess a combination of reason, the potential to attain civility, the ability to acquire knowledge, and the potential to be obedient, which helps people to develop their knowledge and meet their needs as far as habits and acts of worship are concerned.[25]

After this discussion of different aspects of the concept of *fiṭrah*, I shall endeavour to discuss its meaning in light of a discussion of the meaning of the *nafs*. I must first note that the concept of the *nafs*, when mentioned within the context of the aims of Shariʿah, is often reduced to the physical body and its well-being, on the basis that preserving it from destruction is something necessary. But this is clearly drifting from the meaning of the word *nafs* as intended in the Qur'an. When we expand the concept of the *nafs*, we see that it has five aspects – namely reason, emotion, conscience, and will, in addition to the body. And while we can speak of the body as a component, the other four are closer to being floating states; and they interact with each other. As for *fiṭrah* – or the manifestation thereof – it is an essential reality of the human being, and we may envisage it in two ways: (1) We may say that *fiṭrah* is what we mean when we speak of conscience and inner feelings, whether at a conscious or subconscious level; or (2) We may say that *fiṭrah* is connected to all of the aspects of the *nafs* where it represents the God-created inspiring state and the point that the *nafs* defaults to in normal situations.

This understanding of *fiṭrah* and its connection with *nafs* requires an independent study, but some examples may suffice to explain what we mean. For example, emotion is connected to *fiṭrah*, and nothing is more indicative of that than the love we find in all cultures and at all times. The spectrum of *fiṭrī* emotions is indeed broad and includes kindness, hate, jealousy, joy, covetousness, selflessness, anger, forbearance, cowardice, courage, and so on. These emotions are described as *fiṭrī* because they exist in the same way in all people, as a natural reaction to the circumstances and influences to which they are subjected, even though they may vary in their intensity. The very rare cases – such as a mother who feels no compassion for her child – are an exception that proves this rule.

Reason also has a connection to *fiṭrah*, such as asking questions, arguing, observing, analyzing, distinguishing between things, classifying, drawing conclusions, and investigating. As for the conscience, it is the most hidden aspect of the *nafs* and the most difficult to define. Perhaps the conscience is the reflection of the spiritual dimension of humankind. We may regard feelings of guilt that are felt in the heart as a good example of the conscience in action, and the same may be said concerning feelings of regret, which indicate that the *fiṭrah* is sound; the opposite of that reflects deviation and being far removed from sound *fiṭrah*. I believe that appreciating beauty is something connected to the conscience. In sum, I suggest that *fiṭrah* is the default elevated state of all of the aspects of the *nafs* (reason, emotion, conscience, will, and the body) as willed and created by Allah. It is the acts of people when they turn away from the guidance of the Prophets and revealed messages that dull the sensibility and receptiveness of *fiṭrah*.

In his book Ḥujjat-Allah al-Bālighah, al-Dehlawī confirms that the fiṭrah may atrophy because of three barriers that prevent it from emerging, namely "the barrier of attitude, the barrier of physical inclinations, and the barrier of poor education."[26] What could help to remove these barriers is striving to elevate the nafs, understanding the virtue of spiritual aspirations in overcoming attraction to worldly matters, and reflecting. Elsewhere, he says:

> The three faculties – *ʿaql, qalb*, and *nafs* – are connected to one another, which confirms that the strong person is the one who causes *ʿaql* to control his *qalb* (that is, his emotions), even though his *qalb* is strong, and he causes his *qalb* to control his *nafs*. Such is the one whose character is perfect and whose *nafs* is strong.[27]

Ibn ʿAshur says, "It is no wonder that it is strongly encouraged to seek knowledge, so that people will be able to rectify their thinking, rectify their deeds, rectify their beliefs, and perfect their conscience."[28]

Here we must point out that the materialistic approach to modern sciences and other branches of knowledge tends to reduce human beings and their reasoning, emotions, and conscience to physical structure and genes, on the basis of many new discoveries that show how some psychological faculties or functions fail when there is some physical or genetic defect. But the physical aspect of the human body is like a medium that enables the different psychological functions to manifest themselves in real-life situations, and the physical body does not represent the true essence of those psychological functions. When we do not have a manifestation of some psychological functions, as a result of the lack of any means of allowing them to be manifested, that does not mean that they are not there at all.

The *fiṭrah* is common to all human beings, but there are also differences between the *fiṭrah* of males and that of females, which reflects the variation between them in differences in reasoning, emotions, and conscience, along with the enabling physical make-up. This variation in *fiṭrah* does not contradict the basic idea under discussion here as far as they are part of the willful design of the Creator. Psychological aptitudes of men and women may manifest themselves in different ways, so each sex may have some psychological aptitudes that are more prevalent than others, and thus their aptitudes may complement one another in such a way that life may prosper. The fact that both men and women have the basic underlying *fiṭrah*, even though their aptitudes and inclinations differ, offers additional support for the depth of *fiṭrah* in the human psyche.

5.4 The Concept of Freedom

The concept of freedom in Islam was affirmed by Ibn ʿĀshur in his book *Uṣūl al-Niẓām al-Ijtimāʿī*, wherein he addresses it within different contexts (which we have discussed earlier in this work). For Ibn ʿAshur, freedom can be understood according to two types: freedom in contrast to slavery (i.e., physical manifestation of freedom), and freedom of choice (i.e., in the context of belief and thought).

The historical experience of humanity has witnessed different sorts of servitude, with slavery being the worst type of controlling people's lives. It is well-known that Islamic regulations dry-up its sources, and that there are many regulations and recommendations for freeing people from bondage. However, war lingered as a source since its rules cannot be settled singularly by one party in the conflict. Nevertheless, in effect, Islamic regulations changed the nature of such practice.

Regarding beliefs, we can say that Islam undoubtedly rejects compulsion in matters related to religion, not only on the grounds of freedom, but also on the grounds that the heart should be open to faith and it should be a matter of conviction, for this is what faith should be based on. Freedom of thought may be demonstrated by the fact that the Qur'an presents the views of the disbelievers, not because of any inherent value in them, but in order to highlight the intellectual challenges posed by the disbelievers. The concept of freedom of belief is connected to the preservation of religion, otherwise religion would turn into hypocrisy and empty rituals. Freedom of thought is part of the preservation of intellect, without which one's intellect would diminish. Freedom of speech and freedom of action are connected to speaking the word of truth, offering advice, and enjoining what is right and forbidding what is wrong. All of this indicates that there is in Islam an inherent regard of freedom, distinctively situated within its worldview and its approach to organizing human life. However, I don't think that it is theoretically sound to make the concept of freedom a major principle in *maqāṣid* of *Sharīʿah*—an absolute universal objective that defines all particulars. I will briefly explain what I mean by this in what follows.

However, before we proceed in the discussion of *applied* freedoms, we need to settle the concept abstractly. Conceptually, freedom is ultimately related to *tawḥīd* and stems from within five essential properties of the Islamic belief: (1) The equal creation of humankind by Allah from a single sole; (2) Forming humankind according to the pure natural state of *fiṭrah*; (3) Endowing human beings with the ability to discriminate between right and wrong; (4) The individual responsibility for actions on the Day of Judgment; (5) The absence of intermediaries between a person and Allah. Obviously, such a perspective of freedom has profound implications in all of the aspects of life, be it personal, social, political, or economic. And the implications operate in the positive sense (what a person can and should do), and in the negative sense (what a person cannot and should not do). Furthermore, such conceptualization of freedom traverses between the individual and the collective levels.

Therefore, the concept of freedom in the abstract sense should not be confused with freedom of choice, as the latter is a cornerstone in contemporary liberal thinking. And freedom of choice is necessarily connected to the conditions and stipulations of the social contract between individuals and their communities. The relationships between different human groupings are connected to the Qur'anic principle of *taʿāruf* (knowing one another), which represents God's purport behind pluralism, including that between males and females (cf. Qur'an 49:13). When freedom is thought of in such contexts, then what matters are two-interrelated dynamics: creating harmony among a group of people so that individuals can cooperate and build a community, and creating amicable non-hostile relationships among groupings. On the other hand, individualistic freedom of choice may involve the exaltation of human weakness and an inclination towards self-centredness. Therefore, freedom of choice as an objective of Shariʿah in an absolute sense poses problems – be it related to an individual's freedom of choice with regard to oneself (such as committing suicide or disfiguring oneself, or fulfilling whatever one's desires are), or be it an individual's freedom of choice with regard to others (such as shirking one's duties with regard to family or others). It should be noted that the idea of freedom of choice in the modern discourse intersects with the concept of human rights. But human rights can turn narcissistic if not coupled with responsibilities and obligations. In fact, they are not separable; they are the two faces of the same social reality, for responsibility liberates and liberty invokes responsibility.

In considering the concept of freedom from an Islamic perspective, we can note five operative aspects: a cognitive aspect relating to the Islamic idea that the person is a subject to Allah alone, void of comparability and free of any *shirk* (deification of anyone or anything besides or alongside Allah), apparent or hidden; second, an aspect related to conscience and the sense of freedom experienced by true believers who adhere to the exalted unearthly teachings and principles of religion; a third aspect relating to the sense of being free from the control of whims, desires, and whispers of Satan; a fourth social aspect in reference to the relationship among human beings who are all equally free and all equally accountable for their actions; and a fifth political and socio-economic aspect relating to the endeavors of erecting a system of *ʿumrān* that is simultaneously congruent with God's Will and the nature of the universe.

There are undoubtedly issues in the way the concept of freedom is promoted in modern intellectual discourse, where it has acquired three characteristics: (1) it is connected to the individual's whims and desires; (2) it is connected to individualistic culture as a feature of Western societies; and (3) it is connected to the negligence of the collective aspects of life and public goods, as well as tolerating the market's corrupting products.

As for the concept of rights in Islam, it is organically connected to the concept of duties. In the Qur'an, humankind is described in two ways: (1) as weak with the potential to become either righteous or corrupt; and (2) as responsible, and will be brought to account on the Day of Resurrection, having undertook to bear the trust (*amānah* – cf. Qur'an 33:72). It is in light of this that classical Muslim scholars used the well-known phrase "rights of the servants of God (*ḥuqūq al-ʿibād*)," not "human rights." Al-Raysuni holds that the concept of rights in Islam is a unique concept, and that Islam's main concern is to give precedence to taking care of humanity, (i.e., the collective) over human beings' rights (i.e., the individual); what we are facing now is "the human being of rights, not the rights of human beings."[29]

Individual freedom is limited to matters having to do with behavior and conduct; there are limits placed on behavior and duties that are expected of people. The freedom to earn money is subject to guidelines on ways of acquiring wealth and principles of distribution of wealth, and it is also subject to the fact that public wealth is for the public and cannot become the property of an individual. Political freedom of the individual is subject to the principles of giving precedence to the greater interests of society, and it is to be based on the process of *shūrā* (consultation) and choosing representatives from communities or groups.

For the above reasons, I do not see that the concept of personal freedom is fit to be a standalone *maqṣid* or to be one of the universals (*kulliyyāt*). Again, that does not mean that freedom is void in Islamic philosophy or its system. Rather, freedom is conceptualized differently, and it has its unique place in Muslim *ʿumrān* and the architecture of the Islamic system.

5.5 Approaches to Reading Shariʿah Texts

The discussion of *maqāṣid* obviously hinges on the reading methodology of *nuṣus*, the Texts of Shariʿah (namely the Qur'an and hadith), and there are various bases in that respect. Linguistics play an essential role in such reading, and the centrality of the Arabic language, as was reformulated by the Qur'an, is not disputed. Examining the context is another major aspect that preoccupied fiqh; in fact, considering the implications of Qur'an and hadith texts along with the assessment of their context is at the heart of *fiqh*. The *maqāṣidī* reading of Shariʿah Texts, through induction, tried to abstract common goals behind them. Yet, there is an integrative basis in the process of reading Shariʿah Texts, which focuses on the overall design of the Islamic system. Finally, the epistemological basis is another level where reason is deployed to comprehend Shariʿah Texts. These five aspects have been introduced by al-Najjar.[30] Below, I suggest that nesting these five bases forms a potent approach to comprehending texts.

The specific contribution of such an approach lies in defining the effective locus of each basis in serving the overall understanding of the Shariʿah Texts. Furthermore, the model connects the core output of each basis of reading to other basis, which endows the overall understanding of texts with depth and balance. We should remind ourselves here with the known phenomenon in the field of knowledge where specialization deepens the understanding at the expense of a comprehensive appreciation and balanced view of a matter under investigation. And this phenomenon is not a stranger to the corpus of writings about Shariʿah.

Chart: The Nested Reading of *Nuṣus* (Shariʿah Texts)

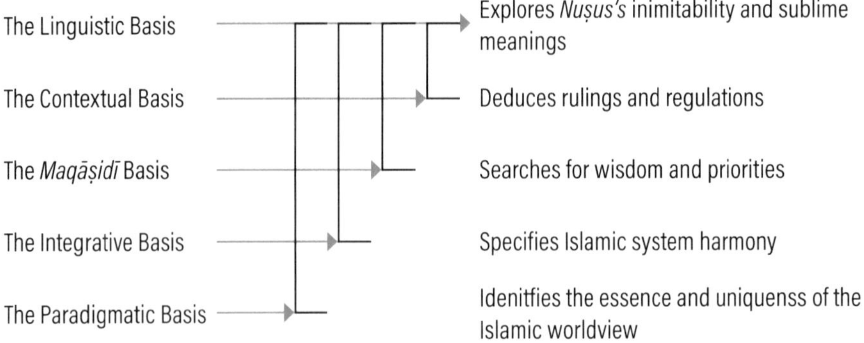

The linguistic approach to Shariʿah Texts (nuṣūṣ) includes deciphering the meaning (both the valid and invalid) of a word or passage. It also clarifies what we may coin as the carrying capacity of the text (i.e., what the text could carry of meanings versus what is considered a runway offshoot meaning). And there is a scholarly agreement that any generated meaning has to stay within the confines of what is acceptable in the Arabic language. However, it should be noted that the Arabic language has been reformulated by the Qur'an itself in a way that the language acquired new potentials, which are, nevertheless, understandable and discoverable. Therefore, words and expressions as signified by the Qur'an take precedence over pure linguistic signification.[31]

The situational or contextual approach involves examining the text for the purpose of determining rulings that could be deduced from it. This approach provides the guidelines and framework for human conduct. *Uṣūl al-fiqh* is relevant here, as it organizes the process of deduction through examining the *khaṣ/ᶜaām*, the *muṭlaq/muqayyad*, and other rules. This approach necessarily accounts for the more immediate level of the linguistic approach.

As for approaching *nuṣūṣ* from the purview of the *maqāṣid* (the aims of Shariᶜah), it concerns identifying the higher objectives and wisdom of the Shariᶜah Text. These objectives and wisdom are ultimately what Islam aims to achieve, and, as such, may go beyond the confines of rulings. At the heart of this approach is the assertion that the guidance of Shariᶜah and its regulations are not void of *maṣāliḥ* that attend to the well-being of people, the interests of individuals, and public interest. Prioritization of *aḥkām* (regulations) is specifically served in this approach. This approach subsumes the above two approaches.

As for the integrative approach, it focuses on the internal correspondence between the different elements of the Islamic system. Analysis at this level goes beyond the specific context at the time of revelation to examine the broad space of a framework in which the system of Islam operates. This level of reading naturally subsumes the above three levels.

Finally comes the conceptual and abstract study of *nuṣūṣ* (what al-Najjar calls the rational approach), which we might call the paradigmatic reading of *nuṣūṣ*. The focus here is on the genetics of the network of meanings that Shariᶜah Texts weave, and the unique nature of the Islamic system that they call for. It is a reading that tries to tune the understanding to a worldview constructed by *nuṣus* meant to be the final divine guidance for humanity.

The above elaboration of the model used the words "basis" and "approach" almost interchangeably. The point is that there are, indeed, different bases of reading Shariᶜah Texts that occupy the process of reflection and understanding. It becomes an approach after the accumulation of scholars' writing adopting one or more of the above schemes. And we specifically note that the nesting idea among the five modes of reading has profound implications, as it allows at once for due diligence in treating the *nuṣus* and expanding the horizon of reading.

Deploying at once the various approaches to Shariʿah Texts, including understanding the connection between them and how they are integrated with one another, is what, on the one hand, prevents the textual horizons from being stifled, restricted, and diminished, as is what happens with the literalists' interpretations, and on the other hand, protects Shariʿah Texts from being liberally interpreted as one pleases (and thus straying from any true or proper meaning) by those who are averse to and afraid of restricting its meaning. Protecting the integrity of the *nuṣūṣ* can be further achieved by setting precise guidelines that have to do with their study from all perspectives, and by setting guidelines to regulate the interaction between different levels and perspectives of study. This is critical, especially considering voices that promote the adoption of Western cultural sensibilities or adopting postmodern hermeneutic methods. The glaring problem with this approach, however, is that it excessively imposes contemporary context and sensibilities to an understanding of the Shariʿah Texts, and camouflages its imitation of modern secular approaches to the bible with creative work.

6

Discovering *Maqāṣid* in Ibn Khaldūn

In order to produce an effective theory of *maqāṣid*, it is essential not to be confined to the areas of *furūʿ al-fiqh* (the branches of jurisprudence or substantive law) and *uṣūl al-fiqh* (the foundations of jurisprudence or legal theory). It is also essential to avoid illusory binaries, the most significant of which is the binary classification of *maṣlaḥah* (welfare, well-being, benefits, and interests, including public interests) into those pertaining to the hereafter and those pertaining to this world; a notion that had been rejected by both Ibn Taymiyyah and al-Ṭūfī.[1] Moreover, and as the greater aim of this study is to offer an *ʿumrānī* perspective on the aims of Shariʿah, it is worthwhile to consider Ibn Khaldūn's thought on the notion of *ʿumrān* as it relates to the aims of Shariʿah. I characterize this present study as "Khaldūnī" as a reference to approaching the topic of Shariʿah through the lens of *ʿumrān*, and wherein we consider system properties that concern social sciences. It would be rather ill-suited for this study to treat the subject of *maqāṣid al-Sharīʿah* without considering how they operate within the Islamic model. This chapter will begin with a discussion of Taha Jabir al-Alwani's methodology to ascertain the major aims of Shariʿah before treating Ibn Khaldūn's thought within the context of *maqāṣid al-Sharīʿah*. This prepares us for the subsequent sections of this chapter, wherein we formulate and discuss in some detail the *ʿumrānī* aims.

6.1 Going Beyond the Framework of *Fiqh* and *Uṣūl al-Fiqh*

The literature review in the first section of this book showed that most attempts to understand and expand the *maqāṣid al-Sharīʿah* have been limited to doing it through the framework of fiqh or *uṣūl al-fiqh*. Thus, most modern research on *maqāṣid* has not developed something conceptually new and has been very careful to adhere to the views of earlier scholars. And though such research has provided some commentary, largely through elaboration or interpretation, it has been without much significant qualitative development. The notion we put forward here of going beyond the framework of a particular science, such as fiqh or *uṣūl al-fiqh*, does not mean setting that science aside or regarding it as fruitless; rather, it is an attempt to reengage with the *maqāṣid* such that they are meaningful to addressing contemporary issues. Regarding this, Hassani says, "But if for practical reasons one is bound by the idea of integration between the science of *uṣūl* and the study of *maqāṣid al-Sharīʿah*, then it behooves them to also recognize that these disciplines are relatively independent of one another, whether at the level of methodology or at the levels of concepts or goals."[2] All of this raises a known problematic in contemporary Islamic thought, that of renewal (*tajdīd*) of a field and the role of classical works therein.[3]

Taha Jabir al-Alwani was at the forefront of calling for non-confinement to what we find in the works of classical scholars. His contribution in the field of *maqāṣid* was the first to offer a methodological change that would go beyond fiqh and *uṣūl al-fiqh* and focus more on the fundamentals of religion (*uṣūl al-dīn*). The subsequent excerpts from al-Alwani's *maqāṣid* work inform us of what he was calling for. He states:

> Within the academic framework that was prevalent in the past, *maqāṣid al-Sharīʿah* were discussed under the subject of *uṣūl al-fiqh*. The scholars of *uṣūl* referred to the *maqāṣid* as: the aims of *sharʿī* rulings; benefits that may be achieved through a *sharʿī* ruling or result therefrom; effective causes (*ʿilal*) that may be referred to when performing analogical reasoning (*qiyās*); or wisdom that gives assurance to the heart and makes one more confident of the soundness of the Shariʿah. Imam al-Ḥaramayn, al-Ghazālī, al-ʿIzz ibn ʿAbd al-Salām, and al-Shāṭibī conceived the *maqāṣid* as being *kulliyyāt* (universal and definitive),

whereby *sharʿī* rulings could not go beyond. However, and for several reasons, the discussion of fiqh and *uṣūl* scholars [regarding *kulliyyāt*] did not take place as it did in regard to *ijmāʿ* (consensus), *qiyās* (analogical reasoning), and *istiḥsān* (juristic preference). Had they done so, it could have led to the further development of the field of *maqāṣid*, turning it into one of the main sources of *sharʿī* rulings and a standard for the evaluation of human actions. It is as such that this discipline of *maqāṣid al-Sharīʿah* remained limited in application to matters pertaining to virtue, or it was regarded as a kind of supplementary evidence for whatever conclusions were reached through other areas of *uṣūl*.[4]

Al-Alwani then says:

Here, we will discuss the higher aims of the Qur'an—namely *tawḥīd* (the affirmation of divine Oneness), *tazkiyyah* (purification of the self and life), and *ʿumrān* (the architecture of the Islamic system)—as being sublime values and major principles that are not restricted to issues of religious duties or particular rulings, and which are not restricted to the notion that the *maqaṣid* are merely an important topic within *uṣūl al-fiqh*. Rather, the aims of the Qur'an go beyond these restrictions and include studying the Qur'anic discourse concerning the divine purpose of creation, and seeking to understand the real nature of human action and how it is to be guided by the aims of Shariʿah.[5]

He then goes on to say:

What is appropriate with regard to the aims of Shariʿah is that they should not be reduced to any one of their components, and that the objectives should embody the message of Islam in such a way as to reflect its most significant features, so that all will be connected in one comprehensive framework.[6]

Al-Alwani defines six characteristics of the higher Qur'anic objectives:

- that the higher Qur'anic objectives are definitive and absolute universals, the sources of which are all to be found in one place, namely the Qur'an;

- that the role of the proven and sound Prophetic Sunnah that is in harmony with the Qurʾan is to explain and elaborate the Qurʾan.

- that the higher objectives cannot be regarded as universal objectives unless they are found in the messages of all the Prophets, because these universal objectives are a demonstration of the unity in the messages and beliefs that came to them, and that the aims and objectives of all the messages are the same;

- that one of the functions of these dominant, higher objectives is that they are able to regulate particular rulings and produce them – when needed – in all human activities, whether spiritual, intellectual, emotional, or physical, so that particular issues will be connected to the universals, and so that the human being in totality will be able to be guided in all aspects by the guidance of God;

- that the higher objectives are like constitutional principles – with regard to the legislative aspect of the matter – in their ability to generate constitutional material and legal guidelines;

- that they would not constitute mere proofs among other proofs, or principles among other principles of *uṣūl al-fiqh*, whether there is disagreement or unanimous agreement on them; rather, they will form the main starting point for an overhaul of the foundations of *uṣūl al-fiqh* and the building of the "greatest fiqh" on this foundation after that.[7]

Al-Alwani points out that most scholars today generally view the humanities and social sciences as being the monopoly of contemporary Western civilization. These fields of knowledge, however, have also played a role in the Islamic sciences, including fiqh and *uṣūl al-fiqh*. In this regard, he quotes Ibn Qayyim al-Jawziyyah as saying:

Thus, they stipulated a condition that the *faqīh*, mufti, qadi, or anyone who would be in a position to judge concerning a case must have two kinds of understanding: an understanding and deep insight of the reality of the situation, and reaching a conclusion concerning it by means of circumstantial evidence, signs, and an interconnection between various matters until one can fully understand what happened. At this point, a determination can be made as to what ruling to apply concerning the case.

Al-Alwani goes on to say:

Based on this, the *faqīh* today needs to be able to understand and employ anthropology, languages, sociology, and perhaps politics and economics, sociology of religion, and other areas from the social sciences. He may also seek the help of the natural sciences and their experts and scientists, according to what he needs and whatever new issues he is facing.[8]

This, as al-Alwani goes on to say, does not apply only to the *faqīh*:

The scholar of *uṣūl*, who sets out the guidelines to help the *faqīh* (whether these guidelines are derived from particular fiqh issues or were formulated before them and led to them), cannot do without being acquainted with the social sciences, behavioral sciences, and psychology, or even the natural sciences. Hence, we find that a large percentage of *uṣūlī* principles are based on these fields and sciences.[9]

This falls under the well-known statement of Taha Jabir al-Alwani regarding the essentiality of studying both the Qur'an and matters of the universe, though knowledge acquired from the study of the Qur'an should take precedence. In regard to studying matters of the universe, for it to be sound and valid, it must be done within the framework of the social sciences and be guided by Qur'anic discourse and Islamic guidelines; it should not be left to gnostic notions.

6.2 *Maqāṣidī* Reading of Ibn Khaldūn's Work

As it is now well-established, the project of revisiting and further developing the *maqāṣid* is one that concerns the entire Ummah, in which all scholars are to be mobilized in order to save the Ummah from wandering aimlessly in darkness and decline. In so doing, it is beneficial to seek the help of other fields of specialization as well as related fields, in which specialists have similar concerns and are motivated by similar goals. It was al-Shāṭibī who referred to "*majārī al-ʿādāt*" (patterns of habits), but Ibn Khaldūn was the one who coined the expressions "*ṭabāʾiʿ al-ʿumrān*" (socio-historical empirical generalizations), "*al-amr al-wujūdī*" (the nature of socio-historical reality, including natural laws), and "*al-majrā al-ṭabīʿī*" (the natural path).

While it is true that al-Shāṭibī and Ibn Khaldūn belonged to the same era and both led intellectual projects towards the purging of deleterious elements in the status quo of Islamic thought, they had radically different approaches but shared similar quests. For al-Shāṭibī, the quest was discerning universal rules from *nuṣuṣ* for the proper understanding of Shariʿah. And the quest for Ibn Khaldūn was discerning universal rules from history to guide Muslim reality in which Shariʿah operates. Therefore, Ibn Khaldūn's field of work was that of history and social sciences. And as this work attempts to develop *ʿumrāni maqāṣid* at the broadest theater of human existence, Ibn Khaldūn's thought stands as a natural mine. Nevertheless, marrying *maqāṣid* to *ʿumrān* is a novelty, and Ibn Khaldūn was not considered among the scholars of *maqāṣid*.

Ibn Khaldūn completed his *Muqaddimah* in 799 AH/ 1377 CE, and al-Shāṭibī completed his book *al-Muwāfaqāt* within the same decade (according to the prevailing view). It is highly probable that the two met in Granada and "learned from one another, either directly or indirectly."[10] Adnan Zarzur notes that al-Shāṭibī and Ibn Khaldūn were contemporaries and experienced the same political and social circumstances, telling us, "It is possible to regard the reform that he [al-Shāṭibī] introduced, or attempted to lay the foundations for in his book *al-Muwāfaqāt fī Uṣūl al-Sharīʿah*, as a counterpart of or complementary to the reform for which Ibn Khaldūn had laid the foundations for in his book *al-Muqaddimah*."[11] However, I consider that the contribution of Ibn Khaldūn is not simply complementary, rather it liberates from the confines of *uṣūl* in a paradigm shift that allows for reformulating the *maqāṣid*, a challenge that this book embarked upon.

A. A Brief Look at Ibn Khaldūn's Innovative Methodology

In considering Ibn Khaldūn's innovative methodology, it is perhaps best to offer a comparison between his introduction and that of al-Shāṭibī's. It was mentioned earlier that al-Shāṭibī commenced his introduction expressing concern that his attempted theorization of *maqāṣid* would be regarded as an adverse innovation, introducing into the Shariʿah that which was not meant to be a part of it. He was concerned that his approach would be perceived as foreign and therefore transgressing against early generations of scholars. Al-Shāṭibī himself acknowledges certain esoteric ideas towards the end of his book which only the learned scholars would adequately decipher.

Ibn Khaldūn, in contrast, did not express such concerns in putting forward his innovative ideas, despite that he was departing from many of the well-known scholarly views up to his time (e.g., that the caliph was to be limited to Quraysh, or the view regarding the Mahdi, or his rejection of certain historical and biographical narratives). Ibn Khaldūn's intrepidness to depart from such widely held views may perhaps be attributed to the dynamics surrounding how various sciences were perceived at his time. More concretely, there was a clear separation between the religious sciences, such as fiqh and *uṣūl al-fiqh*, and other sciences, including those which were complementary or ancillary to the religious sciences, such as history and cosmology. Given that Ibn Khaldūn's innovative ideas pertained to these latter sciences, of which generally did not stir controversy or debate, being innovative in them did not provoke the kind of backlash that would have been directed at him (especially from staunch traditionalists or ignorant common folk) had the innovation occurred in the more explicit religious sciences.

We know that al-Shāṭibī made significant contributions to the advancement of *maqāṣid al-Sharīʿah* in constructing a tight and comprehensive theory utilizing the well-established *uṣūli* principles and rules. However, though he tapped into other areas of knowledge to inform his *maqāṣid* theory, areas such as natural law and history, it was rather cursory and he thus did not fully benefit from such areas by integrating them into his methodology. Perhaps one reason that limited al-Shāṭibī's deployment of other sciences such as history (including historical context and practical lessons from history) to inform his theory is the likelihood that he never traveled beyond his locale (it is not known that he ever left Granada) to acquire knowledge that could be gained through visiting different regions. Al-Shāṭibī's *maqāṣid* theory is thus largely confined to the discipline of *uṣūl al-fiqh*, which in turn limited the extent to which *maqāṣid* thought could develop. As such, one of the things that distinguishes Ibn Khaldūn from al-Shāṭibī is that the former was able to deploy and benefit from multiple disciplines without this leading to great controversy or a negative outcome.

In comparing Ibn Khaldūn's and al-Shāṭibī's discourse on *maqāṣid*, Adnan Zarzur remarks:

> What distinguishes Ibn Khaldūn from al-Shāṭibī in their discourses on *maqāṣid* is that Ibn Khaldūn's discourse is informed by historical and sociological factors. Moreover, Ibn Khaldūn offers a different approach to certain impermissible matters in the Shariʿah by considering them within an economic or sociological framework rather than a religious one, or by attempting to identify a sociological reason (stemming from an *ʿumrānī* basis) for an impermissibility.[12]

Ibn Khaldūn arguably did not stop at framing the aims of Shariʿah within a historical/sociological context; rather, he went beyond that, developing a methodology that would help us understand human development throughout history. Thus, he was trying to develop a methodology independent of his methodological approach to *maqāṣid*, though it was possible to see the connections between them. We find Ibn Khaldūn saying at the beginning of his *Muqaddimah*:

> For example, what the jurists say about giving a reason for some *sharʿī* rulings in their discourse on the aims of Shariʿah, that fornication causes confusion about lineage and thus is harmful to the species, and that murder is also harmful to the species, and that wrongdoing will lead to the ruin of *ʿumrān*, which would lead to harming the species, and other similar discourse about the aims of Shariʿah with regard to rulings, all of this is based on protecting *ʿumrān*.[13]

He also says, explaining the impact that results from changes in circumstances:

> *ʿUmrān* in the east and west has been struck, in the middle of this eighth century, by a sweeping plague that has caused great harm to many nations and has taken the lives of many people, wiping out many of the beauties of *ʿumrān*. It has struck different states at a time

when they had reached old age and were approaching the end of their lives, so it caused their authority to decline and weakened it, and they found themselves on the brink of diminishing and coming to an end. *ʿUmrān* and prosperity on earth vanished with the calamity that befell the people, so doom and ruin spread in various lands; workshops fell idle, roads and landmarks fell into disrepair, neighborhoods and houses became empty, states and tribes became weak, and people died and were replaced by others. It looks as if what happened in the eastern lands is the same as what happened in western lands, but in a manner commensurate with the level of *ʿumrān*.... And God is the One Who will inherit the earth and all who are on it.[14]

Whilst al-Shāṭibī's theoretical approach focuses on the Shariʿah Texts and understanding them in such a way as to derive universal rules from it, in contrast, we find that Ibn Khaldūn's theoretical approach focuses on a few other dimensions. It is as if, in Ibn Khaldūn's words above, he is warning us that the system of Islam and Shariʿah cannot be in good shape and function properly if calamity strikes and ruins people's lives; and that the *maqāṣid* field, if approached and studied within the framework of *uṣul al-fiqh*, will not be able to help the Ummah, because the field of *uṣūl al-fiqh* was shaped and developed at a time of triumph and expansion, not a time of calamity and retreat. Here we may point out that incorporating issues having to do with *ʿumrān* into the field of *maqāṣid* can only be done if the methodology of analysis is also broadened. Ibn Khaldūn was aware of this matter. In the context of mentioning how wrongdoing usually leads to ruin of *ʿumrān* and therefore wrongdoing is forbidden, he says, "There is a great deal of evidence for that in the Qur'an and Sunnah; it is too much to be enumerated and listed."[15]

Abd al-Rahman al-Adrawi believes that "the efforts of al-Shāṭibī and Ibn Khaldūn led to a great leap forward in knowledge and led to the development of a rational methodology that is founded on knowledge and is of a very serious and pioneering nature."[16] He also believes that the methodology of Ibn Khaldūn was an effort to implement the aims of Shariʿah, stating, "The aims of Shariʿah, according to this theory, cannot be looked at only as a means of finding the reason for *sharʿī* rulings; rather it is a means that helps to gain control over the seen world, because these objectives form a guideline that helps us to choose from the various options in the process of building civilizations and societies."[17] This comment is of great importance, because despite the similarity between the efforts of Ibn Khaldūn and al-Shāṭibī in the sense that both of them sought to help the Ummah rise and to correct its way of thinking and acting, the contribution of Ibn Khaldūn stands out as a methodological revolution that went beyond the existing framework which was focused on the linguistic meaning of the texts and the reasons for religious rulings. It set up another framework that encompassed the previous framework and was in harmony with it, while also going beyond it and revising it where needed. Thus, Ibn Khaldūn's contribution was in many ways more expansive than that of al-Shāṭibī's.

Hassan Shahid believes that "both al-Shāṭibī and Ibn Khaldūn have the same academic approach to inductive research and the study of particular matters in this branch of knowledge."[18] He discusses in detail the parallels in inductive research according to the method of each of them, to the point that I fear he is depriving each of them of being unique and thus of being innovative, something they are known for. As such, it becomes difficult to understand the great emphasis on the role of reason according to the methodology of Ibn Khaldūn, in which regard he far surpassed al-Shāṭibī. Undoubtedly, *uṣūl al-fiqh* has provided guidelines which were and still are of immense academic value that cannot be disregarded. But what distinguishes the methodology of Ibn Khaldūn is that he went far beyond these guidelines and did not merely put them into application.

Understanding history, according to Ibn Khaldūn, should be based on a purely explanatory philosophy that is contrary to the Aristotelian understanding of history and fallacious reasoning, and it should be based on a conclusion reached through thorough inductive research that is controlled by the law of causality, the law of continuity, and knowledge of what could lead to prosperity or decline in the life of a society. It is worth noting that the methodology of Ibn Khaldūn goes beyond a dualistic way of thinking, which involves looking at the text then learning from it, because his methodology is based on an interaction between revealed text and real-life experience, to which al-Adrawi refers.[19]

As it was discussed under the topic of *istiqrāʾ*, al-Shāṭibī emphasized repeatedly that Sharīʿah never clashes with *majārī al-ʿādāt*, a concept which subsumes proven social experiences, the judgement of wise people, and the principle of causation in evaluating personal conduct. As valuable and relevant to *maqāṣid* as this concept is, there in nothing in al-Shāṭibī's methodology that would enable studying history and human experience. In contrast, Ibn Khaldūn's concepts of *al-amr al-wujūdī* (an existential matter that is part of what God created and willed) and *ṭabā'iʿ al-ʿumrān* (sociohistorical laws and patterns) subsume a wider set of phenomena, including communal, historical, geographic, economic and political dimensions.[20] Moreover, those concepts have been invoked for different purposes: *majārī al-ʿādāt* helps al-Shāṭibī to situate *aḥkām*, while for Ibn Khaldūn *amr wujūdī* and *ṭabā'iʿ al-ʿumrān* helps in explaining history, social change, and the proper design of the societal order. Al-Shāṭibī's concept stayed close to *ʿurf* (customs and traditions) while the concepts of Ibn Khaldūn stayed close to *sunan* (laws that govern human beings and nature).

There is no one better than Ibn Khaldūn himself to tell us about the connection of *maqāṣid* to *ʿumrān*, or the necessity of the *maqāṣid* having some *ʿumrānī* dimensions. One of the basic principles of Ibn Khaldūn's philosophy is his belief that for humankind to form communities is something essential, and the philosophers refer to that when they say that human beings are social by nature, meaning that they need to come together with others to cooperatively establish and enhance their existence; and this is a major component in the meaning of *ʿumrān*.[21]

Allah made human beings distinct from animals with the ability to reason and make things with their hands, and the ability to communicate with other humans. If there was no such cooperation, then human beings would not be able to produce nourishment and food, and their life would not be the same. If we bear in mind that God never sent any Messenger except to be obeyed, and that obedience is connected to the laws that have to do with *ʿumrān*, then it is inevitable that the laws that govern *ʿumrān* must be connected to the higher aims of Shariʿah. But attaining power and achieving prosperity on earth is possible without religion. People could exist and live without divine law. In fact, the People of the Book and those who follow the Prophets are few relative to other peoples who form the majority of the world. And the latter are able to build states and achieve development and prosperity, let alone meeting the basic needs of life. This is what we can see at present in regions all over. But those who live in disorder, without any purpose at all, will not attain a sound life. This narrative comes through clearly in Ibn Khaldūn's core idea about "the spread of destruction and mischief in people's lives," which can inevitably lead to the end of humankind. Maintaining a sound life for humankind is the aim of Shariʿah and its five indispensables, namely the preservation of religion, human life, intellect, lineage, and wealth.[22]

The methodological contribution of al-Shāṭibī's approach to the *maqāṣid* discipline is manifested in examining particulars in a thorough manner, connecting them to one another in accordance with general guidelines so as to avoid apparent contradictions between them. The methodological revolution of Ibn Khaldūn is manifested in its moving from particular issues to broad, sweeping issues, and in its formulating universal guidelines that are reached through an examination of how the particular issues grow, develop, and change, and through an examination of how the particular issues interact and persist. Based on these two matters, one may derive comprehensive concepts that encompass particular issues but are not restricted by limitations. Hence, what appears to be a contradiction will be resolved through a deep examination of history in light of the Shariʿah Texts, and examining Shariʿah Texts in depth, in light of the lessons of history.

B. Extracting *Maqāṣid* for an *ʿUmrānī* Perspective

The previous discussion only briefly highlighted features of Ibn Khaldūn's methodology. It therefore behooves us to examine his ideas in more detail. The aim here is not to discuss his entire theory or to visit all of his ideas; rather, we want to examine certain issues that he treats in *al-Muqaddimah* from the aspect of their connection to the five indispensable aims of Shariʿah. Despite his ideas being well-known, they are not usually thought of as having any connection to the *maqāṣid* field; this being due to the prevalent methods being used in the study of *maqāṣid al-Sharīʿah*. But, if we shift our focus in the study of *maqāṣid* from the individual perspective to that of society as a whole, we will appreciate the significance of Ibn Khaldūn's views. That is because the life of the individual and the *sharʿī maṣāliḥ* that are connected to the individual could not be attained except through the soundness of the social system on which a society or community is based. And given that many commands and aims of Shariʿah relate to collective efforts, the concept of *ʿumrān* should be regarded as fundamental to the aims of Shariʿah.

At this point we will not repeat the definition of the term *ʿumrān* (that was discussed in the introduction and will be discussed again in the coming last chapter); we will let the reader get a sense of it from Ibn Khaldūn's own words. Yet, we hint that such a concept is expansive and attends to the wider dynamics of a civilization. *ʿUmrān* is not civilization per se, neither is it economic development; rather, it is more about the socio-historical laws that produce civilization. Therefore, it should be of no surprise that the implied conception of *maqāṣid* for Ibn Khaldūn is qualitatively different in its nature and in the methodology of their derivation.

Ibn Khaldūn did not claim that he was writing on *maqāṣid*. The academic hegemony of fiqh methods would not have allowed such a claim. Also, we should remember that when al-Shāṭibī died, his now celebrated work on *maqāṣid* was not yet looked highly upon, even that his work was deeply rooted in *uṣūl al-fiqh*. The intellectual field on *sharʿī* subjects were not ready to admit that Ibn Khaldūn's contribution had *maqāṣidī* implications. Ibn Khaldūn's contribution is not simply an expansion upon an idea that already existed in the field of *maqāṣid*, but laying a new kind foundation for the aims of Shariʿah, though from an *ʿumrānī* perspective. What follows is a discussion of certain *ʿumrānī* aims in the thought of Ibn Khaldūn that gives credence to this work's reformulated *maqaṣid*, namely: having a sound understanding of religion, well-being of the self, balanced societal order, economic vitality, and a just system of government. These are the outlines that we will further discuss in the last chapter.

Sound Worldview

If we expand the concept of religion to include soundness in understanding the universe and natural laws, then it would be inclusive of the ideas already expressed (explicitly and implicitly) by Ibn Khaldūn in his *Muqaddimah* regarding the concept of natural laws, the purpose behind the creation of the universe, and human being's role in this universe. In regard to the treatment of natural laws in Ibn Khaldūn's thought, Adnan Zarzur tells us that the focus of Ibn Khaldūn's theory was not confined to *ʿaṣabiyyah* (social cohesion) as al-Husari suggested, or *dawlah* (the state) as Taha Hussein suggested, or *al-badāwah wa al-ḥaḍārah* (nomadism vs. civilized life) and the conflict between them as Ali al-Wardi suggested; rather, Ibn Khaldūn's discourse on these matters came in the context of his discourse on the natural laws governing society.[23] In other words, natural laws encompass all of these matters. Hence, we may say here that the focal point in the *Muqaddimah* of Ibn Khaldūn is natural laws, or that his theory is essentially about natural laws.

We referred earlier to the concept of *al-amr al-wujūdi* (laws and regulations to which society is subject, including natural laws) in the work of Ibn Khaldūn. This concept has many decisive consequences in our understanding of Islamic issues. With this concept false dualities will be rejected, and deceiving ideas about compulsion (*jabr* – i.e., denial of human free will), or denial of the divine decree, and talking about contradictions between reason and the Shariʿah Texts will become futile. Studying the revealed Book and studying this open universe, or simultaneous study of the Qurʾan and the universe, is what Ibn Khaldūn attempted to promote and it is the basis of his vision. There is no doubt that this conceptual dimension is not sufficiently present in the books of *maqāṣid*.

Ibn Khaldūn paid a great deal of attention to the concept of the unseen and the essence of Prophethood, as he said in the *Muqaddimah*:

> The Qurʾan itself is the revelation from God, and it is a miracle. The proof of that is in the Qurʾan itself, and there is no need for external evidence, as is the case with all other miracles that could accompany the revelation. Hence, it is the clearest of proofs, because the evidence and what it points to is the same. This is the meaning of the words of the Prophet (ṢAAS), "There was no Prophet who was not given signs (miracles) on the basis of which people believed; what I have been given is revelation that Allah has revealed to me, and I hope that I will be the one with the greatest number of followers on the Day of Resurrection."[24]

Thus, Ibn Khaldūn confirms that the Qurʾan is the ultimate reference point, which should not be subject to any doubtful argument that found its way to the Muslims after their mixing with neighboring civilizations. What we are trying to highlight here is that preserving religion involves staying away from the mythological thinking. Preserving religion includes the appreciation of the God-created natural laws and the laws of causality, turning to Allah alone, and affirming that the Qurʾan is the only reference point and that the Sunnah explains it. This should not prevent from thinking of that which is subject to different interpretations and that which is to be subject to rational thinking, without going to extremes in such a way that undermines the nature of our belief in Islam.

Emotional and Psychological Well-being

Ibn Khaldūn's discourse was aimed at producing a theory in a systematic and cohesive manner. He complained about blind following and the fact that there was no longer any interest in engaging in ijtihad, and all that was left was mere imitation. Hence, he says, "These four *madhhabs* and their views came to be regarded as fundamentals of Islam, and disputes arose among those who adhere to them and follow their rulings as if disputing Shariʿah texts and the [universal principles] of *uṣūl al-fiqh*."[25] In other words, taking the views of the imams as being the fundamentals of Islam led to misunderstanding of the rulings and it also led to undermining ʿumrān, which is the basis for the well-being of the system of Islam. Ibn Khaldūn expressed concern about the mixing of what is part of Islam with some of the practices of the Prophet which come under the category of customs and habits. As an example is the issue of medicine, which falls under ʿādiyyāt (ordinary empirical experiences), that is part of human endeavors. He tells us that the Prophet Muhammad was sent to "teach us Shariʿah and was not sent to instruct us on medicine or other *ʿādiyyāt*."[26]

Al-Shāṭibī held that everything in the Sunnah has a basis in the Qur'an. Ibn Khaldūn offered a more elaborate understanding of the Sunnah's place vis-à-vis the Qur'an and Islam. Ibn Khaldūn not only links the Sunnah to the Qur'anic text, but he also connects it to the higher objectives with respect to *uṣūl al-dīn* and the mission of the Prophets. Ibn Khaldūn's approach to understanding the Sunnah parallels the concept of the *maqāmāt* (the various roles) of the Messenger which was referred to by al-Qarāfī (with Ibn Khaldūn's approach being even more elaborate in many ways).

As Ibn Khaldūn's concern was to correct the understanding of causality at the level of popular culture, he also paid attention to doing so at the institutional level and the role of "movers and shakers," pointing out the relationship between those with executive authority ("people of the sword") and the scholars ("people of the pen"), and the possibility that the politicians may gain the upper hand and that the scholars may come under the control of those in authority, at which point, "the pen would become like a servant and promoter of those in authority" and "the people are followers of those in authority and follow their way."[27] Ibn Khaldūn criticizes the way of later scholars and their going to extremes in discussing and explaining fiqh matters, saying:

> It should be noted that what undermines people's efforts to acquire knowledge and gain proper understanding of what they learn is the fact that so many books have been written [on the same issues] and there is such a variety in terminology and approaches to teaching. The student and seeker of knowledge is then required to remember all of that, and only after learning all of that will he be regarded as one who has acquired knowledge. Hence, the student needs to memorize all or most of this information, and to learn and recognize different approaches and styles of learning. Even if a student spends their entire life trying to read all that has been written about a particular subject matter, they would still not cover everything of that subject. Hence, he will inevitably fail to reach the level of being recognized as one who has acquired knowledge.[28]

In other words, the system of education in Islamic fiqh causes a person to fail to learn what he is striving to learn, which is in contrast to how it would be if the education style was "more reasonable and straightforward."

The phrase "*al-amr al-ṭabīʿī*" ("the nature of things") is regarded by Ibn Khaldūn as one of the basic concepts in his theory. We may examine the implications of this concept on two levels: the individual level, and the collective or societal level, including the natural laws governing human society. With regard to the individual level, Ibn Khaldūn examines it from three perspectives: (1) from the perspective of the physical make-up of human beings; (2) from the perspective of the human psyche and the innate nature of humankind (*fiṭrah*); and (3) from the perspective of people's upbringing and the habits and customs with which they are exposed to during their upbringing.

With respect to the first perspective, this includes matters such as the effect of pollution or hunger on the physical well-being of people. There is of course more detail pertaining to this perspective. The second perspective pertains to the *fiṭrah* (innate human nature), concerning which Ibn Khaldūn has some interesting views. There is a well-known debate concerning human being's inclination towards good and evil and whether their innate nature (*fiṭrah*) is equally inclined towards good and evil or is more inclined to one or the other. Ibn Khaldūn offers a unique perspective on innate human nature (*fiṭrah*), holding that, "Human beings are more inclined to develop good characteristics than evil ones by their innate nature and by their innate ability to speak and understand because their evil inclination is a result of animalistic forces in them (physical desires). As for being human, they are more inclined towards good and more inclined to develop good characteristics."[29]

The third perspective regarding *al-amr al-ṭabīʿī* (the nature of things), according to Ibn Khaldūn, has to do with people's upbringing. Here, Ibn Khaldūn focuses on the impact of the surrounding environment on people's behavior, and it is on the basis of that outlook that we should understand his discussion of the *ʿumrān* of the Bedouin and savage nations, not from a deterministic perspective. Along the same line, Ibn Khaldūn places an emphasis on the importance of *ʿurf* (custom and tradition) in shaping people's lives, but he states that *ʿurf* should be subject to Islamic teachings and values. The formation of a noble class that distinguishes itself from the rest of society is something common in human societies. Although the customs and traditions of the noble class may elevate the manners and behavior of society as a whole, self-admiration and arrogance (on the part of the noble class) may ultimately corrupt it, reducing their actions to mere boasting that is unable to promote any kind of good behavior and manners.[30]

Ibn Khaldūn's view about living a life of luxury and ease, and the consequences thereof, is a basic element in his theory. Living a life of civility is the ultimate goal of the Bedouin that he strives his utmost to attain. The city dwellers, because of what they suffer of indulging in all sorts of physical pleasures and luxuries, focusing on worldly matters and the physical desires of this world, have developed many blameworthy attitudes and characteristics, and they indulge in evil deeds, thus drifting away from the path of good commensurate with the extent to which they indulge in pleasures.[31]

Ibn Khaldūn also points out the effect of behavioral reinforcement and becoming accustomed to good deeds and conduct, and the impact that has on rectifying a person's character; because the impact of deeds will inevitably be reflected in a person's character. Therefore, righteous deeds will have a good impact on character, increasing one in wisdom; and evil deeds and foolishness will have the opposite effect. These consequences will become deeply rooted if the deed in question is done repeatedly.[32]

Understanding the aims of Shariʿah is thus important in thinking about issues such as this, especially wherein deeds that are generally permissible can, in their repetition, lead to foolishness on an individual level, which may in turn lead to mischief and social ills if they become entrenched among a group of people. Such people may be influenced by their professions and ways of earning a living, and other habits and customs of which the mischief and negative impact do not become apparent except over time when it develops into something serious.[33]

We can observe that the way in which children are raised has an impact on their character. For instance, if punishment is commonly resorted to when raising a child, this could lead to the child losing resilience, because carrying out the punishment can lead to the child feeling humiliated, which undoubtedly reduces resiliency. But if the focus in raising the child is discipline and education from an early age, this will not lead to loss of resilience, because the child will have been raised to observe proper decorum and listen to instruction; thus, the child will not be so overly resilient or confident as to overstep the mark. We see from the aforementioned Ibn Khaldūn's concern about the method used in raising and educating children that was prevalent in his time. He was aware that the way in which a child is raised, educated, and disciplined could negatively impede upon the goals behind that education, including religious education.[34]

Balanced Societal Order

The concept of ʿaṣabiyyah is central to Ibn Khaldūn, and its general meaning is cohesiveness and solidarity. This concept does not only apply to political matters; rather, it can apply to anything having to do with the notion of maintaining the well-being of society and the coherence of its components. Ibn Khaldūn discusses what people have in common at the level of thinking and belief, and how that could help to form a solid community, as well as bringing the different components of society together. The religious content is what purifies the social structure and creates balance between the different components of society. This is because the religious spirit takes away negative competition and envy that are usually found among people of pure ʿaṣabiyyah, and instead causes them to focus on the truth. Once a community develops that higher purpose into what it wants to achieve, nothing can stand in its way, especially because they are all heading in one direction. Such a community will have a unified goal, and the members of the community are prepared to sacrifice in order to achieve this.[35]

When sound religious teachings become entrenched in people's minds, it leads to the development of civilized character. Therefore, the preservation of these religious teachings becomes a goal in and of itself, as this will be what the masses accept and are willing to follow, even at a subconscious level. Moreover, this civilized character will produce a general framework for different components of society to meet, including non-Muslims. In other words, what is needed is not only preserving religion in the sense of rules and decrees, but also to preserve it on the basis that it is a general framework in which people come together and can agree with one another, so that the moral teachings of religion become teachings that dictate cooperation that people follow by way of customs and traditions, and teachings that people refer to in the event of differences.

We should highlight here Ibn Khaldūn's view that when a nation becomes accustomed to humiliation and being submissive, it will lead to loss of innovativeness and strength. One of the obstacles that prevent a nation from obtaining strength is when it feels humiliated and submits to others, the reason being that these feelings of humiliation undermine the strength and intensity of the sense of solidarity (ʿaṣabiyyah). The way in which this is connected to the ʿumrānī objectives is the manner of cultural adaptation followed by the nation when impacted by events and calamities. Therefore, what needs to be included in the ʿumrānī objectives is protection of the general culture from weakness, so that it will be possible to preserve the cohesion and solidarity (ʿaṣabiyyah) of the Ummah, at times of both ease and calamity, victory and defeat, and any situation in between. As for his saying, "Therefore, you see that those who are prevailed over try to imitate those who prevailed over them in their clothing, mount, and weaponry, and in the way in which they use them and shape them, and in all matters,"[36] this may be understood as not only being by way of approval, but also being by way of seeking to compete and stand up to them.

There is a correlation between social harmony and the establishment of homes, including the way in which homes are organized within a certain residential area. To have a home to dwell in which is a refuge for physical safety in cities is something that humankind has an inclination towards and strives to attain, because it is part of his nature to think of the consequences of the conditions in which he lives. Those who have homes to live in may increase in number, such that more homes are needed to be built in the same area. A community thus arises that needs to be protected (e.g., by setting up a barrier around it), and hence, forming a city. The preservation of human life and honor, and many other everyday interests that carry weight in Shariʿah, dictates the way these homes are designed, which should be done in a manner suitable to offer protection from external enemies or harm.[37]

The notion of social harmony does not only concern attaining kinship among fellow believers but includes examining the causes that lead to differences and resentment. Great attention should be paid to these causes because it will be beneficial for people at the communal level. It is thus very important that [bringing harmony among people] be considered among the aims of Shariʿah. And what Ibn Khaldūn established as the things that are essential for ʿumrān must be included in the theory of *maqāṣid*.

Economic Vitality

We find in Ibn Khaldūn's work much discussion pertaining to economics and people's financial matters, and the idea of striking a balance in dealing with the bounties of Allah when developing the economy. His contributions in this field came before the emergence of heavy industry and the service economy that are widespread nowadays. He discusses in precise terms the issue of generating wealth for the state when the state reaches its peak and has different institutions and departments. Taxes are lower in the early stages of a state's development, but the total revenue collected will be greater; whereas, at the end of a state's development, taxes will be higher, but the revenue collected will be smaller. Hence, the challenge is to create a balance in tax collection so that the state will have sufficient funds to function and carry out its duties, without burdening people unfairly to the point that they lose motivation to work. When the taxes imposed on people are light, they will be motivated to strive and work, so that their economic activities will increase and the state's revenue will increase as a result of the lower taxes. And when economic activity increases, it will generate more wealth in people's hands, thus increasing the total revenue.[38]

Something similar may be said regarding social systems and organizations. When they are simple and straightforward, it is easy to keep the public wealth in view and see how it is spent, and there is no need for a great deal of effort to identify appropriate ways of spending it. Hence, the poor, needy, and widows will be obvious deserving cases, in a society that is organized in a simple fashion; whereas, when it is complex, the need for bureaucracy arises, which itself incurs public cost.

Ibn Khaldūn discusses how serious the matter is if people in authority and the ruler get involved in trade and business. That is because when the people are equal in terms of economic status and compete with one another, it serves the interests of all. But if the ruler joins them in this competition, when he has much greater wealth than they do, hardly any one of them will be able to earn a living. Thus, Ibn Khaldūn points out the need to protect livelihoods and all opportunities of earning a living, to create an environment in which wealth can grow, and to protect it from the transgression of people in authority. That is because the state has too much power, of which it could create imbalance in the markets and ways of investment. Everyone is competing by striving hard in the field of his expertise to bring benefit for himself, and this brings benefit to others who are working for him. This is in contrast to the situation when people of authority and people with power engage in trade and farming.[39]

Just System of Government

Before discussing this *ʿumrānī* aim, we should note two methodological points pertaining to Ibn Khaldūn's discourse:

1   The focus of Ibn Khaldūn's theory is not *ʿaṣabiyyah* (social cohesion) per se, the state, Bedouin life, or civilized life. Rather, his focus is the natural laws that govern societies; that is, his stress on *ʿaṣabiyyah* should be understood as pointing to a social law that is often forgotten.

2   It is important not to confuse normative standards with social laws. Normative standards have to do with ideals, whereas social and natural laws have to do with what usually happens with regard to humanity's actual situation.[40]

However, focusing the discussion on the natural laws as societal factors that support *ʿumrān* does not mean to Ibn Khaldūn the dismissal of normative standards, because they represent the principled high standards that human effort should strive to attain.

Keeping these two methodological points in mind is important, so that we do not think that the ideas of Ibn Khaldūn are applicable only to the conditions and circumstances of the 8th AH/14th CE century when he wrote his theory, as he was attempting to write a theory that was appropriate to the prevalent conditions of his time. In examining Ibn Khaldūn's ideas, we realize that his theory encompassed very broad concepts having to do with the state, such as: the intellectual basis for politics, the qualifications required of the one who is to be in charge of the state, on what causes wealth from the state's treasury may be spent, and the concepts of cohesiveness, stability, and change.

The intellectual basis for politics

To the cursory reader, Ibn Khaldūn's theory appears realistic and pragmatic. However, the intellectual foundation of the state, according to his theory and how he envisaged the legitimacy of authority and its role, is informed by and deeply rooted in an Islamic worldview. It is as such that he repeatedly affirms that, "The religious spirit takes away [negative] competition and envy that are usually found among people of ʿaṣabiyyah, and causes them to focus on the *ḥaqq* [i.e., truth, or what is just and right]."[41] The ideal is to attain *ḥaqq*. At the same time, and according to natural laws, there is a need for a strong and cohesive solidarity (*ʿaṣabiyyah*). However, the latter should not supersede or cancel out the former, even though there is a possibility that the latter may fail to achieve what is required by the former. It is the religious spirit that always purifies the group feeling of its dross and malevolence, because the latter may lead to corruption and mischief if it is left without cleansing and being subjected to certain ideals.[42]

Qualifications required of the one who is to be in charge of the state

Repeated mention of a strong social cohesion (*ʿaṣabiyyah*) in the context of discussing dominion and power should not make us overlook what Ibn Khaldūn was emphasizing, that it is essential for those in authority to be qualified to manage the affairs of the state. Thus, the ruler and people in authority are a functionary class, and they are the ones to take care of the people or subjects. Ibn Khaldūn affirms that running the affairs of state (*siyāsah*) is an art that cannot be merely based on having vast knowledge, whether that is knowledge of Shariʿah or other types of knowledge. Similarly, that the ruler be very rich, such that people are impressed with his wealth, does not make him qualified to rule. What really matters with regard to people of authority is the ability of a good character, which leads to gentleness and kindness.[43]

If the ruler is oppressive and cruel in punishment, seeking out people's faults and mistakes, the people will be controlled by fear and will feel humiliated. They will try to protect themselves from the ruler by means of lies, deceit, and scheming; thus, they will acquire those bad characteristics and become corrupt.[44] In other words, the style of ruling and the characteristics of the subjects are interconnected, and the impact of the resentment that may exist between the ruler and his subjects does not only harm the latter; rather, it also harms the former, because the resentment may make the subjects disloyal at times of war and when fighting enemies, undermining state security because of ill feeling (between ruler and subjects). They may even plot to kill him because of that ill feeling. Thus, mischief will spread and chaos will prevail. And if he continues to rule and suppress them, social cohesion will be undermined.[45]

Therefore, even though having strong social solidarity (*ʿaṣabiyyah*) is something essential for the stability of the state, when it is diverted from its purpose and is used to achieve the goals and desires of politicians or those in authority, "the type of social and political dynamic will prevail that leads to civil war and much killing."[46] If running the people's affairs is an art, that does not mean – according to Ibn Khaldūn – that the people in authority should be cunning or exceedingly clever, "because that could result in wrongdoing and bad conduct."[47] The intellectual basis for the person in authority being in charge of people's affairs is justice and other great Islamic virtues, but attaining the *ḥaqq* and achieving other ideals should be done in accordance with *al-amr al-wujūdī* (laws and regulations to which society is subject, including natural laws). These are general and natural laws to which all communities are subject.

If these laws are put forward by intellectuals, statesmen, and those with deep insight, then their basis will be rational thought. In addition, if these laws are rooted in divine Islamic values and Shariʿah principles, then they will procure benefit both in this world and the hereafter. In other words, running the affairs of the state in accordance with religious teachings and based on the natural law of *al-amr al-wujūdī* will direct the state towards attaining the ultimate ideals that the *Shāriʿ* intended. The teachings of Islam thus provide the rationale for people to base all their affairs, both those pertaining to acts of worship (*ʿibadāt*) and those pertaining to human interactions (*muʿāmalāt*), on a foundation that reconciles revelation and reason. This includes running the affairs of the state and the people—a matter that is both critical and natural for human society.

Ibn Khaldūn had thus offered an integrated theory of the aims of Sharīʿah and the ways to attain these objectives. For Ibn Khaldūn, the aim of a political system is to ensure that all people behave in accordance with the dictates of reason. And the aim of Islamic governance is to ensure that all people behave in accordance with the values and teachings of Sharīʿah. In fact, Islamic governance should uphold what the Prophet had upheld in safeguarding religious teachings and governing worldly affairs in accordance therewith, there being no contradiction between the two.[48] An Islamic system of governance would thus identify higher goals to achieve and prescribe ways to achieving them, while those in authority would strive to achieve those goals on the basis of rational thinking, according to the law of *al-amr al-wujūdī*. Hence, the Muslim state operates simultaneously according to *sharʿī* rulings and guidelines on moral conduct, and natural laws that pertain to human society. Furthermore, Ibn Khaldūn notes that governing in a Muslim state involves specialization and division of authorities and functions according to skills, all of which, nonetheless, be grounded first and foremost in Islamic teachings, then on the recommendations offered by those with requisite experience, and lastly on lessons learned from previous leadership.[49]

Ibn Khaldūn leaves no room for doubt about the type of people who should be in charge of running the affairs of the state or community from an Islamic perspective, and that the nature of their rule should not be theocratic. Ibn Khaldūn concludes that his purpose in this discourse is to explain the institutions that the state needs in order to carry out its duties. Discussion of the duties of rulers and people in authority is from the perspective of *ʿumrān* and the role of human beings therein, not from the perspective of *sharʿī* rulings. This is so because discussion of the duties of rulers from a *sharʿī* perspective has already been sufficiently presented in various books. Our discourse here is from the perspective of *ʿumrān*.[50]

The treasury (*bayt al-māl*) and where wealth is to be spent

The third matter that is of importance for the political stability of the Ummah is the state's ability to secure what it needs of wealth so that it will be able to function and carry out its duties. We have noted above, in the context of preserving wealth, that people in positions of political authority who are running the affairs of the Ummah should not be involved, as persons, in trade, business, and other investment activities. The point of discussion below focuses on two aspects related to state finance: spending too much, which leads to deficit; and the causes on which the money in the public treasury (*bayt al-māl*) of the Muslims deserves to be spent. I pointed out earlier the challenge that arises when society increases in numbers and becomes more complex, which calls for bureaucracies and ministries that, themselves, consume public funds. Under exploitative regimes, such administrative departments do not do their job properly because of what they suffer of mismanagement or autonomy in the running of their affairs. In other words, increased complexity of society leads to two things, one of which leads to the other: (1) the increased need for departments or ministries to organize the people's affairs and serve their needs; and (2) increase in the number of ministries or departments with the passage of time. When the rulership turns into a dictatorship, there will be more taxes imposed on people.

Ibn Khaldūn adds the term *mukūs* (levies) to the terminology of duties and taxes, a term that invariably carries negative connotation.[51] While he acknowledges that expanding ministries do need funds that are secured through taxation, later on excessive taxation and levies takes place as the furtive administration indulges itself in extravagance luxury. And because this increase is very gradual, no one notices it and no one knows who imposed it in the first place. The matter then reaches a critical point and goes beyond "the balanced threshold."[52] In other words, we find that there is a need to create a balance between two important *maṣāliḥ* or interests recognized by Shariʿah: the need for the state to collect funds from people in order to be able to carry out its duties and provide services for the public, and the financial well-being of individuals. These two important matters are interconnected.

Mishandling of public funds could happen indirectly or unintentionally by increasing the funds allocated to different ministries or departments over time. That is because if the ruler becomes powerful and the people running the affairs of the state feel secure due to the stability and prosperity of the state, then the ruler in that case will have exclusive control over the taxes that have been collected, or most of them, and he will accumulate wealth and keep it for his own spending in various ways. Thus, his wealth will increase and his own coffers will be filled, and he will increase in power and prominence; he will look down on his own people, so the people around him and his relatives – such as his adviser, scribe, doorkeeper, associate and police – will increase in prosperity, and thus they will gain status and accumulate wealth.[53]

We should point out that this is not something that simply happens to some individuals who are motivated by love of wealth; rather, the attitude and behavior of those who are in charge of the state slowly change after the state becomes powerful. Moreover, spending in this extravagant manner increases the prestige of the state, which is something that could be justifiable and acceptable when the entire nation is living in a state of prosperity. Increasing spending to give prestige to the state and giving generously to those who are working for the state may reflect the power of the state at the beginning, and whilst the state is still young and powerful. When the state then begins to decline with the diminishing of social cohesion (ʿaṣabiyyah) and the demise of the first generation who built the state, at that point the ruling elite will need helpers and supporters, because there will be many rebels and revolutionaries who dispute its authority, and it will be afraid of losing power. The ruler will therefore give much of public funds to his helpers and supporters, who are people with strong solidarity (ʿaṣabiyyah) willing to fight to support him. Thus, the government will be spending a significant share of public treasury and what has been collected of taxes to protect the state. Eventually, tax revenue will decrease and the need of the state for wealth will increase. The inner circle, bodyguards, and scribes will become less prosperous and will lose prestige, and prestige will be restricted to a smaller circle of the ruling elite.[54]

With regard to the appropriate causes on which to spend the money of the Muslim treasury (*bayt al-māl*), Ibn Khaldūn refers to some of them and stresses the need of an overall balance. He affirms that the central government of the state needs wealth, and that it is risky to allow different provinces to keep all wealth to themselves, for that will lead to political repercussions that could go as far as the secession of some provinces, and cause division among the Muslims. What is required is moderate taxation on a reasonable basis, and a balance between revenues collected and government spending. Furthermore, Ibn Khaldūn acknowledges that what the state spends plays a major role in energizing the economy, the reason being that the state is the greatest driving force for the economy, and the major player in social and economic development. The state is the driving force for different economic activities, so if it undergoes stagnation and its spending is reduced, then that will affect other sectors of the economy, which will slow down even more. Ibn Khaldūn made the connection between political stability and economic prosperity, and he referred to the accumulation of knowledge, skills, and experience in different crafts and industries, and the traditions connected to that; all of this could become well-established and well grounded by means of repetition over time, with the result that it would become second nature for subsequent generations. The state plays a role in all of this. Ibn Khaldūn notes:

> Here, there is another subtle issue, which is that the main customer for these crafts, and the high-quality ones among them, is the state, for it is the state that will buy these products and will place orders for these products. Whatever the state does not buy, other people in the city will buy it, but not on the same scale as the state, because the state is the main driving force behind the economy, so the state will buy everything; whether it buys a little or a great deal is all the same for the state.[55]

Cohesion, stability, and change

It is nothing strange that in the theorization of Ibn Khaldūn we see a great deal of attention paid to the concept of stability. That is not only because there was something unique about the circumstances of the 8th AH/14th CE century; rather, it represents a basic need in human society. Nothing can be achieved without stability, and having power and authority to bring society together is something that is required for the purpose of *'umrān*, because humankind cannot live and exist except by living in community and cooperating so that they can maintain physical well-being and the basic necessities.[56] To have effective political authority, those who are in authority should be surrounded by people with a strong sense of solidarity (*'aṣabiyyah*) in order to preserve the system. The issue of solidarity is universal and is even applicable to the Prophets. Such was the situation of the Prophets (blessings and peace be upon them) when they called people to God; they were protected by means of their clans and relatives, and we know that they were supported by Allah, Who could have supported them by means of everything in the universe, if He had so willed. But Allah wanted things to take their natural course. And Allah is Most Wise, All-Knowing.[57]

Solidarity is not a mere tribal connection among some people; rather, it is a connection that could be limited to people within a tribe, or it could go beyond the tribe, as it must do when the state develops further. Thus, a new solidarity may emerge that is based on some pre-existing solidarity, and that new solidarity prevails over all others so that it brings them all together and unites them under a new social cohesion that encompasses existing groups.[58]

Agreeing with Abū Bakr al-Baqillānī, Ibn Khaldūn elaborates further noting that the Arabs all acknowledged the high status of Quraysh, and that if leadership was not given to Quraysh in this new state, then the expected result would be division in the leadership of the new forming state. But with the passage of time, being of Quraysh became irrelevant. He then concludes his discussion by saying:

> Moreover, history testifies to that, for no one could lead a nation or a generation except one who seizes power and authority over them, and it is very rare that *shar'ī* instructions are contrary to *al-amr al-wujūdī* (laws and regulations to which society is subject, including natural laws).[59]

Ibn Khaldūn's view concerning this matter is clear and decisive. He reached his conclusion on this issue in light of a collective understanding of the *maqāṣid*, despite that there is a clear text and a claim of scholarly consensus on the matter to the contrary of his conclusion. He introduced the concept of *maqāṣid* into an issue of politics and ruling in which the *maqāṣid* had not been introduced, and he broadened the scope of *maṣlaḥah* from an individual to a societal level. Thus, we may conclude from the way in which Ibn Khaldūn understood *al-amr al-wujūdī* (socio-historical laws to which society is subject) that he rejected the theocratic concept of authority and the concepts of nationalist and dynastic authority. Instead, he introduces new concepts, based on his understanding of the aims of Shari'ah, and highlighting in his discussion the nature of *'umrān*. He guarded his theory from being based on imaginary notions that could not be applied in real-life situations.

We should understand the details of Ibn Khaldūn's theory on the basis of an idea that he referred to throughout his book, namely the dynamism and ongoing change that are inherent in human existence. He says:

> That is the situation of people and nations, and their customs and sects. They do not settle and remain static; rather, they differ with the passage of time, moving from one condition to another, as happens in the case of individuals, eras, and countries. Similarly, there occurred changes in the nature of things in all regions and all times: "That was Allah's way with those who passed away of old" (Qur'an 33:38).[60]

For Ibn Khaldūn, social cohesion (*'aṣabiyyah*) is a prerequisite for the ability to lead. And "once leadership of the state is established for those who are entitled to it, the successive generations of leadership form a closure on it."[61]

The role of institutions becomes clearer with the passage of time, which makes them more established and accepted by people, who willingly obey them. The strength of social cohesion and of state authority determines how long that state will abide, "because how long something lasts is connected to the driving force behind it, and the driving force behind a state is social cohesion. If social cohesion is strong, then the driving force that results from that will also be strong, and it will last for a long time."[62]

If this is the case with regard to the issue of social cohesion, then states usually face the issue of expansion and the limits thereof. The survival of states is connected to the efficiency of the administrative structure that runs its affairs and which is in charge of making the state function. So long as sufficient numbers of soldiers are still available, and their numbers have not been thinned by distribution to the borders and regions, the state will remain strong and able to expand further, until it reaches a point beyond which it cannot continue to do so. The ultimate limit for that expansion is influenced by many factors, the most important of which is the availability of abundant wealth for the state and the strength of those who are resisting its expansion from without.[63]

Ibn Khaldūn emphasized the importance of the comprehensive political idea that is promoted by the opposition – as we say nowadays – because "the well-established state develops customs and traditions that make people accept obedience to the state and believe it to be a necessary duty."[64] Similarly, "the stable state will have a great deal of income .... Therefore, they will own a lot of forces and buy good quality weapons, and will demonstrate their majestic power."[65] But victory cannot be attained by means of physical might only; rather, it takes place "by means of illusion and psychological factors. Even though the numbers of weapons and sincerity when fighting could guarantee victory, that may not be sufficient on its own."[66] But when the state begins to decline and diminish, the opposition will begin to grow stronger by means of what they gain of territory, so they will become united and fight the state, and they will no longer be under the influence of the thoughts that were demoralizing them and sapping their resolve. Then their stand-off with the state will reach its ultimate goal, and they will finally defeat the state by fighting.[67]

Even though Ibn Khaldūn affirms that natural law is that power changes hands, that does not mean that any call for change is a valid call – even if it is well-founded – unless this call follows the right course of action. For example, if the revolutionaries who have taken it upon themselves to change corruption are from among the masses and religious scholars, they may take a wrong course of action. There are many people who appear to be devoted worshippers adhering to the teachings of religion, but when they decide to stand up to unjust rulers, seeking to change their corruption, forbidding it and enjoining what is good in the hope of earning reward from God, it is like seeking reward from God in an inappropriate manner. Their actions may be hindered by two things, the first of which is that they may gather a lot of followers and supporters from among the thugs and riffraff, thus exposing themselves to great danger, with the result that many of them are killed in their attempt to change corruption. Thus, they incur sin instead of reward.[68]

What we have presented here is but a brief discussion about Ibn Khaldūn's contribution and his approach to the aims of Sharī'ah at both the societal and *'umrānī* levels. Ibn Khaldūn states:

It should be understood that this is the wisdom behind the prohibition on injustice, because of what injustice leads to of ruin and mischief, and the undermining of *'umrān*, which in turn could lead to the extinction of humankind. This is the underlying wisdom behind all five indispensable aims of Sharī'ah, namely preservation of religion, human life, intellect, procreation, and wealth. Because injustice, as noted above, could lead to the extinction of humankind, as it leads to ruin and the undermining of ʿumrān, this was the reason for the prohibition on injustice and thus it was very important to prohibit it [from a religious perspective]. There is a great deal of evidence to that effect in the Qur'an and Sunnah, but which cannot be subject to a definite and exhaustive rule.[69]

I conclude by pointing out that the basis of Ibn Khaldūn's concept is the eminence of natural laws, specifically social and historical laws. But they are not inevitable because human understanding is relative, and because throughout history various new factors may arise. Therefore, we may assume that the phrases with which Ibn Khaldūn concluded his chapters, such as the phrase "God always prevails in His purpose" and the like, were quoted for a reason and not merely for blessing. These phrases are intended to highlight the limitation of human understanding, no matter how hard people strive to reach the right conclusion.

PART III

ʿUMRĀNĪ AIMS OF SHARIʿAH

Preamble

Part Three presents a theory of the aims of Shari'ah from an *'umrani* perspective. Part One affirmed that the study of *maqāṣid al-Sharī'ah* is an intellectually critical as well as practical endeavour for the Ummah, and it is through the *maqāṣid* that the Ummah can address real-life issues that arise with the passage of time. In that part, we discussed prominent contributions of classical scholars in the field of *maqāṣid*. We also discussed distinct contemporary contributions, expounding on them and offering commentary. In Part Two, we discussed methodological issues and tried to shed light on certain concepts with the aim of laying a foundation for reshaping the *maqāṣid* from an *'umrānī* perspective. This final part introduces a novel theory, through benefits from the contributions of earlier and contemporary scholars, in an attempt to form a *maqāṣid*-based vision of Islamic *'umrān* that has a unique formation with a distinct character. That vision would give rise to an *'umrānī* outlook that is based on the concept of *tawḥīd*, a system in which individuals, as agencies, are intellectually and psychologically shaped in a particular manner, and who are connected socially on the basis of a communal social system, supporting one another in a self-sufficient economic system, and all under the umbrella of a political system that is based on consultation and justice. This type of *'umrānī maqāṣid* focuses on issues that pertain to the Muslim Ummah as a community and is not limited only to issues pertaining to individuals.

At this point, it is appropriate to remind the reader of the horizons of the term *'umrān*, as was discussed in the introduction. It is an expansive concept on which different authors stress different aspects. At its core, *'umrān* signifies the architecture of social reality. As such, it addresses the social system, both at the structural and cultural levels. Therefore, religion, language, and social ties are basic dimensions, as well as polity, economics, and society. While ʿumrān is not civilization, yet at the end it points to civilizational aspects where historical, cultural, socio-economic, and political patterns are present. One important reason why Ibn Khaldūn's approach to ʿumrān is celebrated is because it does not ponder on Shariʿah solely in terms of exerting ijtihad in the possible meanings of texts, but also in terms of an empirical societal system where historical laws are operative.

Naturally, exploring and ascertaining ʿumrānī aims of Shariʿah have to be based on an overall reading of Shariʿah Texts, the Qurʾan and Sunnah, beyond specific aḥkām and rulings governing the conduct of the individual Muslim. As is well known, much of the Shariʿah Texts (nuṣūṣ) emphasize the importance of having sound perception in philosophical questions regarding the Creator, sending prophets and messengers to guide humanity, the role of human beings on earth, and responsibility in the hereafter. And there are many nuṣūṣ that pertain to acts of worship (ʿibadāt) and matters of morality and proper conduct (akhlāq). But with regard to the area of human transactions (muʿāmalāt) and matters related to planning and management, there are fewer nuṣūṣ, especially pertaining to areas that are prone to change or evolve, such as in matters of politics and economics. Therefore, simple induction of the Shariʿah Texts related to aḥkām is not sufficient for such an endeavour. And we cannot miss that al-Shāṭibī himself noted continuously that the Shariʿah ways do not contradict majārī al-ʿādāt, the general patterns known in human conduct.

The approach to the aims of Shariʿah in this work acknowledged Ibn ʿAshur's attention to the political, financial, and social dimensions in his theory of maqāṣid; but the logic of the inclusion of such dimensions is akin to Ibn Khaldūn's thought more than that of al-Shāṭibī. This work also tried to stay as close as possible with the terminology and the categories used by al-Shāṭibī as to allow for continuity and comparison.

However, from a methodological point of view, this work has been inspired by Taha Jabir al-Alwani in his call for a new approach that would go beyond the maqāṣid having to do with the accountable individual (maqāṣid al-mukallaf). Al-Alwani suggested three supreme governing values: tawḥīd, tazkiyyah, and ʿumrān. I regard tawḥīd as the guiding ray for all branches of maqāṣid, and *tazkiyyah* (purification) as the means by which the *maqāṣid* are pursued. I regard them as such so that the notion of striving to be guided might be actualized. However, I departed from al-Alwani's approach of linear theorization; from my perspective, *tawḥīd* cannot be put at the same plain with what it guides (*tazkiyyah* and *'umrān*). Ultimately, this book adopted a multi-dimensional model of *maqāṣid* that has precedence in Ibn Khaldūn's work more than any other work. Therefore, this work neither kept the fiqh and the legal-like approach of handling the aims of Shari'ah, nor *uṣūl al-fiqh*; indeed, and as I have discussed elsewhere,[1] the approach of *uṣūl al-fiqh* is barren for analysis in the *'umrānī* perspective.

Nevertheless, I tried to keep points of correspondence with the classical *maqāṣid* theory. Namely, the well-known five indispensable aims were maintained, but after collapsing together two of them (the self and the intellect) and adding a new one (that is related to polity). I divided each goal into four sub-objectives, such that we could cover all human activities that are subject to the guidelines of Shari'ah, and that they may be rectified. I did not limit myself to using the term *ḥifẓ* (preservation), because today it has acquired a meaning of stagnation, not renewal. Therefore, I added to it the concept *tazkiyyah* (refinement, purification, and evolvement).

The theory that I shall present does not refer to the three well-known levels of *maqāṣid*, that is the indispensable, the exigent, and the enhancement—granted that these levels are among the most valuable aspects of *maqāṣid* theory. Defining these levels in a precise manner would be rather challenging, especially as it pertains to social issues, wherein the dynamics of society are subject to ongoing change. I have therefore avoided altogether discussion of them in this chapter. I also believe it is more appropriate to regard the higher aims as general objectives, and to regard the nature of a real-life matter as being what determines which of the three levels that matter corresponds to. It is left to scholars to determine the practicality of an aim and how it corresponds to the different levels, all the while understanding that an aim may overlap between different levels. Nevertheless, the three levels are relevant to the issue under discussion, namely regarding where they belong on the continuum between individual and communal (i.e., in terms of the number of people who are affected), and the area in which they may have an impact, and the extent and intensity of that impact.

Table: *Maqāṣid* from an *'umrānī* perspective

Major aim	Minor aim
I The preservation of religion and the refinement of its worldview	1 Guarding against belief in incarnation (*ḥulūliyyah*)
	2 Guarding against thinking of Allah in physical terms (*tajsīd*)
	3 Guarding against transcendent nationalism
	4 Guarding against denial of the hereafter (*dahriyyah*)
II The preservation and the refinement of the holistic self and its intellect	1 Sincerity and mindfulness of Allah
	2 Trust in Allah and certainty of faith
	3 Patience and striving
	4 Learning and education
III The preservation of family and the refinement of the societal order	1 Familial tranquillity
	2 Mutual support
	3 Mutual advice
	4 Reconciliation
IV The preservation of wealth and the refinement of livelihood	1 Taking possession of material wealth as a trustee
	2 Circulation of wealth
	3 Emancipation
	4 Sustainability and sufficiency
V The preservation of polity and the refinement of governance	1 Justice in rights and obligations
	2 Perfecting consultation
	3 Jihad for peace and security
	4 Transcendental communication and elaboration of the Islamic universal message

Thus, we see that the first aim is purifying one's worldview, because no aspect of life can be sound unless there is sound perception at such abstract level, and because people's worldview may be subject to contamination, leading their perception to drift away from the unique perspective of Islam. The second aim is the preserving and purification of the self, broadly understood, which includes the emotional, cognitive, conscientious, and the human will; it also includes the physical self without which such four aspects seize to exist. Such a conceptualization of the self avoids separating its different interacting dimensions. The third *ʿumrānī* aim is preserving the family system, the very basic social unit, and refining societal order. Pointedly, the concept of societal order surpasses the realm of interacting individuals and involves the realms of institutions within which individuals operate. Thus, this refers to the broad space within which all human activity occurs, namely politics, economics, and education; it also includes cultural developments. As for the aim of preserving wealth, it goes beyond individuals' property and include all the resources in the universe that mankind can utilize. Finally, I have added the aim of preserving the political order and refining its institutions of governance, this being an aim that is absent or often neglected in *maqāṣid* discourse.

The aforementioned are aspects without which the study of any human society cannot be sound. Ijtihad should be deployed to address those matters which are influenced by and thus vary according to time and place. Analyzing matters within this approach allows us to take into account what is constant and what is subject to change.

Our discussion in what follows will aim to highlight the connection between different parts of *maqāṣid* theory in an orderly and interactive manner, highlighting the impact of each part of the theory on other parts so as to coalesce them in a framework that reflects the nature of Islam, which is comprehensive and balanced. This approach is based on full awareness of the changes and developments that have taken place in this world, and seeks to address them in a critical manner that goes beyond merely recognizing them; a manner that is not swayed by the new developments and does not compromise on the distinct features of the Islamic *Weltanschauung*.

The diagram below attempts to capture in simple terms the *maqāṣid* theory that will be presented subsequently. It places religion at the center, which reflects an important aspect to the theory: it is not appropriate to place the aim of "preserving religion and the refinement of its worldview" on the same footing with any of the other aims. This is so because a sound understanding of Islam and the concept of *tawḥīd* is central to all activities of life. There is no individual conduct, no social organization, no financial system, and no political structure that is not in some way impacted by religion, guided by its teachings, and shaped by its principles. All activities, social, economic, and political, revolve around the core of Islamic conceptions and their understanding thereof.

Diagram: The five *maqāṣid* realms[2]

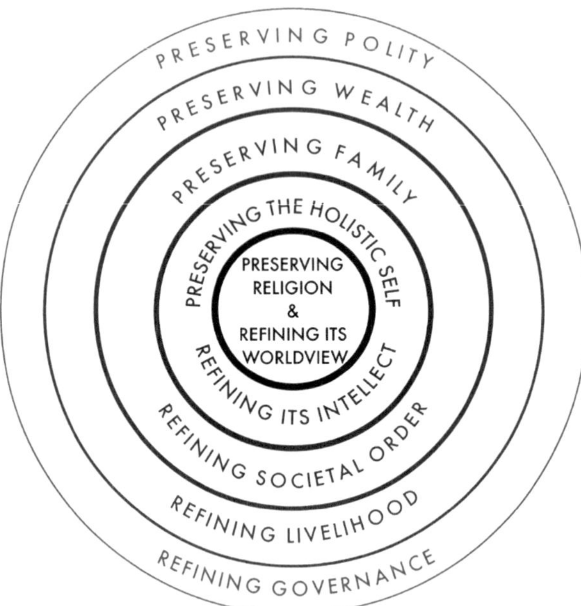

Finally, I made a commitment to be brief, as my primary aim was to highlight certain general and concise guidelines. Those who should be most concerned with learning about the ʿumrānī maqāṣid are the educated Muslim masses and those working in the fields of politics, economics, and sociology.

7

ʿUmrānī Maqāṣid

We have sufficiently introduced the five *ʿumrānī maqāṣid*, which maintained affinity with the classical *maqāṣid* but expanded their horizons and reformulated their substantive content. The *ʿumrānī maqāṣid* are the preservation of religion and the refinement of its worldview, the preservation and the refinement of the holistic self and its intellect, the preservation of family and the refinement of the societal order, the preservation of wealth and the refinement of livelihood, and the preservation of polity and the refinement of governance. This chapter is the culmination of the contribution of the book and elucidates those five aims of Shariʿah.

7.1 The Preservation of Religion and the Refinement of Its Worldview

Religion is the greatest guide in human life, and it is the core and spirit of all matters, the framework within which all issues are organized and placed on a straight path, so as to protect against misconduct that could lead to misguidance. As religion could be subjected to lack of understanding and distortion, understanding of religion needs to be monitored, otherwise it may lead to error and deviation. What is required is to attain a faith that is not confused by any misunderstanding. This requires study of issues that could affect the understanding of religion and cause one to deviate from achieving its objectives. It also requires discussion of ways of the refinement of the individual that can preserve the purity of *tawḥīd* and the purity of understanding the religion without adding or subtracting anything, deal with the misconceptions regarding the concept of causality and natural laws, and that also urges the individual to reflect upon the names of Allah in a comprehensive manner whereby the meanings of these names and attributes complement one another.

The first *ʿumrānī* aim is the preservation of religion and the refinement of its worldview. Fundamental to this is therefore *tawḥīd*. *Tawḥīd*'s impact is reflected in the formation of a worldview. It is reflected in the formation of a methodology of thinking and appreciating the principle of causation. It is reflected in shaping the feelings and emotions which form the conscience of human beings. It is reflected in the shaping of people's conduct and activities. And it has an impact on all aspects of life, including aesthetics. All this leads to influencing the culture of a people and becomes part of their thinking and feelings pattern; they imbibe it and it becomes deeply entrenched in the social milieu.

The deviation in understanding experienced by religions can be summed up in four points: belief in divine embodiment (*ḥulūl*), incarnation (*tajsīd*), transcendent nationalism, and denial of the hereafter (*dahriyyah*). In the discussion below, there will be references to different religious beliefs, and it should be clear that it is not the intent to assess them; rather, they will be invoked as "ideal types" in the Weberian sense. Therefore, some practices within other religions may exhibit some of the qualities of those ideal types, even if not in the purist form.

A. *Ḥulūl*: Guarding Against Belief in Divine Embodiment

Among the distortions of religion is belief in divine indwelling. If people properly reflect upon the beautiful names of Allah, which provide guidance and clarity in belief, they would not believe that God indwells in His creation. Yet, there are religions that completely embrace the notion of indwelling. Their way of life is shaped by such beliefs, and they divide humans into castes, describing the highest caste as having divine indwelling and the lowest as cursed. They reduce humankind, whom God created and honored, to a cycle of reincarnation. Some of these ideas influenced some Muslim groups and distorted their understanding of the teachings of the religion.

Without understanding the relative independence of causes, human beings cannot be held responsible for their actions. And without understanding that the Creator is not bound by the causes that He created—even though He willed that they should exist—and that the universe is operating as God caused it to operate, according to constant laws, it is not possible to understand the way to achieve an Islamically inspired *'umrān*; and efforts to bring about reform on earth, without falling short or overstepping the mark, will falter. It comes as no surprise to see that people who believe in indwelling are very fond of the ambiguous verses in the Qur'an, whilst they ignore the clear verses. And while those who believe in indwelling claim to rise above whims and desires, their beliefs and practices ironically don't appear to provide the support for this.

Allah has created humankind and instilled in people inclinations and desires which, if they were to be given free rein without any restraint at all, would control their life and destroy them. Yet, if they were to be suppressed completely, they would fester and then leak out and cause mischief. It is as such that deviation from the proper understanding of religion leads to deviation in behavior and conduct. The Qur'anic criticism of some monks for consuming people's wealth unlawfully is a warning to all and is applicable to all religions (9:34).

Belief in divine indwelling typically attracts two diametrically opposed groups: the poor and oppressed, and some of the wealthy. The motive for the first group is to obtain some relief from rather desperate conditions, and the motive for the second is belief that a sense of guilt for the perceived sin of being wealthy may be expiated through certain ritualistic practices and mystical ecstasy. It is often the case that people of authority see these distortions of religion as a means of distracting people from rectifying the status quo and from trying to resist oppression and wrongdoing. It is no wonder that times of concurrence of prosperity and need have witnessed the popularity of distorted Sufism.

Belief in indwelling can be taken to extremes when it reaches the level of *al-ḥulūl al-bāṭinī*, wherein those who believe in indwelling also adopt esoteric beliefs whereby the verses of the Qur'an and clear instructions in the religious texts become – in their minds – laden with hidden symbolism that is controlled by imagination and whims and desires, then it is claimed that the verses of the Qur'an are speaking of those esoteric meanings. The esoteric ideas derived from belief in indwelling cancel out fundamental Islamic concepts and transgress against them; this includes the concepts of creation, accountability, and requital.

B. *Tajsīd*: Guarding Against Incarnation

Another distortion found in religion is incarnation (*tajsīd*). Incarnation usually leads to division of divinity because no physical entity can encompass all the attributes of the Divine. Thus, those who believe in incarnation resort to distributing the divine attributes among various physical entities. This in turn leads to undermining the law of causality, with some physical entities being regarded as having certain divine attributes to the exclusion of others. This division of divinity leads to competition between different aspects of belief among themselves, and to competition in what people imagine of some attributes of good or evil. Thus, people will be inclined towards one deity or another. All of that is, in effect, like ascribing attributes of created beings to the Creator, and imagining that just as the attributes of created beings are imperfect, the Divine is susceptible to imperfection.

The notion of incarnation has unfortunately crept into the thought of certain Muslim groups. We see its manifestation in various ways, such as in the idea of intercession, wherein a person is afforded the ability to intercede and save a person from hell. Some groups have taken such views to deviant excesses, leading to other kinds of extreme beliefs and practices. Case in point is the belief in and practice of monasticism and extreme asceticism. In these we find inappropriate claims of human beings, and certain religious duties being waived. More concretely, there is the notion that the rules and regulations of Shariʿah were revealed for the common folk, while certain individuals are exempted from them, having supposedly attained a level that is even greater than that of the Prophets. The views associated with *ḥulūl* and *tajsīd* may at times be intertwined, leading to further deviancy and ultimately the undermining of *tawḥīd*.

C. Guarding Against Transcendent Nationalism

The third distortion of religion is the physical manifestation of transcendent nationalism; that is, ethnocentrism stemming from the belief of being divinely "chosen" and therefore superior. This is the understanding that ignores the hidden unseen and the unknowable (*ghayb*) whilst trying to give a physical manifestation to what is unseen, and then turns both of them into attributes that are unique to some specific people. Some religious understandings distanced God from life on the grounds that His mission has been fulfilled due to the success of His chosen people.

This distorted claim—that religion is the special privilege of a select group—crept into the thought of some Muslim groups, resulting in their disregard of Islam's universal message. Thus, there appeared people who thought that they were the only ones who were guided to the right way, and that guidance could be passed down like inheritance. As with other distortions of religion, this distortion perhaps arose out of negligence, and those who succumbed to it did so out of weakness and not due to ill intentions on their part. The inclination towards anti-universalism and the human inclination to bond with one's kin and friends can cause people to cast aside what is right and to believe that righteousness does not go beyond their own privileged group. This leads others to resent and want to avoid those who espouse such beliefs. But this resentment may also carry over to undermine the latter's rights. It leads the latter group, in turn, to invent for themselves distinctive characteristics and traditions to compensate for the negative experience that results from being shunned and resented by others. Within the Muslim historical experience there are several groups who can be identified with such. Certain Shiʿah and Nasibi groups stand as examples of a gradual slipping into error because of socio-political circumstances. Kharijite and Rafiḍī groups stand for reactive extremism that ascribed sanctification to their ideology and group. And several *bāṭinī* groups branched off from early Shiʿism despite the warning of Shiʿi ulama.

D. *Dahriyyah*: Guarding Against Existentialism

The fourth distortion is existentialism and the denial of the hereafter (*dahriyyah*). The basis of this distortion is the delusion that humankind and life are not beholden to an infinite God Who is absolutely perfect in all His attributes and Who sustains the universe constantly, without faltering or absence. This is seen in elements in the beliefs of Zoroastrianism, Gnosticism, Buddhism, Confucianism, and modern humanism, all of which drowned in the eternal mystery with regard to the relationship between reason and religion. The symptoms of this distortion manifested themselves in the Muslim experience in the work of philosophers, and exacerbation of the distortion may vary between negligence resulting from human weakness and extremism resulting from human arrogance.

Some think that religion and illumination are two aspects of the same truth. And some believe that religion is the outer manifestation of truth, whilst its core essence is philosophy. They may even say that religion is the tool of philosophy and is secondary to the eternal facts of the universe. According to their view, religion is no more than a means that is appropriate for ordinary people to understand the dictates of reason. Some go to extremes in inappropriately emphasizing the role of reason to the extent of denying Prophethood and divine guidance. Perhaps placing such a great emphasis on reason is a reaction to superstitions and denying the causes and means that are part of bringing about prosperity and building civilization. But understanding the tangible world whilst denying the world of the unseen leads to a dichotomy that brings trouble and a difficult life.

Given the aforementioned distortions, we should note at this point the interconnection among them, for it is as if they are placed in a circle that has no beginning and no end. Thinking of the Divine in terms of a physical entity (*tajassud*) is a kind of belief in incarnation (*ḥulūl*), and partitioning the Divine leads to its fragmented incarnation in symbols. Transcendent nationalism implies that the Divine is incarnated in some specific people, just as thinking of the Divine in physical terms (*tajassud*) is a belief in the unseen taking physical shape.

As distortions in religious belief affect all religions, guarding against them should be the aim of preserving religion. If it is asked why such distortions were unable to change the main course of Islam, the obvious simple answer is that Islam has been divinely preserved as the last of the revealed messages. Nonetheless, if there are distortions in religion that have affected humankind throughout all ages and times, then what is required is to guard against the infiltration of such distortions.

The emergence of distortions in religions is often connected to politics, in the sense that a group may seek the help of political authorities, so they subject their thoughts and ideas to the pressure of those in authority. Or this group may try to escape and hide from the authorities and their politics, and go underground, hoping to protect itself from the harm of the deviation of those in authority, in which case the group will be afflicted with the ailments of hiding and being far removed from proper checks and discussion. In this case, there is the possibility of it developing into a strange cult.

As for measures to protect the proper understanding of the faith and guard its fundamentals, one of the requirements is that the scholars should be independent of the political authorities, and should have a secure income to preserve their dignity and protect them from the humiliation of having to ask of others. It also requires showing respect to knowledge and people of knowledge, and devoutly acknowledging that "God knows best" (*wa Allahu a'lam*). It requires warning against preachers who are no more than storytellers swayed by their whims and desires as a result of seeing people attracted to them and infatuated with their narratives.

Part of guarding, protecting, and purifying the perception of Islam involves understanding the Arabic language properly, and knowing when it is to be taken literally or metaphorically, or knowing the limits of the metaphoric elements in the understanding. What distinguishes and makes the Arabic of the Qur'an unique is that it combines subtlety and expansiveness. Thus, meanings are not confined and limited, but that does not leave meanings open to various mis-interpretations that could undermine the core intended meaning of the text. Furthermore, the Qur'anic use of Arabic language reformed its meanings and set forth new integrated conceptual horizons. In this regard, we should note that the philosophical infiltrations that historically adulterated the originality of the Islamic concepts proceeded through language and terms.

We should further note here that since failing to have a proper under-standing of the message of Islam could lead to corrupt deeds and behavior, the contrary also holds true—that corrupt deeds and behavior can lead to a corrupt understanding of the message of Islam. There are certain attitudes and behavior, in fact, that directly link to a perverted understanding of religions, namely the following seven ailments:

1   Fatalism and the failure to attend to the laws of causality embedded in the universe, which lead to poverty and injustice.

2   Self-promotion and undermining of others. And it is a natural outcome of self-admiration based on one's supposed righteousness, which leads to arrogance.

3   Sectarianism and converting the virtuous strong bonds of the religious community into wholesale rejection of the other.

4   Extremism (*ghullū*) and obstinacy in religion to the point of exhausting oneself, and failing to appreciate forgiveness that is an inherent value in religion. And to the opposite of extremism, some slip into seeking loopholes in rules and regulations, adherence to which is essential to the well-being of the community as a whole, and is also essential to individual well-being.

5   Ritualism, where the exteriority of the acts of worship overtake the intention behind them.

6   Esotericism and making religion a mere flight that is removed from life.

7   Literalism in understanding texts and failing at contextualization.

The last point deserves further clarification. Literalism suffocates religious texts and prevents them from attaining what they are meant for—guiding human behavior and elevating its conscience. Contextualization involves taking into consideration the relationship between the scope of possible meanings and implications of the text and the specific issue it may have addressed.

Such concerns apply to Islam's two sources, the Qur'an and the Prophetic Sunnah, but in different ways. That is because the miraculous style of the Qur'an establishes core ideas and concepts whilst maintaining the potential to generate new meanings that radiate from the text, in congruence with its direct meaning but not limited to it; therefore, we can speak of concentric meanings that emanate from the original root. In addition, the Qur'anic discourse goes beyond any specific "reason for revelation," if there was one. On the other hand, hadith by its very nature is context laden, since it is the elaboration on and the application of the Qur'anic meanings in a specific moment in time and space, which makes contextualization critical in treating hadith in particular. However, that does not make hadith irrelevant; rather, proper contextualization converts the specificity of the case into behavioral protocols to be emulated.

Furthermore, we need to remember that while the letter of the Qur'an was exactly preserved as revealed, in the case of hadith it was the meanings that were relayed, despite that we can consider that the statements of "strong" hadiths were narrated verbatim or very close to what Prophet Muhammad actually uttered. Hadith has an elaborative role in the overall Islamic guidance, and its style is qualitatively different from that of the Qurʾan. Because many hadith texts are direct commands, they tend to be specific. Therefore, the challenge is in the proper contextualization of hadith more than in avoiding a literal reading of them. Although there are general statements in some hadiths, most hadiths are connected to an incident or issue, so a kind of literalism (in the sense of pointing to a direct meaning and a concrete matter) is expected. However, there is still a need to account for context as for a specific hadith to be applicable for future situations. In fact, the whole intellectual plain in which the scholars of fiqh worked was estimating the context of hadith, its original intent, how it is situated within the universals of Shariʿah, and how its purport could apply to different situations. Literalism and failing at contextualizing hadith distort its original intent and precludes the appreciation of its wisdom. Such dwarfing of hadith becomes more consequential with the passage of time and the changing of circumstances.

7.2 The Preservation and the Refinement of the Holistic Self and its Intellect

The second *ʿumrānī* aim of Shariʿah is to preserve and refine the *nafs* along the lines of the elevated state of *fiṭrah*. *Fiṭrah* is the natural state according to which Allah has created humankind's intellect, emotions, conscience, and will power, as well as the physical body. The *nafs* in Islamic conceptualization is not just the self as desires and wants; rather, it is a holistic self, endowed with potentials. The concept of the *nafs* includes five dimensions: intellect, emotions, conscience, will, and the physical body. Here we may point out that although wickedness and piety are both inherent tendencies of the *nafs*, humankind can stay close to the original standards of the refined state of *fiṭrah* by heeding the guidance of religion. Whether an individual becomes wicked or pious is dependent on whether such a person, capable of differentiating right from wrong, goes along with the call of desires or restrains them. And humankind is not alone in this competition, as worship and following the commandments of religion enable the good to overcome the evil. Felicity is the lot of the one who purifies the *nafs*, and loss and doom is the lot of the one who corrupts it.

Just as it is required to take care of one's physical well-being and health, and to give them their due of care, the same is also required with regard to the intellect. Developing one's intellect and maintaining its capacity may be achieved by seeking knowledge. The same applies with regard to emotions and feelings as they thrive through reciprocation. And when the conscience and sub-conscience are examined and watched they become cleansed. As for a person's willpower, it is tuned by the continuous resolve to uphold the values of religion. Part of the natural state of the intellect is to be enriched in knowledge and to draw lessons from experience. Part of the natural state of emotion is that people have an inclination to show compassion towards others, and they appreciate it if others show compassion to them. Part of the natural state of conscience is that people feel at ease with those who are sincere, righteous, and honest. Part of the natural state of the willpower is to gain trust through successful action. Part of the natural state of the body is that it feels good when it is cleansed. These aspects of the *nafs* are interconnected and interact; purification of the *nafs* in all of its dimensions is an essential aim that becomes rightly enforced through worship and adhering to the teachings of religion.

A. *Ikhlāṣ*: Sincerity and Vigilance

Ikhlāṣ, sincerity, is a central concept in the Islamic faith as it is a necessary condition for the acceptance of deeds on the Day of Judgement. The aim of purifying the *nafs* dictates that individuals should take stock of themselves and their deeds, for human beings will have nothing but what they strive for. As the condition for attaining reward from Allah is that deeds should be done purely for His sake, the Muslim's overriding attitude is striving his/her utmost to attain sincerity, and to keep striving for that. As the individual's lower inclinations always try to make the person drift away from that sound motive, such a person can stay the course by being ever vigilant and watchful for the quality of deeds. By means of striving for sincerity, the motives of the deeds are consistently questioned and, thus, refined. Deeds that are not completely sincere for the sake of Allah, or at least try to be as such, will soon corrupt the individual and corrupt the community. Therefore, the benefits that result from sincerity and vigilance are not limited to purifying the souls of individuals; rather they rectify the condition of the community as a whole. Thus, through piety in the heart, deeds are cleansed of selfishness which could cause harm to society and be detrimental to the public interest. By emphasizing the fact that people will be judged on the basis of their deeds, and their deeds will be judged by their sincerity, people are encouraged to rise above arrogance and selfishness, and people should become conditioned to account for the consequences of their overt actions and covert impulses.

Individuals will be brought to account for obligations at the individual level on the Day of Resurrection, and justice would be delivered accounting to what means such an individual has been availed. Furthermore, the concept of accountability at the individual level will be reflected in social norms at the communal level. But social norms might not be in total congruence with Islamic standards. Here is where two-way dynamics takes place: conscientious individuals are expected to feel their responsibilities toward refining the norms for a better match with the Islamic quest, and individuals are expected to modify their behavior, out of sincerity, in accordance with the refined norms. In other words, sincerity and vigilance traverse the individual and the collective levels. Therefore, while personal behavior is basically the person's responsibility and it is hard to imagine that standards can be forced upon from without in the absence of personal appreciation, nevertheless, the collective element in not absent since there social input gets internalized. And when the communal corrective flow is expected by individuals and internalized as part of sincerity and vigilance, then social harmony would not be compromised, and the overall quality of the society becomes gradually refined.

B. Trust in Allah and Certainty of Faith

The second means by which purification of the *nafs* may be attained is strengthening one's trust in Allah and attaining certain faith in Him. Giving in to despair and hoping for more worldly gains are two feelings that may find their way into the heart of the weak individual and exacerbate the person's weakness. Hence, developing trust in Allah and making it second nature, on the basis of rational conviction, is one of the most powerful means of rectifying people's lives. By surrendering to Allah, one may attain the fruits of faith and develop a sense of contentment and conviction. At that point, it will become easier for the individual to handle the difficulties of life, and whatever sense of constraint and stress would be eased and replaced with a sense of comfort and being sheltered.

One of the areas in life that requires the check of faith is the aspiration for ample provision, which is something natural in humankind. However, being content with one's lot is what makes the believer feel independent of other people. Contentment with one's lot may be felt in more than one aspect of life, and is not limited to feeling content with one's provision or wealth, and includes feeling satisfied with one's physical build and appearance. Therefore, for the purpose of fostering the quality of contentment in individuals, the religious culture places a great emphasis on what is in the heart and on the purity of intention. People would not become angels, but higher standards become reinforced and expected, thus more likely to materialize and less likely to face the pressures of disapproval.

At the societal level, the quality of trust in Allah and contentment includes being content with the color with which Allah has created one, and with the grouping and social category to which one belongs; this contentment is coupled with the rejection of claims to superiority. Contentment also includes not wishing to be of a different sex, for men shall have the reward for what they earn, and women shall have the reward for what they earn, as the Qur'an affirms. Those with strong faith would be contented with the place and circumstances in which they have found themselves. To a great extent, a person's lot – in terms of abundance of provision and good living conditions – has to do with circumstances beyond the control of the individual; therefore, being angry over that is irrational and self-defeating. Moreover, trust in Allah, contentment, and certain faith are balanced out by Islam's requirement that a person should take appropriate measures and not surrender to hopelessness and inaction. On the one hand, it is not possible for human beings to know with certainty what the future will bring them, and on the other hand, a person is required to plan and take proper measures. Without proper trust in Allah, a person cannot plan properly for that which is unknown and concealed from him.

C. *Ṣabr* and *Mujāhadah*: Patience and Striving

Ṣabr, patience, is a highly recognized attribute in the Qur'an and Hadith, and frequently the concept of *mujāhadah* (striving the utmost) is associated with it.

For the purpose of purifying the *nafs* and keeping it aligned with sound *fiṭrah*, it is required to develop patience and train oneself to adhere to it. It also requires understanding, on a rational basis, the nature of this world and realizing that the life of this world necessarily involves stress, troubles, and problems. Because this world is a realm of test and trial, not a realm of reward, one will inevitably be faced with tests, which requires one to be prepared to face them and think wisely with an attitude of confidence and perseverance. A person may dislike something in which there is much goodness, and he may like something in which there is much harm, as the Qur'an states.

The life of people is filled with all kinds of tests, such as loss of loved ones and friends, and physical illness or loss of good health. Human beings cannot do anything about this, and whoever feels discontent will suffer the consequences of their discontent. Here, we see a connection between the idea of a striving patience and the concept of accountability on the Day of Judgment, which is central to the Muslim's mindset.

Developing and strengthening patience is connected to the idea of reward, and to the idea that this world is the realm of trial. The interconnection of these two concepts highlights the balance visible in the Islamic faith, for having patience that is based on faith in Allah is qualitatively different from callous willpower and disregard of others. The patience that is based on striving for the sake of Allah is the patience of one who is sincere and content with whatever Allah decrees, and striving in His cause strengthens and perfects patience.

D. Learning and Education

The fourth element connected to preserving and purifying the *nafs* is taking care of the intellect and protecting it through education and learning; and we are using the term education here in its general meaning of being cultured, not simply in the technical sense of certificates and formal education. Islamic teachings encourage people to improve their intellect through thinking and contemplating the signs in themselves and in the universe, and this is regarded as an act of worship and a means of developing God-consciousness. The more humility in their knowledge that a person has, the more he can see the miracles in Allah's creation and notice the wonders in the creation of the universe and the blessings of Allah in the way in which He created humankind. The more comfortable a person is with abstraction, the more such a person will be able to feel free from the constraints of the physical realm and be further removed from reducing sublime acts of worship to empty routine rituals. And by abstraction we do not mean pure philosophical abstraction; rather, a common-sense type of abstraction. Herein lies the brilliance of Islamic *tawḥīd*—it is at once straightforward and profound.

With regard to causes and measures that are part of Allah's creation, humankind is instructed to travel through the land and examine the universe, and to reflect upon human beings' own creation and learn lessons from history. Islam considers that reflection is as an act of worship for which a person will be rewarded. By establishing the fact that causality is a law that is embedded in all creation, and by connecting that fact to the belief that the Divine Will is not restricted to such causes (that are part of Allah's creation), a balance is created in the Muslim mindset. In turn, that would lead to the development of a culture that rejects the split between the dictates of reason and the dictates of faith. The connection between belief in causality and belief that nothing escapes Allah's knowledge or counters His will is a connection that has an equal impact on the development of abstract knowledge (such as philosophy) and of applied knowledge (such as science), just as it has an impact on social life and individual behavior.

There is a correspondence between taking care of the intellect and the maintenance of human order, because people of mature thinking will understand, through reflection, the normality of diversity in human life. Among the areas in which diversity among humans is most prominent are the ways in which they manage communal affairs, the ways in which they earn a livelihood, and the ways in which they manage their shared resources; diversity in customs and traditions, life experiences, and skills; and diversity in historical experiences and the impact that has on their subconscious. Human life is filled with mysteries and wonders, and when people understand the subtleties of these mysteries and wonders and seek to crack their codes, that enriches their lives, making them strong and beautiful. But if they fail to do this, diversity would turn into something incomprehensible, and lead to doubt, disputes, and misery. People tend to feel at ease with that with which they are familiar, and to feel comfortable with that to which they are accustomed. People who grow up with certain traditions accept them without question; this is something that is deeply entrenched in human nature, as those traditions affect the formation of human communities. Hence, people have no alternative but to gain sufficient knowledge about the cultures of other human group formations (referred to as *tribes* and *peoples* in Qur'anic terms), in order to broaden their horizons and become more inclusive.

The less cultured people are, the more narrow-minded they may become and unable to tolerate those who differ from them, even with regard to the most insignificant issues. Islam, and religions in general, has a clear mandate in regard of diversity, as it differentiates between God-created diversity in which persons themselves have no control, on the one hand, and differences of behavioral conduct on the other. In Islam's view differences in personal conduct are respected insofar as they are in harmony with moral standards. And moral standards are the ones that the Prophets of God have preached, and are thus shared among different religions. In other words, the mode of Islam's appreciation of diversity is starkly different from diversity understood in contemporary liberal culture and the postmodern view in which anything passes, as if there exists no essence to the human self and there is no absolute moral dictum.

Humbled knowledge makes human beings aware of their weakness, and alert to the ways in which Satan creates disharmony and undermines the love between people. Nothing can weaken a sense of security and social harmony like narrow-mindedness, attachment to trivial matters, and paying too much attention to outward appearances, for that has a more harmful impact on unity and cohesion among people than the schemes and conspiracies of their enemies. Even friction could erupt within the faith community because of superficial uneducated precepts toward religion. Ignorance can lead to rigidity regarding issues in which there is room for leniency, with the result that they become a point of conflict; a consequence of not understanding the Shari‘ah's aims and goals. What could help in such situations is not only an attitude of forgiveness and tolerance, but also mature thinking that is based on knowledge and understanding the nature of human life.

Within the functioning of the social system, it is critical to protect thought and freedom of thinking from the distortions of political and financial power. Therefore, knowledge and people of knowledge deserve respect to the extent that they rise above trivial matters and pursuit of worldly gains. Such respect is a form of protection, and it is to be granted on the basis of social customs. In order to protect people of knowledge from the domination of people of wealth, it is useful to have funds allocated to them in order to preserve their honor and dignity, and to grant them some income so that those who are devoted to knowledge will be spared the need to ask people for help. The most difficult task is to protect people of knowledge from the dictates of political authority, because almost invariably political power focuses on immediate needs and is constrained by conflicting demands, so its holders feel annoyed with the advice of people of knowledge and may try to silence or harm them.

The aforementioned are aspects of the *nafs* (the holistic self) that the Shari'ah seeks to purify. There is no need to elaborate on preserving physical well-being, because that is something instinctive. It is known that Islamic teachings support maintenance of the body and protecting it from harm. The particular formation of different Muslim cultures supports this preservation of good health by the distaste of risky behavior. Moreover, sponsoring the needy and the institutions that facilitate such efforts also plays a role in protecting physical well-being.

'Umrān and the thriving of Muslims' efforts in enriching life along the lines of *fiṭrah* cannot really be maintained except when people put their trust in Allah and proceed in their attempt to rectify the condition of society, without accounting to what may lie ahead of obstacles, showing patience in putting up with difficulties as they strive, and having strong resolve to bring about reform that will prevent dispute and division. The community will gain strength and power so long as people adhere to the straight path and so long as they control their base inclinations mindful of the day of reckoning.

To activate the goal of purifying the *nafs*, the process goes through many avenues, starting with giving children a proper education by means of curricula and teaching methods that stimulate their minds to think creatively, and not limiting education to memorization and repetition; instilling a public culture that emphasizes the individuals' responsibility for what they learn; establishing media that transmits content which balances teaching and informing, motivating and directing, and highlighting art, good taste, and entertainment. The aim of purifying the *nafs*, holistic self, is further achieved in all aspects by creating a Muslim culture that incorporates these meanings in such a way that they become part of people's habitual lifestyle.

7.3 The Preservation of Family and the Refinement of the Societal Order

Maintenance of societal order and the very reality in which human activities take place is the third ʿumrānī aim of Shariʿah. The focus here is on the collective side of human life; therefore, the word societal, not social, is used to highlight that the institutions of society are the matter of concern, not simply the individuals. There are four dimensions of this aim of Shariʿah: seeking tranquillity, mutual support, mutual advice, and correcting what is wrong. In the absence of the shelter of the family unit, life becomes ruined. Without mutual support, human beings are unable to carry the burden with which they have been entrusted. Failure to engage in mutual advice leads to disorder and trouble. Without mending and correcting its diversions from the straight moral path, society will decline and become dysfunctional. All of this operates within a specific culture of the people, which in turn is largely informed by religion and its worldview. Through the cultural prism, ideas flourish, expectations and hopes are shaped, and behavior and conduct become modulated.

The family system forms the smallest and most essential institution in society, as affirmed by humanity's historical record. There is a quality of exceptionalism in the institution of the family. That is because it is at once deeply personal and deeply social. It has a significant bearing on the psychology of individuals and it is the incubator of values. The preserving of lineage is both part of *fiṭrah* and a biological necessity. Through the family, most rudimentary and crucial education takes place early on in life, and has long term impact. The family setting was for long an economic unit, and despite the massive changes that modernity brought, family still has significant ties to the economic aspect of life including the transfer of wealth. Lastly, family experiences have a significant role in forming political orientations and in prepping for activism and joining social movements. It is no wonder that Islam, as well as religions in general, have given utmost importance to the family unit.

A. *Sakan*: Tranquil Stability

Sakan is a Qur'anic term that includes the meanings of repose, comfort, peacefulness, shelter, and stability. Assured stability is a crucial property in all of the institutions of the society, especially the family. Promoting the measures that lead to stability is clearly a matter of importance, because the family is the framework that brings together the two sexes, which are the brilliant creation of Allah. The male and female are both honored by Allah and given the responsibility of *khilāfah* (viceregency). But Allah has willed to make them differ in a wide spectrum of qualities and tendencies, so as to cooperate in knitting the nest of life and establishing its foundations. The historical record of humanity attests to such varied qualities, and Islam, as well as religions in general, are attuned to this aspect of life. For Shari'ah, the family is an existential fact, *amr wujūdī*, and in the language of Ibn Khaldūn it is part of *ṭabā'i' al-'umrān* (socio-historical empirical generalizations) to which the *'umrān* of life and the architecture of the Islamic system closely attends to. However, the differences between males and females do not suggest any inherent superiority of any of them. And while the differences in qualities, or their depth and intensity, propel toward differentiated roles, such roles are not Shari'ah ordained except in the sense of attending to *fiṭrah* and to the pulse of social life. The collective affairs of the community cannot be sound and lineage cannot continue except through kinship ties, which are natural, organic, and psychological.

Social reality cannot find tranquillity and fulfilment until the two sexes come together within a framework of love and compassion. Their living together cannot be sound and good, and family life cannot continue, except on the basis of a solemn covenant. The most important type of stability is that which one finds within the framework of a family, an institution that is rooted in the *fiṭrah* of males and females. And while it is true that there are legal rights and duties connected to family, they come secondary in the organization of human life and are to be invoked only at the time of stubborn discord. Otherwise, conventional cultural ways and norms are what govern family expectations, with variations among the different social groupings.

One of the strongest means that leads to stability is the promotion and enhancement of the qualities that are specific to each sex, on the basis of mutual understanding and support. Thus, everything that is masculine by *fiṭrah* (natural God-created disposition) should be subject to refinement and enhancement, and everything that is feminine by *fiṭrah* should be subject to refinement and enhancement, and any transgression or imbalance from one side will undermine stability and will lead to undermining the well-being of the other, and will prevent the other from carrying out the duties entrusted to him or her. That in turn would affect the whole society and plague it with contentiousness and misplaced competition atrophying the fabric of life.

Attaining stability requires understanding the qualities of the opposite sex and appreciating how amazing is what Allah has created and perfected. That way of appreciation operates in society through the culture that acknowledges such special kind of diversity at the interpersonal level, and caters to it instead of trying to fit the behaviors of females and males into a fabricated form, as the case is with modern popular culture. The chivalry of manhood and the tenderness of womanhood are mutually expected from males and females. And this is primarily dictated by nature, not religion, though Islamic culture recognizes such qualities because the *sharʿī* does not conflict with natural laws. Obviously, this includes the varied responsibilities and roles involved in raising children and maintaining the smooth functioning of the family and its stability. Within such a light, the concept of *qawāmah* of husbands (roughly, maintainers) toward wives should be understood, for the special responsibilities that a man feels toward women is what allows both masculinity and femininity to flourish.

Indeed, human history is filled with precedence which highlights the importance of the differential roles of men and women in accordance with the relative heightened qualities of each sex in terms of toughness, carefulness, and other sensibilities. The precedence shows that when protection is no longer expected of man, maleness becomes inappropriately bloated, thus suppressing women and trying to control their lives.

It is noticeable that the Qur'an mentions together, in the same *ayah*, the differences between male and female along with the diversity among tribes and peoples (and we stress again that the structure of tribes/people is a universal one, far from the modern negative attributes associated with the term tribe).[1] Failing to properly cater the nature of femininity and masculinity will lead to falling short in regard to *taʿāruf* (getting to know one another). The claim that one sex is superior to the other is contrary to Qur'anic discourse, that the most honored is the one who is most righteous or most mindful of Allah, and that each soul will be dealt with according to what it has earned.

The above discussion has gone into detail in regard to the relationship between the two sexes and the family as a system, but stability is crucial to all social institutions, and the refined ethics of religion would naturally enhance such stability. However, stability cannot be secured by good will alone. Rational laws and regulations play a crucial role, and stability would not be attained if the quest for fairness was not pursued. This dimension will be discussed under the *maqāṣid* pertaining to political life.

B. Mutual Support

Human beings are inherently weak, but this weakness turns into strength through cooperation with others. The newborn is weak in the most comprehensive sense, but with love from parents and their cooperation in raising them, those vulnerable beings become young adults with capabilities of their own. Because newborns and minors are so vulnerable and susceptible to harm if they are not properly cared for and nurtured, there is instilled in the parents' hearts love which protects them from being exposed to such harm. As for the adults, even though they may need help, not having help and support will not lead to loss of life. Therefore, cooperation between adults cannot be sufficiently maintained by natural inclinations; rather, in addition, it needs ties based on rational thinking and mutual interests.

Social cohesiveness is to be fortified and purified through the bond of religious faith, because although bonds of blood and ethnic ties are natural, they need to be disciplined by religion and high principles. Faith here points to moral and ethical standards that are sanctioned by the main religions in human history; and contrary to the secular claim, these standards are universal. Furthermore, when people who happen to fall under a certain religion categorically violate such moral standards, their actions do not nullify those standards. We can speak of concentric arrangements that are conducive to social harmony. The smaller circles invest in familial, kinship, and friendship ties, while the larger circles invest in more abstract based ties, all of which are to be infused with a religious moral sense. As such, the believers all have roles to play in maintaining the structure of society, and they are all required to strive against their lower inclinations, so that resentment will not cause them to drift away from the path of justice.

Mutual support in this sense is what protects people from the *jāhilī* (ignorant) type of tribalism and from supporting one another on the basis of falsehood and stubbornness. Mutual support cannot be achieved unless the believers strive to attain it, and they have to collectively develop customs and traditions that strengthen the building blocks of the community. Throughout their lengthy history, Muslims developed many customs and traditions that could form the basis for mutual support and cooperation. But customs and traditions on their own are not enough to maintain mutual support in the society at large. Policies and regulations need to guard and encourage cooperative settings. Thus, the most damaging to society is when formal bureaucratic policies conflict with social mood. When political authorities fall short in meeting the special needs of the different segments of people, that will undermine cooperation in society and may result in conflict. The same applies if resources are not used in such a way as to strengthen social bonds or when the national culture focuses on narrow interests, failing to account for the collective priorities and affairs. In other words, the attaining of mutual support cannot be based on the mere goodwill of individuals and their good character and behavior; rather, it is also dependent on their collective work and proper planning. Civil society and *natural institutions* play a crucial role in that regard. Natural institutions are the family, kinship, neighborhood, places of worship, and local informal education activities, which can be justifiably termed as *fiṭrah institutions*.

C. *Naṣīḥah*: Mutual Advice

The third aspect of strengthening societal order is enjoining what is right and forbidding what is wrong. *Naṣīḥah* is an Islamic term of expected behavior of Muslims in all affairs, and it is to be understood in its widest implications not limited to personal advice. As it is normal for people to lapse in their conduct, it is essential to make social space for advice that reminds with what is more appropriate and proper. Every nation and community has a moral code that they follow to some extent, and if people do not try to stop the wrongdoer, forbid harmful actions, and remind people of noble deeds, then cultural standards deteriorate in the society as a result of the actions of a minority of wicked people.

Despite the fact that this principle of mutual advice is something that is found in every nation or community, and despite the fact that the need for it is clear, there have developed some doubts about its validity and importance, because of its misapplication on the part of some Muslims, and because the notion of individual freedom is often excessively invoked to condone irresponsible behavior. The practice of advice becomes corrupted in two ways. One, when it becomes hollow of moral backing and based merely on personal preference; in such a case, the validity of the advice cannot be ascertained. The second is when the delivery of advice is used to put down the receiver. According to Islamic ethics, not only does the way of delivery have to be courteous, but also those who offer advice should doubt the advice they are giving, because the conduct of the other person (the receiver of the advice) may have been based on some valid ijtihad of which the one who is giving advice is not aware. There is also the danger that the habit of preaching to others may be inflicted with self-admiration.

Enjoining what is right and forbidding what is wrong in Muslim societies is the duty of relatives, friends, neighbors, and the community as a whole. But the concept of advice, which implies sincerity, wisdom, and care for public affairs, is sometimes confused with reinforcement by the formal means of the state. Thus, the idea of advice became closely connected to compulsion in matters of religion. Obviously, compulsion is of no benefit in the realm of values, understanding, and morality. The backing of official authorities is only applicable to major issues and cases in which few people openly commit transgressions that could lead to the spread of immorality; it is not applicable to minor errors and small misdeeds. The role of authorities is specifically needed when spreading deviant behavior becomes systematic, such as part of a commercial enterprise. And the role of law enforcement agencies and the scope of their mandate should be predicated upon the approval of society.

The concept of enjoining what is right and forbidding what is wrong cannot be restricted to mere rebuking and preaching. Rather it is a form of social responsibility. Civil society and *fiṭrah institutions* naturally participate in mending the shortcomings within the society, and they motivate people to do good and facilitate voluntarily adherence to righteousness and resisting deviant paths. Moreover, institutions that research social ills and seek to address them with the help of those with experience and academic knowledge, draw up general plans appropriate to the society according to its prevailing culture and its historical backdrop.

D. *Islāḥ*: Maintenance of the Social System

The Qur'anic term *iṣlāḥ* is a generous term where it carries the meanings of improvement, mending, suitability, acting morally with religious consciousness, and agreement and mediation. Islam inspires people to engage in the rectification process in all situations, and to plant the seedling even if they have doubts that it will mature and bear fruit. People in Muslim communities are encouraged to do righteous deeds of different types, from the simple act of smiling at others, to feeding people at times of food shortages, to preparing and equipping those who are battling and contending for the sake of Allah, to offering financial help to seekers of knowledge. In this regard, individuals and social groups may do their utmost in putting their trust in Allah without neglecting to take appropriate measures, yet not pinning their hopes on those measures, and showing patience in the face of adversity, avoiding despair and hopelessness, and always hoping to be spared tests and trials.

This inclination towards *iṣlāḥ* is the basis for the universal nature of the message of Islam, as Islam confirms the messages of religions that came before it. We can trace such a repairing impulse throughout history, as Muslims did not seek to destroy human societies or annihilate culture, language, or tradition except the elements thereof that were corrupt by nature. The dynamics of the movement of Islam in the international theatre defeated tyrant rulers and their attempts to act as gods, and abolished *ribah* (usury), thereby protecting people's right to their capital and properties. This was at the political and economic levels.

With regard to the social level and people's customs and traditions, the matter is more delicate. That is because cultural systems encompass a mixture of qualities, including undesirable elements. Thus, they may be left so that the passage of time may purify them, after changing the organizing frame in which such elements operate. In other words, rectifying customs and traditions is to be contingent on the full comprehension of Islam itself. Thus, the mode of the Islamic system in mending social reality is to dissolve structures that are completely corrupt and beyond redemption. But as for elements which are not overwhelmingly corrupted, they are left to gradual improvement with the passage of time. The Islamic system combines at once measures that try to uproot depravity, and measures that are left to have their impact in people's lives gradually. It was by means of this moderate approach that Muslims proceeded throughout the world, carrying a vision of justice. Thus, the Islamic movement benefited from what other people had of goodness, and the Islamic civilization was shaped by the various cultures of the peoples of the earth, each people contributing something and serving the overall aim of Islam.

I will end this discussion by highlighting some practical measures which could strengthen societal bonds and protect them from becoming eroded. These include the following:

- Designing residence settings in which spouses and their children will reside in a manner conducive to honoring parents and caring for those who reach old age and begin to need assistance.

- Designing roads and walkways in neighborhoods in a manner that helps people to do their duties towards their neighbors.

- Designing urban spaces in such a way that will bridge the gaps between people of different social statuses.

- Designing public transport in such a way as to make it feasible for people to stay interconnected.

- Designing means of communication and news services in such a way that support social cohesiveness and prevent the spread of mistrust among society's fissures.

- Establishing *awqāf* (endowments) for many purposes, so as to meet people's collective needs apart from the state and formal authorities as well as apart from the dictates of capital and for-profit and enterprises.

- Establishing communal groups in which there is exchange of ideas on local issues, which are issues where political authority is not suited to play that role. That includes professional organizations that advance standards and specialized knowledge away from political dictates and pressures.

7.4 The Preservation of Wealth and the Refinement of Livelihood

This is the fourth aim of Shariʿah regarding *ʿumrān*, where the focus is on maintaining *rizq* (bounties) of Allah, which includes both visible and hidden wealth, both individual and collective wealth, and wealth that could be achieved directly by individual effort or that already exists, having been bestowed upon humankind and entrusted to it. It is no secret that abundant provisions may affect people's lives, for Allah has described it as a means of support for us, without which life will fade away and can never prosper. This aim (preservation of wealth and purification of livelihood) has four aspects: individual ownership in the sense of it being a trust from Allah, circulation of wealth, emancipation, and conservation.

A. Individual Ownership as a Trust from Allah

Within the Islamic worldview, wealth belongs to Allah, and human beings are entrusted in what they own. The Qur'anic term regarding this concept is *istikhlāf*, and it spans the realms of politics as well as the economy, all as part of humankind's mission on earth as a *khilāfah*, viceregency. Ownership of wealth in the Islamic view, and whatever a person may possess, is not regarded as ownership in an absolute sense. Such a view is reflected in regulations and instructions that made the idea of being a trustee something manifested in real-life situations.

Divine wisdom dictated that humankind should have an inclination towards wealth, which is a means of preserving that without which life cannot be sound. But because wealth is something to which people are attracted and like to accumulate, Islamic teachings regarding wealth are two-tier: the Shariʿah encourages charitable giving (*ṣadaqah*), and in contrast to this voluntary spending it requires individuals to annually pay zakat on surplus wealth and income in the form of due shares to specific categories of people and causes worthy of financial support. And since the second kind is obligatory spending, it stands as a major element in the Islamic financial system on the collective level, and we should remind ourselves that zakat is considered a pillar of Islam, confirming the importance of the economic dimension in the Islamic system.

The teachings of Islam clearly aim at preventing transgression and stopping people from depriving others. In examining human history, we find that there is no nation in which a small segment of people accumulated and hoarded wealth but that wealth was accumulated by means of usurping it and taking it by force, or obtaining that wealth in an unjust manner, or else it was acquired by means of deceit, wrongdoing, and cheating people.

Islam considered the enjoyment of Allah's bounties as something human, expected, and even encouraged. However, since the enjoyment of provisions may fall into excess, Islamic teachings also encouraged thriftiness and moderation. And as personal spending cannot be managed from without, it was left to the conscience of the person, coupled with the encouragement for charitable spending, eschewing extravagance (*isrāf*), and exhorting against squandering resources (*tabthīr*) in wrongful channels. Thus, avoiding extravagance is personal and connected to the mindfulness of Allah's discretion, while squandering is liable collectively. And to the degree we move from the individual realm to the public realm, spending becomes subject to societal and state controls.

All of this is congruent with the core Islamic concept of ownership being a trust, which is the opposite of ownership in absolute terms that gives individuals the right to do whatever they wish with their wealth. Wealth belongs to Allah Who gave people the right to dispose of it. Ownership as a trustee requires giving precedence to public rights, whether the right is that of a small community or a large society, over individual rights.

From a *maqāṣid* perspective, one of the issues that is important to highlight with regard to the evaluation of zakat is that sources of wealth differ from one time to another, for people are constantly introducing new ways of making money and earning a living. Hence, the due portion of zakat and the types of wealth on which zakat is due should be the focal point of purifying wealth. If the scholars of ijtihad fail to note the new ways of generating wealth and do not work out what rate of zakat is applicable on that new wealth, then the public will be deprived of a source of income that is essential to meeting the needs of the public. It should be noted that the appropriate category for zakat, in terms of the categories of Islamic regulations, is *muʿāmalāt* (transactions), even though at the individual level it is an act of worship (*ʿibādat*) and an individual obligation. That gives a wider latitude for reason and deliberating the appropriate rates, exemptions, and other zakat related issues, because unlike *ʿibādāt* that are stationary in nature and have exemptions only in unusual situations, the normal affairs of *muʿāmalāt* is variation.

Paying zakat on different types of wealth requires scholars to activate *maqāṣidī* thinking in order to work out the percentage required in the case of different types of wealth, and to work out the *niṣāb* (minimum threshold at which zakat becomes due) in a particular time and place, below which wealth is exempted from zakat, because it is necessary for meeting the needs of the individual, and above which is regarded as surplus that the individual can do without. Another issue critical to the subject of zakat is how it is to be collected and distributed, and there is a connection between the two. Concerning this, there are significant differences of opinion among the fiqh schools. And from a *maqāṣid* perspective, it seems that neither a totally centralized system of zakat serves the purpose nor a totally decentralization one, as some areas of the country and segments of the economy might be either prosperous or much in need, and frequently due to conditions unrelated to people's efforts. The *maqāṣid* perspective seems to point to a stratified system of zakat that matches the organizational layers of communities, districts, and provinces.

There is a great need for state income other than zakat in modern times. As populations are increasing in numbers, and there is increasing specialization in ways of earning a living and ways of production, co-dependency across different segments of the economy has significantly increased. Furthermore, the existence of a number of different skills, industries, and experiences has become a necessity without which life cannot function. As people have become focused on subtle areas of specialization, the scope of public goods has broadened. In turn, the areas that public funds are needed to take care of have expanded; otherwise, if there is no spending at all on such areas, that will have a negative impact on the strength and soundness of the community as a whole. And since there is public spending, public supervision and administration is required.

We can safely assume that the areas that are crucial for the society and worthy of public spending are of six types: food supply, security, education, health, transportation, and communication. As for food supply, this is an ancient and constant need. In the past, it was possible for individuals to obtain what they needed by means of cultivation that they did themselves, and from what was produced by keeping flocks, hunting, and the like. But when cities became places of residence for large numbers of people, and their skills became limited to matters that had no direct connection to cultivation and animal husbandry, the issue of food supply in cities became an issue of communal concern; people who live in cities need to bring water through pipes and not waste it, and there is a need to create a balance between what they need as a matter of necessity, what they need as a matter of luxury or leisure, and what is needed for agriculture.

As for spending on security and protecting the community, this is obviously a public responsibility. The need to maintain security is an ancient need that increases with the increase in complexity of societies and when there is sudden change in living conditions. Regarding education, it was an individual or localized matter that took place more or less within the circle of the family and the community, or the case that a few individuals might frequent circles of knowledge and even travel for the purpose of seeking knowledge. But nowadays, the issue is very different, especially since the acquisition of knowledge has become based on learning some branches of knowledge in great detail.

As for maintenance of public health, it has become a collective concern, and the massive increase of human density in liveable areas has heightened the danger of contamination. Generally speaking, densely populated areas require more of public spending and administration, and those who live in large communities need different types of public services. Increase in population density leads to the spread of epidemics, and the transportation of food supplies and goods from one part of the world to another helps to spread germs and health problems. Many new industries have become synonymous with hidden diseases that were previously unknown and which must be watched carefully.

As for transportation, modern realities faced people with the irony of the much-increased ability to move long distances and the need to do that, in addition to dependency on what lies faraway. And mediated communication is connected to transportation in terms of the kind of need, but it has become an empowering tool and a source of critical information. From a *maqāṣid* perspective, these six avenues require partial or full public funding, in addition to public overseeing who operate them.

B. *Tadāwul:* Circulation of Wealth

Circulation of wealth (*tadāwul*) is a Qurʾanic term and a basic principle in the Islamic system. Most of what is mentioned about the possession of wealth as a trust is applicable to what the individual owns of wealth, and zakat is the major tool to achieve that. On the collective level and from a *maqāṣid* viewpoint, this would be applicable to public wealth which is aimed at preventing concentration of wealth in the hands of small groups of people. It cannot be imagined that it is appropriate for all the resources of the earth that Allah has created, such as the treasures of rivers and seas, with their fish, and what is buried in the earth, to become the property of individuals, because that could lead to giving too much control to some individuals, which would lead to a great deal of mischief. With the passage of time, there have developed brilliant methods of utilizing the resources of the earth to benefit people, such as desalination of water to make it fit to drink, or the generation of electricity by harnessing the energy of waterfalls, or by burning oil and coal, and other things, as is well known. Therefore, regarding these matters as coming under the same three categories that were identified by Prophet Muhammad's largely accepted hadith "People are partners in three: water, grass, and fire" (reported by Imam Ahmad), of which people have common ownership, is something very clear and essential from a *maqāṣid* perspective.

Life is dependent on water, and the environment in which humans live is dependent on vegetation produced by the land. Similarly, many professions practiced by people depend on generated energy. Within this general framework, it is possible to set out some guidelines concerning the fiqh concept of ownership privilege to that who revives a dead land. Ownership in that case becomes like ownership on behalf of the community, controlled by the interests of the community. Otherwise, we will find that people who have the means to usurp land will rush to do so, and they will usurp the best land and keep for themselves all the opportunities to own land, thus depriving those who are in greater need of the land. Moreover, land could be seized by rulers who will give it to people close to them, and the original objective of this principle (namely, the Shariʿah principle of revival of dead land) will not be achieved, which is to encourage making use of land and producing a harvest from wasteland.

In sum, because there are so many new ways of earning a living and producing wealth, a *maqāṣid* perspective needs to be adopted to account for the following: what rate of zakat is applicable (2.5, 10, or 20 percent), *nisāb* (the minimum wealth amount above which zakat applies), *ḥawl* (the annularity condition), and what constitutes surplus, thus, zakatable. On the collective level, because of the increasing density of human population and the contraction of space, there have arisen public needs having to do with organizing life that has dictated reliance on public funds to be spent on new public goods and interests.

C. *Iʿtaq*: Liberation

Iʿtaq is freeing the enslaved, and it is a term that frequently appeared in hadith. It is a counterpart of the Qurʾanic term *taḥīr raqabah* (literally, freeing a neck). The term is used below to denote a *maqṣid* of Shariʿah for the liberation of bondage, where bondage is also broadly understood and not restricted to slavery.

Allah has created people free and bestowed blessings upon them, both manifest and concealed. The concept of freedom has already been discussed earlier in this work, stressing that within the Islamic worldview this concept is situated within a network of five essential fundamentals of creed: the equal creation from a single soul, forming humankind according to the pure state of *fiṭrah*, the ability to discriminate between right and wrong, individual responsibility on the Day of Judgment, and the absence of intermediaries between individuals and Allah. Such an account of freedom has wide implications in all aspects of life, and we specifically point here to its relationship with *i'taq* (liberation) in terms of the attempt at securing the livelihood of people, individually and collectively.

As humankind is a trustee with regard to what they own of wealth and are entrusted to manage, and as circulation of wealth is the basis of public wealth, then, in principle, there should be complete equality among all individuals is such an economic aspect. But the reality of life is that people differ with regard to the kind of trials and tests they face. Moreover, people vary in their ambitions, intellect, abilities, and strengths. They may also live in different areas that vary in the standard of living, and different communities may have different ways of dealing with their circumstances; what befalls some people may not befall others, and what some may achieve of success and prosperity, others may not.

Among people there is what may be described as horizontal variation and vertical variation. Horizontal variation is where different people or different categories of people are equal but endowed differently. This is more pronounced in the varied contributions of men and women to life. And we find that the Qur'an reminds us of such social fact and that the recognition of their contributions is recognized relative to their endowment on the Day of Judgement—"For men is a share of what they have earned, and for women is a share of what they have earned" (Qur'an 4:32). But such horizontal variation is not restricted to the differences between males and females; regardless of sex, different people are differently endowed, and some endowments might not be fairly rewarded. What matters in this case is their righteous deeds in adequately carrying out their responsibilities along with cooperation among each other.

The second type of variation is vertical, where different people or different categories of people are more apt in contributing to life, regardless of whether such aptitude is by nature or nurture. The reality of life is such that there are different classes of people, so that they may serve one another (Qur'an 43:32) and this life may become prosperous by means of various skills and potentials. But when unethical standards are attached to such variations and when they are associated with arrogance and greed, then we are speaking of servitude that calls for *i'taq*/liberation.

The relevance of this sub-*maqṣid* can be further appreciated with the consideration that life has developed into a form where there is an increasing need for people to cooperate and support one another as their numbers increase. In the past, it was possible for people to be self-sufficient, as most of what they needed was available in a stream of water, or by picking the fruits of nearby trees and catching fish and game. Later on, local agriculture as well as fishing and hunting could, in many cases, suffice the basic needs of a locality. In different historical epochs, large plantations appeared, and were frequently associated with harsh conditions. With the spread of modern machines and the introduction of new ways of generating wealth and provision, the concern of those who had capital turned to securing a large number of industrial workers and agricultural laborers. The quest for more profits introduced new and subtle ways of controlling these crowds of workers. All of this attests to the continuous relevance of the goal of *i'taq*/liberation, especially in relationship to economic activities.

D. Sufficiency and Conservation

Islam regards wealth, resources, and provision as belonging to Allah, and teaches that people are merely entrusted with them. They are regarded as blessings which are subjugated to people's use for the purpose of bringing prosperity, and are entrusted to people, generation after generation. Allah has bestowed upon humanity the blessing of reason; hence, they were able to learn of the secrets and wonders of this universe. Allah criticizes those who forbid the beauty which He has produced for people (Qur'an 7:32), and He calls for moderation in spending and enjoying life. If contentment is the quality of the believers, then this quality should also be the quality of the community as a whole, not only individuals. The challenge then lies in actualizing such personal and communal qualities and making them part of the socio-economic system.

Allah invites people to travel through the earth and to look at the horizon, so that there will be development on earth and life will prosper. With the passage of time, people would be able to accumulate different types of knowledge, skills, and ways of making use of natural resources so as to be able to meet people's needs. This is part of His blessings and a sign of His miracles in His creation. As we are discovering more of the earth's treasures these days, the dominance of utilitarian philosophies has served to legitimize greed and turn it into a right that is protected by law. The matter has gone so far that some people and nations would devour their own share and the share of others, and the race to extract resources has ravished the environment and led to the poisoning of shared resources, all of which threaten the very sustainability of life.

Hence, the objective of acquiring wealth dictates that enjoyment of good things should be controlled by the principle of moderation, taking into consideration the share of those yet to come of subsequent generations, which is a broad Qur'anic principle. The wealth that people own and acquire through their efforts is regarded as wealth belonging to Allah with which they are merely entrusted; that is more so regarding the resources of the earth. Consequently, there is a need to examine and ensure the soundness of the ways that enable extracting the resources of the earth, and the return on investment in these resources should be used in such a way as to bring long-term benefits for successive generations. The depletion of the environment to the extent that it cannot be renewed is a clear transgression against the creation of Allah, humans and animals, as well as transgression against nature.

This aim cannot be achieved except by striving to examine human activity and its impact at all levels. Purifying livelihood and preserving wealth and resources is critical for maintaining the stability of life and social peace. If the goal of the individual with regard to his/her private wealth is to invest it and generate more wealth from it, then the goal with regard to public wealth and resources owned by the Ummah is that they should yield continuous benefits, and those benefits should reach everyone.

7.5 The Preservation of Polity and the Refinement of Governance

This is a fundamental aim that deserves to be addressed on its own, almost absent in the classical writings on *maqāṣid*, but appears prominently in the writings of Ibn Khaldūn. Bad practice of politics and falling short in taking care of the Ummah's affairs leads to a great deal of mischief and trouble in all aspects of life, which in turn may lead to turmoil and bloodshed. If that persists, the Ummah becomes weak and loses power. No stability can be achieved in society unless there is a political system that attends to the collective welfare of people and society. People's efforts cannot be united and focused on the sublime goals of the Ummah unless politicians and those in authority plan for that; and the Islamic system of government cannot reach its goals without mature leadership who have sophisticated understanding of the intellectual foundations of such a system. As Islam is a comprehensive religion, this dictates that it must have guidelines on the running of political affairs, and the universal nature of its message may be manifested when its people have a stable political system. It is most appropriate that this Ummah should pay great attention to this requirement, because falling short in this regard was the first step towards the weakening and undermining of the Muslim Ummah.

This *maqāṣid* aim may be divided into four objectives, as follows: (1) achieving justice with regard to rights and duties; (2) managing a multi-layered system of consultation; (3) striving to achieve security and peace; and (4) creating means of communication among people so that they may get to know one another and convey the message of Islam.

A. Justice with Regard to Rights and Duties

This is the most important requirement in politics and running the affairs of the Ummah, and is the most prominent reason to give power to people in authority. The area required to be covered by this aim, and the need for various departments for political administration, grew and became varied. One of the reasons for that was the great increase in the size of human groupings and societies. In the distant past, people lived on hunting and picking fruits, which did not require more than the teaming of a few locals. Small societies then began to engage in herding and horticultural activities based on small gardens around their dwelling places in which some communal help may be needed. At that time, the numbers of a single tribe could be counted in the thousands at most. Then, as a result of the discovery of fire and the smelting of iron, the taming of animals and the invention of the plough, the inhabitants of the plains became able to cultivate large areas. Thus, the size of harvests increased greatly and accumulated until they became sufficient for large numbers of people, reaching into the tens and hundreds of thousands. Then the populations of human societies grew to what we know now of millions. Achieving justice in such societies centred around the informal judgement and arbitration efforts of tribal chiefs and wise men, well-versed in the affairs of their communities and who, in effect, practiced an organic form of consultation.

Paying attention to population in human society is important for two reasons: firstly, if the number of people increases, it becomes difficult for their affairs to be run by a single leader; and secondly, the more diversity there is in economic activities, and the more complex and interconnected people's interests and relationships become, the greater the need for a large administrative apparatus. *ʿUrf* (custom, tradition) plays a major role in the organization of smaller societies and communities, but when numbers increase and people's relationships and connections become more complex and intense, there is a need, alongside local traditions, for written laws. Although traditions may be good enough to deal with some private issues in people's lives, public life still requires laws and regulations to organize people's different activities. Designing a workable Islamic system in modern societies, a challenge since the late Ottoman era, is one of the most delicate challenges for *tajdīd* and invigorating *maqāṣid*.

The concept of justice is a central aim of all Islamic teachings. The one who reflects on the condition of peoples throughout the ages will realize that justice is the key to goodness, and the absence of justice is the key to mischief and corruption. But there is nothing in human life that is more strenuous to achieve than attaining absolute justice in all times and in all affairs. Although pure justice and extreme injustice are both clear, and no one would dispute concerning them, trying to work out what is regarded as the middle path between the two extremes in various issues is something that could be very difficult. Therefore, achieving justice is something relative most of the time because the middle path is not quite clear and it is difficult to have a final judgment on different priorities, let alone exhausting the identification of such different options. As such, there is always a need for continual reflection and mutual advice between people of experience.

We should point to an irony with regard to politics, which is that when prosperity becomes widespread and people become preoccupied with enjoying their lives, they give up following how the political affairs of the people are run. When people become no longer aware of hidden injustices and wrongdoing, and justice no longer prevails, then wrongdoing becomes widespread in all aspects of life, which is followed by the collapse of societal balance. Justice cannot be achieved when relevant institutions fall short in carrying out their duty. And justice cannot be achieved when theoretical issues related to justice are not reconsidered in light of changing circumstances. Another irony is that when the state monopolizes guarding security and maintaining justice, flexibility becomes lost and the formal departments that were assigned those functions become, themselves, a source of mischief trampling justice and security. That brings us back to the centrality of *ʿurf*, which fiqh effectively invests in and which is seriously considered in *maqāṣid*.

Speaking of justice, we should assert again that the proper approach for claiming rights is to be matched with corresponding duties; by creating the balance between rights and duties, justice could be more closely achieved and has more chance to prevail. From a Shariʿah perspective, there are some rights and duties that are clear and unambiguous, as they are explicitly enjoined in the Islamic texts, and anything other than that is based on ijtihad and the process of ongoing trial and error. On the other hand, there are rights and duties that have become part of people's customs and traditions. While most rights and duties could be maintained in a social reflexive manner, without having to give the matter much thought, there are some rights and duties that require the watchful eye of the law (*qānūn*). The law is entrusted to the judiciary, and the judiciary is protected by custom and perpetuity on the one hand, and by the power of those in authority and the awe in which they are held by people, and their ability to enforce the law, on the other hand.

By striking a balance between rights and duties on the one hand, and customs and laws on the other, people will be able to enjoy assured freedom that is neither incomplete nor leads to transgression. There can be no freedom without justice, and freedom without rights and duties is selfishness that leads to conflict and less freedom. Think of how, when liberalism gave a definition of freedom that has no limits and is not controlled by justice, it turned into freedom of desires and pointless activities that lead to chaos. Absolute freedom is a myth; there is no human behavior but it is constrained by some social custom or legal ruling. In both cases, freedom is connected to responsibility for the consequences thereof. We can be certain that any freedom that is not situated within the framework of justice leads to selfishness. There is overwhelming evidence that organizing society is a human challenge that was faced by all societies regardless of culture, numbers, or circumstances. This is the case if what we mean by freedom has to do with human conduct. But if what we mean by freedom is freedom in a purely philosophical sense, then it is a natural outcome of *tawḥīd*, one of the most significant implications of which is equality among people in servitude to Allah and rejection of the notion of any group having a special status, whether that group is religious, national, or political.

From this belief (*tawḥīd*), and in harmony therewith, stem three types of freedom:

1 Disallowing compulsion in matters of belief, and it is not simply disallowing compulsion on changing one's religion;

2 Freedom of thought and creativity; having this type of freedom allows people to focus their minds, examine and study the world around them, and contemplate the natural laws that govern society; the opposite will happen when political authority adopts a particular school of thought or ideology and forces it upon people;

3 A subtle type of freedom which refers to the believers feeling a sense of transcendence because of the dignity that stems from rising above physical desires.

And since the idea of freedom is frequently invoked, three matters should be clarified:

1 Disallowing compulsion in religious matters does not mean condoning relativity toward truth.

2 Freedom to reflect and reason does not negate the virtue of humility toward what reason might reach.

3 Freedom in conduct does not absolve from the responsibility toward such a conduct.

At this point, let us consider some of the applied issues connected to freedom, justice, and organizing human societies beyond the mere concern of individuals. Justice dictates that the judiciary should have power and have a clear structure and way of operating. Historically, Muslim nations were distinguished by having many scholars whose main focus was fiqh and the branches of knowledge connected to it, and by a diversity of juristic schools, each of which was completely independent of the authorities. We have noted in the introduction that the term fiqh is much wider and distinctive from the term law, although laws can draw on fiqh. The role of the political and administrative authority was merely to assign a group of people of knowledge to advise them on the basis of the knowledge they had of the aims of Shariʿah and other rulings. This type of relationship between scholars of Shariʿah and the political authorities was regarded as something unique in the civilization of Islam, because it made fiqh, *uṣūl*, and *maqāṣid*, which approximate a theoretical framework of the law, separate from politics. This way of separating authorities (executive and legislative) is one of the main assurances for the protection of freedom and justice at once; it is not possible to achieve balance between rights and duties without ensuring that the judiciary is independent and is not influenced by political authority. But that is not to say that the relationship between the political and the literary classes was not tense, for political authorities always drift into consolidating power and bringing all of society's activities under its auspices.

As rights cannot be protected from the transgressions of wrongdoers except with a set of laws to deter them, it should not be assumed that mere promulgation of laws could do away with the necessity of basic decency, for there is no law that is not subject to different interpretations as to whether it is applicable in certain cases or it is appropriate to refer to that particular law or some other law. Widespread litigiousness is a sign of meanness and selfishness at the communal level and is indicative of the breakdown of the fabric of society, because in most human societies, people of prominence and authority are able to manipulate the law and interpret it and apply it. Thus, the law alone will not be able to completely and effectively protect what it is meant to protect.

There is a painful paradox with regard to the position of law in the life of nations, for the need for it is well-established, but the law by nature falls short of achieving what it is hoped it will achieve of the highest level of justice. This shortcoming is exacerbated and becomes clearer when lawmakers go to extremes in promulgating laws that regulate minor issues; the reason being that the law, by its very nature, is incapable of encompassing the detailed context of various cases, and without understanding the context of a problem and the many aspects connected to it that make it stand out from other similar cases, justice cannot be achieved. Therefore, it is appropriate that referring the case to court should be the last resort, and whenever it is possible to resolve a problem through mutual understanding and referring the matter to local advisers or to custom, this is more likely to achieve justice. The advantage of resorting to arbitration through communal, informal, or semi-informal means for settling disputes lies in: (1) being more in touch with the reality at hand; (2) staying away from the built-in rigidity in legal procedures; and (3) keeping away the rough edges of law enforcement agencies.

The preceding contextualization of the proper role of the law does not mean that it is not central to political authorities in running their affairs. It is not possible to protect people's rights and make sure that people receive their dues without resorting to written documentation. Hence, the setting up of official departments and records, and organizing their work and activities, is something that is urgently needed. With increasing numbers of people and the increasing variety of professions, there is a need for different types of departments and professional associations that can be attentive to behavior and conduct that is not congruent with the interests of the Muslims and does not meet their needs. Again, achieving justice is a balance between rights and duties. And achieving that aim (and refining it) requires continually thinking of the ultimate Shari'ah goals.

Finally, the reader should have noticed that while this theorizing approach to *maqāṣid* did not make freedom a stand-alone goal of Shari'ah, the implications of freedom were considered within all of the four applied *maqāṣid*, for we believe that this is its proper place within the unique perspective of Islam.

B. Shūrā: A Multilayered System of Consultation

The consultation (*shūrā*) process should be promoted and made effective by making consultation the basis of various societal activities. *Shūrā* is not limited to the realm of politics, although it has a primary place there. The Qur'an considers *shūrā* as the default nature of communal affairs. Since *shūrā* is encouraged for individual and private matters, it follows that mutual consultation should be adhered to with regard to issues of concern to the community as a whole. Mutual consultation with regard to such communal issues is something known to humanity from the most ancient times. In ancient communities, the process of consultation took place among prominent figures and those who were known for their wisdom. Consultation took place in a spontaneous manner and was not subject to formal guidelines or rules and regulations. The only guideline was the customs and traditions that were known to and accepted by all. Consultative councils at that time were distinguished by their direct contact with the common people and were fully aware of the aspirations and concerns of members of the community.

This type of consultation did not take place only among small communities; surprisingly, it also took place in larger political formations, such as some kingdoms and empires. We should note here that there is a common misperception in understanding the political structures of kingdoms and empires, as they did *not* resemble the modern nation-states of today. While a solid center of political authority did exist in such kingdoms, it did not replace local authorities and the society. Small social formations retained their authorities, whether that was the clan, the neighborhood, or the religious group. People continued to bond and form communities on the basis of local interests and local economic activities, and along the basis of living in the same neighborhood and being tied to religious worship practices and conventions. The role of the central political authority was mainly focused on macro issues in addition to taxation.

The system of *shūrā* is necessarily related to the type of the social formation in which it operates. As the nature of the Islamic system gives significant attention to the micro and meso social formations, a point that has been stressed all along in the presentation of this book, the *shūrā* system it envisions (and it practiced) is multilayered to match the structure of society. Below is a brief discussion of the relationship between consultation processes and social structure; and since the absence of consultation is usually associated with political oppression, we will also discuss the issue of rebellion against authorities.

The Connection between the Shūrā Process and the Type of Human Community

The type of *shūrā* may vary according to the three characteristics that human communities may have:

The Degree of Diversity in the Social Make-up of the Community

Diversity is of three dimensions: ethnic, linguistic, and religious. When the political system acknowledges these dimensions, it puts forth a realistic basis for managing differences and tensions. Identities related to those three dimensions and the sense of belonging is but human, as they resonate with peoples' culture, values, and historical memories. However, such attachments do not necessarily clash with or cancel the national identity based on the political framework. Therefore, an effective *shūrā* structure would naturally take such diversity into consideration, which in the end would lead to more harmony and to reducing grievances.

How People Come Together and Form a Single Political Entity

There are two factors at play here: one having to do with changes that affect demography, and the other having to do with geopolitical matters. Nations do not stay the same with regard to demographics, because migrations are a consistent part of human history, and they result in the formation of human societies made up of different components. The expansion of some states and political domination of new territory and its population is something that never ceased. However, the formation of new entities (societies with different make-ups) could occur through hostile means or through peaceful or quasi-peaceful means, and privileges and opportunities may be distributed among the people in ways that may be pleasing to them or otherwise. Obviously, the less confrontational political formation was, the smoother the development of the *shūrā* process and its institutions could materialize. Here we can note that since Islam acknowledged the Abrahamic religions and deferred judgement of people to the Day of Judgment, such quality puts forth a value-based acknowledgment of the other and creates a common ground for *shūrā* at the appropriate and relevant realm of social relations.

The Need of Different Sections in Society for One Another

This has to do with the topography of the land, its geographical location, and what it has of resources. All of that will have an impact on many human activities, including ways of earning a livelihood that will be reflected in the bonds and connections within that society, and may lead to various types of bonding. Usually, each region has different resources and different ways of earning a livelihood, and that leads to the *shūrā* process in that type of society being different from the *shūrā* process among people who are compacted in a small area with a high density of population.

The Basis on Which Human Groups Form

There are five common types of human groups in which the *shūrā* process may take place:

1   Friendship groups, because there is affection and compassion among them.

2   Neighborhood groups.

3   Associations of small groups among those who practice the same profession or share common interest.

4   Cities that typically house a large number of inhabitants. The nature of group formation in cities is different from that of small groups' localities, as the system in cities is composed of different levels among which there is interaction and overlap.

5   The Ummah as a whole.

Except for the first type of human groupings (friendships), there is a need for a suitable *shūrā* mechanism and institution. And only a multi-layered system of *shūrā* may effectively respond to the overall need of consultation between political authorities and societies. We can think of different types of *shūrā* with different mandates, some of which are principally coordinative.

The *shūrā* process at the Ummah-wide level is aimed at discussing larger issues of concern to the Ummah, such as maintaining security, issuing currency, guarding borders, collecting zakat, distributing surplus provisions, and keeping all of these matters in order. Promoting and developing all of that, and keeping it in good shape, requires keeping an eye on the *shūrā* process and regularly checking on it to ensure that it is functioning properly, so that the system of *shūrā* would not be reduced to a mere formality that does not achieve what is expected of it.

Moreover, the *shūrā* processes at the above four levels (neighborhood, associations, city, and Ummah-wide) are strongly interconnected; any shortcomings at one level will have an impact on the other levels. If there is any shortcoming in the *shūrā* process at the lower levels, then people may be left with no choice but to refer issues belonging at the lower level to the higher level, and this may lead to stiff authoritarianism if it continues. When issues that belong at the higher levels are delegated to people at the lower levels, it becomes very difficult to reach agreement on these issues, because local interests would take precedence over wider interests, and with the passage of time this may lead to the disintegration of society. Therefore, *shūrā* systems become stronger, more deeply rooted, and more well-founded when *shūrā* is practiced at many levels and is not concentrated at a single level (whether at the top or at the bottom).

The process and structure of *shūrā* has a relationship with the basis of legitimacy of authority. The legitimacy of authority in the Islamic perspective is based on its ability to serve the community interests that are essential in order for people to fulfil their role as vicegerents and to live the way God intended. Religion-based *sharʿī* commands begin with the individual, so people are accountable for their deeds, then there are *sharʿī* instructions that are addressed to the family, then the neighborhood, then the clan or tribe (which is simply a larger form of social organization typically misunderstood because of our modernist stereotypical impressions), and so on. In other words, from a political point of view, the smaller units of society are what give the state and its institutions their legitimacy; it is not the state that does a favor to the smaller units of society when it gives them their rights. This process of multisegmented *shūrā* practiced at various levels of society is one of the characteristics of Muslim societies in the past. It is a unique characteristic that some observers may overlook, because they are completely focused on formal consultation through bureaucratic bodies, namely that which occurs at the political level.

The process of *shūrā* invariably requires the assignment of representatives to act as brokers on behalf of their social units. The *shūrā* process can be set up and carried out in a manner that is separate and distinct from the process that leads to the higher positions of power and authority in the state, and such an arrangement functions as a buffer in turbulent times. In normal circumstances, the process and activities of *shūrā* can be carried out in a manner parallel to authority, but at times of crisis the matter of authority is very often settled by a force that seizes power by force, moving first, or having an advantageous position and resources. In such a situation, it is not possible for the *shūrā* process to take place through normal channels at the higher levels, and parallel consultative structures compensate for such a lack.

Historical experience teaches us that *shūrā* and the general processes of consultation are more durable and meaningful if the structure of the state is not steeply hierarchical. And the existence of overlapping and integrated system with several layers in its administrative structure is certainly advantageous.

Then if some layers or levels fall short or become corrupted or dysfunctional, that will not lead to the collapse of the entire structure. Moreover, these overlapping layers of administration, in which responsibilities, rights, and duties are distributed (among different layers), will create barriers which will protect against injustice and excessive control.

Rebelling Against Authority

Implementing the *shūrā* process in a manner that is appropriate to the time and place will enable the Ummah to benefit from the best of what it has of expertise and resources. But what should be done when there is widespread injustice, the *shūrā* process is not implemented, and people want to get rid of a regime and replace it? And if justice is one of the aims of Shariʿah with regard to *ʿumrān*, and if freedom from oppression or suffocating control is entrenched in human nature and is something that is protected and promoted according to Islamic teachings, and if injustice is a precursor to social and economic ruin, then what are the guidelines for rebelling against the established political order? It is very difficult to give precise guidelines on this matter because it is strongly connected to circumstances, and because it is also connected to how dreadful the injustice is and of what type it is. However, that should not prevent us from developing some general guidelines, a matter that will be discussed in the following section.

Wise people of various cultures are inclined not to encourage rebellion against authority for the slightest reason, and they think that revolution is the last resort. There are two reasons for this: (1) that the motive for rebelling against authority is often no more than political aspirations and the desire to compete, so the main goal behind rebelling is to attain power, not to achieve justice and reform; and (2) it is easy to stir up the common folk because of some shortcomings on the part of those in authority, even if that is in matters in which shortcomings are not of such an extent that would call for rebellion and revolution. However, having reservations about revolting against authority is not applicable in the case of tyranny and injustice; rather, these reservations are applicable to the type of shortcomings that are inevitable in any political situation, where revolution could lead to disintegration of society. Undoubtedly, following the teachings of Islam and complying with the commands to be just and fair take precedence over obeying the one who is in charge of the Muslims' affairs. Moreover, people in authority should be people of mature thinking and understanding, people whom the Ummah trusts, not people whose overriding quest is accumulation of worldly gains.

When people in authority are not qualified to be in that position and fail to serve the vital interests of the Ummah, this creates resentment among the people towards those in authority. Thus, the people will begin to look for someone who has the aspiration to lay the foundation for a new vision and a new plan. In that case, if the *shūrā* process is based on a sound foundation in various levels of society and at various levels of administration, those in authority will have no alternative but to accept the plans for reform, and there will be no need to replace the political system. But when there is no *shūrā* or the means of implementing *shūrā* are corrupt, then a need will emerge for total overhaul of the political system, altering its structure and the way in which it operates. If the existing political system allows for the necessary changes, the Ummah will gradually regain its vitality and strength. However, replacing the political system is difficult due to three reasons: (1) that political dictatorship weakens the nation, siphons the resources, and precludes the very conditions that are needed for changing the regime; (2) the existing regime has an advantage in mobilizing soft powers to thwart the momentum of change; and (3) that the political regime protects itself with well-trained forces and resorts to violence on the part of the police, the army, and the like of forces in order to silence the opposition.

Revolution against injustice and oppression is something dictated by the inner logic of *ʿumrānī* dynamics themselves, beyond the anger of individuals and groups. Even though the conditions required for the revolution to begin may be delayed because the injustice and oppression are so overwhelming that the people find themselves helpless and with no power to resist, when revolution erupts, especially after a long period of oppression, there is the fear that internal conflict may arise due to the large numbers of demands too difficult to respond to at that moment. Hence, the primary demand when rebelling against authority should be to restore the *shūrā* process, and that should be the motive for change, which will open the way for gradual reform.

When people decide to change the ruling system, it is inevitable that there will be different visions of reform. If that happens in the absence of the *shūrā* process, it may lead to turmoil and never-ending disputes, and people may divide into factions supporting different views. But if the *shūrā* process is implemented in the proper manner, and the people involved in debating and exchanging views agree to show lenience concerning the minor issues whilst agreeing on some major issues that will bring them together, that will pave the way towards reform. Any plan for reform will take time to put things in the proper order and rebuild. However, when there is serious deviation in the way in which people in authority are ruling the country, confrontation becomes inevitable, and violence usually takes place.

All of this highlights the importance of weighing up the issue of rebellion and revolution in light of the *ʿumrānī* aims, and it is essential to determine the causes that led the political authority to drift away from *maqāṣidī* guidelines: is it due to shortcomings and lack of resolve, or is it a deliberate act based on rejection of these guidelines? In the first case there should be demands to rectify the situation, and in the second case there should be resistance and standing up to authority.

Namely, the lack in actuating the *maqṣid* of maintenance of religion and its worldview could range from laxity to the systematic adulteration of the belief system. The lack in actuating the *maqṣid* of maintenance of human life and intellect could range from negligence, such as not supporting enough the institutions of learning, to deliberately spreading ignorance, corrupting individuals, and leading them to indulge in immoral pleasures. The lack in actuating the *maqṣid* of maintaining the societal order could range from shortcomings in supporting social harmony to stirring discord, deepening divisions, and inciting conflict among the different segments of society. The lack in actuating the *maqṣid* of maintenance of wealth and livelihood could range from shortcomings in propelling economic activities to causing poverty to become widespread, raiding public funds, and making the national economy dependent on foreign hostile nations. Lastly, the lack in actuating the *maqṣid* of maintenance of the political order could range from favoritism and narcistic political positions to tyrannical oppression. Reform demands are what is suitable for the first state of affairs; and structural change, which might call for rebellion and the use of force, is what is needed for the second state of affairs.

This *maqāṣid* approach to political change and rebellion is of utmost importance and supposedly fills a gap in relevant literature. Classical Islamic literature on the matter became paralyzed in the animosity of political events that circumvented and stymied the development of a balanced theoretical approach to the matter. The classical fiqh argument was so fixated on a binary position in the discussion of the subject: accepting the status quo versus rebellious annihilation of political legitimacy (*khurūj*). The first position justifies its stance by fears of social discord and the disintegration of the Muslim order, and the second position justifies its stance in rejecting any deviation from the immaculacy of political affairs at the time of Prophet Muhammad. The *maqāṣid* approach could solve this impasse as explained above by taking into consideration the degree of deviation. Furthermore, the three levels of *maqāṣid* could be included in the theory of *khurūj*: *ḍarūriyyāt* (indispensables), *ḥājiyyāt* (exigencies), and *taḥsīniyyāt* (enhancements)—discarding the indispensables justifies and calls for rebellion and total change, while overlooking the enhancements calls for pressuring authorities through political activism, and in the middle is the neglecting the exigencies which calls for stern political opposition.

C. Jihad: Striving to Achieve Security and Peace

Jihad is a Qur'anic term, which has suffered much abuse and controversy from within and without. It means literally, striving, and refers to any earnest striving in the way of God, involving either personal effort, material resources, or arms for righteousness and against evil, wrongdoing and oppression. Where it involves armed struggle, it must be for the defense of the Muslim community or a just war to protect even non-Muslims from evil, oppression, and tyranny. Therefore, the abuse of the term "jihad" does not justify discarding it. Establishing and maintaining security and peace is an important aim of politics, and certainly should have a place in the *maqāṣid* of Shariʿah. No affairs could be sound, no soul could have any joy, and no harmony could prevail in society if there is no security. Achieving security and peace is to take place at three levels: local, regional, and national.

Maintaining the security of the locality may be achieved by protecting it from the ignorant acts of thugs. A police force is usually sufficient to carry out that task. It is appropriate for the police force to consist of people from the neighborhood itself. In this way, the members of the police force will be from among the same people of the community, and therefore the people will not feel that there is any bias against them. This will restrain the police from transgressing against the people, because in that case they would be transgressing against their own people, those with whom they have ties and among whom they live, which would be going against the customs and traditions on which the neighborhood is based. The police force should be under the supervision of councils from within the respective communities.

At the regional level, it is wise if the security forces consist of a mixture of people from different ethnic and religious groups that constitute the region, so as to leave no room for suspicion of bias or enmity. The security force at this level would naturally fall under the supervision of councils that share in running regional affairs.

At the national level, jihad is needed in the interests of peace and security, as well as for self-defence maintained against foreign aggression of foreign powers. And a critical question arises in this matter: should the nation have a standing army or not? I think that the *maqāṣid* of Shariʿah, in light of historical experience, generally point to not having standing armies. That is because having such permanent force pushes, through slippery institutional dynamics, into unnecessary conflicts. That is apart from two concerns: the toll on the national treasury that a standing army incurs, and the possibility of the army aspiring to play a political role transgressing its mandate of protection from foreign enemies. However, the need for a small, able, and well-trained permanent force seems to be a practical necessity. Moreover, such determination is necessarily connected to the geopolitical conditions of a nation. Both weakness and too much power invite aggression, and there is no one-way aggression.

D. *Taʿāruf* and *Balāgh*

Taʿāruf and *balāgh* are two Qurʾanic comprehensive terms, and among their meanings are creating means of communication among people so that they may get to know one another and conveying the message of Islam. The duties of *taʿāruf* and *balāgh* span from the individual level to the top collective level.

Allah has created people as different nations and tribes/ethnic groups, as well as different religious groups and communities, and He has made the coming together (in marriage) of male and female the basis for the ties of kinship and ties among people in general. If Allah had so willed, He could have made people all one nation, but it was His will to create diversity so that life could develop and prosper. Here, we have to note that the negativity surrounding the term tribe and assigning it to narrowness, rivalry, and senseless conflict is a modern, conceited, and reductionist understanding incapable of appreciating history. I have elsewhere suggested that "tribes" and "peoples" (which both are mentioned in the same *āyah* in the Qur'an) are universal structures in human existence. Furthermore, as the All-Knowing willed that humans should vary in their languages, tribes, and peoples, and in their colors and other differences, and He made all of that among His signs, then it is appropriate to consider that knowing one another is a sub-objective *maqṣid* of Shariʿah and a goal to be sought.

We note that the differences in languages and colors may refer to differences in cultures and traditions; the differences in tribes and peoples may refer to the differences in ethnic groups, nations, and the overall societal setting and its design. These two dimensions are among the most visible aspects of *ʿumrān*.

The aim of keeping political affairs in good shape is one of the main *ʿumrānī* aims. Ensuring that political affairs are run properly and maintaining the well-being of the Ummah requires constant effort to ensure that justice is achieved, because justice means creating balance between rights and duties, and protecting people's freedoms from being transgressed against. As such, people will be able to think and be creative in an atmosphere of freedom.

Ensuring that political affairs are in good shape requires implementing the *shūrā* process extensively at all levels. The locus of authority of the officials in power should be constrained by the consultative councils, so as to prevent them from turning into dictators and tyrants. Finally, at the abstract level of politics, the most important point is rectifying the concepts that form the foundation of the political system. Thus, the political system will gain credibility, which will reinforce its stability and allow reform to take place and prevent tyranny.

Conclusion

This book has introduced an *ʿumrānī* perspective of the aims of Shariʿah. The first and foremost of these aims is preserving the essence of religion and its pristine worldview, and to rectify the process of being guided by religion. The second *ʿumrānī* aim lies in the preservation of the holistic self and refining its multiple dimensions, reason, emotions, conscience, and will, in addition to the physical body, along the lines of *fiṭrah*. The third *ʿumrānī* aim that the *maqāṣid* of Shariʿah maintain is preserving the family system and refining the societal order with its overlapping institutions and the very reality in which people live. The fourth *ʿumrānī* aim has to do with wealth, property, resources, provision, and the economy. The fifth *ʿumrānī* aim lies in the maintenance of polity and rectifying the governing ways of running and managing the collective affairs of people.

The interactive dynamics of the five aims should not be missed. Beliefs and concepts have an impact on the individual's behavior, emotions, conscience, and thoughts, and will have an impact on shaping the social, economic, and political system. The aim of preserving the societal order is connected to the aim of preserving resources and livelihoods. Similarly, it cannot be imagined that there could be harmony in society if there is corruption with regard to provision and livelihood or the distribution of wealth. And in the opposite direction of influence, it is tortuous to earn a living if there is no social cooperation and no political stability. And in order to maintain a healthy political system, it is essential to have funds available to its institutions and to operate within a reasonably harmonious social system.

Whatever *ʿumrānī* aims have been introduced in this book may be regarded as a reformulation and an extension of the five classical aims of Shariʿah. The aim of the preservation of religion and the refinement of its worldview is parallel and complementary to the aim of preserving religion in the classical theory. The preservation and the refinement of the holistic self and its intellect is an *ʿumrānī* aim and an expansion of two aims in the classical formation: the preservation of *nafs* (self) and the preservation of *'aql* (reason). As an *'umrānī* aim, the preservation of family and the refinement of the societal order is an expansion of the classical aim of preserving lineage. The preservation of wealth and the refinement of livelihood is also a broadening of the classical aim of preserving property. Lastly, the preservation of polity and the refinement of governance is an *'umrānī* Shari'ah aim that was added as its realm is virtually absent in classical *maqāṣid.* And in all of these aims, the collective dimension was specifically stressed, an important feature for *maqāṣid* from an *'umrānī* perspective.

Studying both the Qur'an and Sunnah and deepening the understanding of their horizons are a sure duty upon the serious believer, and learning from human experience as it accumulates knowledge with the passage of time would help in furthering the *'umrānī* perspective of Shari'ah. The comprehensive nature of the discourse of *'umrānī* Shari'ah *maqāṣid* is the key to rectifying the Muslims' affairs. And so long as life is constantly changing, there will be a constant need to think about how to expand the framework within which the aims of Shari'ah are to be achieved. That is the responsibility of the vicegerent, who is obliged to use reason, to read and understand Allah's revelation, and to reflect on the creation of the universe and the history of humanity.

Notes

INTRODUCTION

[1]   Gudrun Krämer, "Islamist Notions of Democracy," *Middle East Report* 183 (July-August 1993): pgs. 4-5.

[2]   Louay Safi, "Islamic Law and Society," *American Journal of Islamic Social Sciences* Vol. 7:2 (1990): p. 177.

[3]   Nimat Hafez Barazangi, *Women's Identity and the Qur'an: A New Reading* (Gainesville, FL: University of Florida Press, 2004), p. 6.

[4]   Khaled Abou El Fadl, *The Great Theft: Wrestling Islam form the Extremists* (San Francisco: Harper, 2005), p. 35.

[5]   Mazen Hashem, "Muslim Friday *Khutbas* in America: Veiled and Unveiled Themes," *Institute for Social Policy and Understanding* (October 2009), p. 23.

[6]   Mazen Hashem, "Contemporary Islamic Activism: The Shades of Praxis," *Sociology of Religion* 67 (2006): p. 25.

[7]   Taqī al-Dīn Aḥmad Ibn ʿAbd al-Ḥalīm Ibn Taymiyyah, *Al-ʿUbūdiyyah* (Al-Iskandariyyah: Dār al-Imān, 2003), pp. 14-15.

[8]   ʿAbd al-Malik Ibn Muḥammad al-Thaʿālibī, *Fiqh al-Lughah wa Asrār al-ʿArabiyyah* (Beirut: Dār Maktabat al-Ḥayāh, 1999), p. 116.

[9]   It should be noted that the English use of the term Bedouin with a capital is rather strange to its semantics in the Arabic language.

[10] Malek Bennabi, *Mushkilat al-Thaqāfah*, translated by Abdel-Sabour Shahin (Damascus: Dār al-Fikr, 1984), p. 101.

[11] Mona Abul-Fadl, "Contrasting Epistemics: Tawhid, the Vocationist and Social Theory," *American Journal of Islamic Social Sciences* 7, no. 1 (1990): pp. 15-39.

[12] Saif AbdelFattah, "Bayn Al-Nasaq Wa al-Manhaj:Al-Manẓūmah al-Fikriyyah Li Munā Abū al-Faḍl," in *Al-Taḥawwul al-Maʿrifī Wa al-Taghiyīr al-Ḥaḍārī: Qirāʾah Fī Manẓūmat Fikr Munā Abū al-Faḍl*, ed. Nadia Mahmoud Mostafa, Saif AbdelFattah, and Majidah Ibrahim (Cairo: Dār al-Bashar, 2011), pp. 78–85.

[13] Haldun Karahanlı, "Al-Tadāfuʿiyyah: Transcending the Imperial Concept Of 'Civilization': Recalling the Concept of Al-ʿUmrān" (Master's thesis, Istanbul, Turkey, Ibn Haldun University, 2020).

14   For a detailed analysis of the concept of *ʿumrān*, see: Salih ibn Tahir Mushawash, *ʿIlm al-ʿUmrān al-Khaldūnī wa Athar al-Ruʾyah al-Kawniyyah al-Tawḥīdiyyah fī Ṣiyāghatihi* (Herndon, VA: International Institute of Islamic Thought, 2012).

PART I

CHAPTER 1

1   See: Abī al-Walīd Muḥammad ibn Aḥmad ibn Muḥammad ibn Aḥmad Ibn Rushd al-Ḥafīd, *Bidāyat Al-Mujtahid Wa-Nihāyat al-Muqtaṣid*, ed. Muhammad Subhi Hassan al-Hallaq (Cairo: Maktabat Ibn Taymiyyah, 1994); Muḥammad ibn Isḥāq Ibn Khuzaymah, *Kitāb Al-Zakāt* (Beirut: al-Maktab al-Islāmī, 1980).

2   Ahmad al-Raysuni, *Muḥāḍarāt fī Maqāṣid al-Sharīʿah* (Rabat and Cairo: Dār al-Imān and Dār al-Islām, 2009), p. 77.

3   Shihāb al-Dīn al-Qarāfī, *Al-Iḥkām fī Tamyīz al-Fatāwā ʿan al-Aḥkām wa-Taṣarrufāt al-Qāḍī wa-al-Imām*, ed. ʿAbd al-Fattāḥ Abū Ghuddah (Halab: Maktab al-Maṭbūʿāt al-Islāmiyyah, 1967), p. 231.

4   Abū Isḥāq Ibrahīm al-Shāṭibī, *Al-Muwāfaqāt fī Uṣūl al-Sharīʿah*, ed. Muḥammad ʿAbd Allāh Darrāz (Beirut: Dār al-Maʿrifah, n.d.), vol. 2, p. 307.

5   Ibid., 4:233.

6   Muḥammad Ibn al-Qayyim al-Jawziyyah, *Iʿlām al-Muwaqqiʿīn ʿan Rabb al-ʿĀlamīn* (Dammam: Dār Ibn al-Jawzī, 2002), vol. 3, p. 14.

7   Abdullah Muhammad al-Amin al-Naʿim, "Itijāhāt al-Naẓr fī al-Taʾsīs al-Maqāṣidī li al-ʿUlūm al-Ijtimāʿiyyah," *Maqāṣid al-Sharīʿah: Naḥū Iṭār li al-Baḥth fī al-ʿUlūm al-Ijtimāʿiyyah wa al-Insāniyyah*, ed. Abdullah Muhammad al-Amin al-Naʿim (Damascus: Dār al-Fikr, 2009), p. 52.

8   Al-Shāṭibī, *Al-Muwāfaqāt*, 1:35.

9   Ibid., 2:306.

10   Qays Mahmud Hamid, "Maqārabah Falsafiyyah li Maqāṣid al-Sharīʿah al-Islāmiyyah," *Maqāṣid al-Sharīʿah: Naḥū Iṭār li al-Baḥth fī al-ʿUlūm al-Ijtimāʿiyyah wa al-Insāniyyah*, ed. Abdullah Muhammad al-Amin al-Naʿim (Damascus: Dār al-Fikr, 2009), p. 85.

11   Al-Shāṭibī, *Al-Muwāfaqāt*, 1:87.

12   Muhammad al-Awad Abdullah, "Al-Maḍāmīn al-Manhajiyyah li Muqadimāt al-Shāṭibī fī al-Muwāfaqāt," *Maqāṣid al-Sharīʿah: Naḥū Iṭār li al-Baḥth fī al-ʿUlūm al-Ijtimāʿiyyah wa al-Insāniyyah*, ed. Abdullah Muhammad al-Amin al-Naʿim (Damascus: Dār al-Fikr, 2009), p. 85.

13   Al-Shāṭibī, *Al-Muwāfaqāt*, 1:46.

14   Ibid., 1:62.

15   Ibid., 1:99.

16   Ibrahim Mohamed Zain, "Al-Istiqrāʾ ʿinda al-Shāṭibī wa Manhaj al-Naẓar fī Mudawwinātinā al-Uṣūliyyah," *Islāmiyyat Al-Maʿrifah* 8, no. 30 (October 2002): p.40.

17   Ibid.

CHAPTER 2

1.   Shah Walīullah al-Dehlawī, *Ḥujjat Allah al-Bālighah*, ed. Sayyid Sabiq (Beirut: Dār al-Jīl, 2005), p. 22.

2.   Ibid., 1:49.

3.   I define "human universal" as an element, pattern, trait, or institution that is common to all human cultures worldwide, throughout the ages.

4.   Shah Walīullah al-Dehlawī, *Ḥujjat Allah al-Bālighah*, 1:186.

5.   Ibid., 1:84.

6.   Ibid.

7.   Ibid., 1:92.

8.   Ibid., 1:94.

9.   Ibid., 1:99.

10.   Ibid., 1:87.

11.   Ibid., 1:90.

12.   Ibid., 1:93-94.

13.   Ibid., 1:154.

14.   Ibid., 1:164-166.

15.   Ibid.

16.   Ibid., 1:57.

17.   Ibid., 1:255, 2:208.

18.   Muḥammad al-Ṭāhir Ibn ʿĀshūr, *Maqāṣid Al-Sharīʿah al-Islāmiyyah* (Tunis: Maktabat al-Istiqāmah, 1946). p. 50.

19.   ʿAllal al-Fasi, *Maqāṣid al-Sharīʿah al-Islāmiyyah wa Makārimuhā* (Beirut: Dār al-Gharb al-Islāmī, 1993), p. 47.

20.   Ibid., p. 55.

21.   Ahmad al-Raysuni, Muḥāḍirāt fī Maqāṣid al-Sharīʿah, p. 94.

22.   Ismail Hassani, *Naẓariyyat Al-Maqāṣid ʿind al-Imām Muḥammad Ibn ʿĀshūr* (Herndon, VA: International Institute of Islamic Thought, 1995), p. 435.

23.   Ibrahim Zain, *Al-Istiqrā' ʿinda al-Shāṭibī wa Manhaj al-Naẓar fī Mudawwinātinā al-Uṣūliyyah*, pp. 47-48.

24.   Ibid., p. 49.

25.   Ibid.

26.   Ibn ʿAshur, *Maqāṣid al-Sharīʿah al-Islāmiyyah*, p. 6.

27.   Ibn ʿAshur, *Maqāṣid al-Sharīʿah al-Islāmiyyah*, p. 51.

28.   Ibid., p. 50.

29   Ibn ʿAshur, *Maqāṣid al-Sharīʿah al-Islāmiyyah*, p. 10.

30   ʿAllal al-Fasi, *Maqāṣid al-Sharīʿah al-Islāmiyyah wa Makārimuhā*, pp. 45-46.

31   Ibn ʿAshur, *Maqāṣid al-Sharīʿah al-Islāmiyyah*, p. 89.

32   Ibid., p. 98.

33   Ibid., p. 48.

34   Ibid., p. 65.

35   Ibid., p. 133-134.

36   Ibid., p. 49.

37   ʿAllal al-Fasi, *Maqāṣid al-Sharīʿah al-Islāmiyyah wa Makārimuhā*, p. 127.

38   Ibn ʿAshur, *Maqāṣid al-Sharīʿah al-Islāmiyyah*, p. 57.

39   Ibn ʿAshur, *Maqāṣid al-Sharīʿah al-Islāmiyyah*, p. 79.

40   Ibn ʿAshur, *Maqāṣid al-Sharīʿah al-Islāmiyyah*, p. 125.

41   ʿAllal al-Fasi, *Maqāṣid al-Sharīʿah al-Islāmiyyah wa Makārimuhā*, p. 56.

42   Muḥammad al-Ṭāhir Ibn ʿAshur, *Uṣūl al-Niẓam al-Ijtimāʿī fī al-Islām* (Tunis: al-Sharikah al-Tūnisiyyah li al-Tawzīʿ, 1985), pp. 20-21.

43   Ismail Hassani, *Naẓariyyat al-Maqāṣid ʿinda al-Imām Ibn ʿĀshūr*, p. 267.

44   Ibid., pp. 430-431.

45   Ibn ʿAshur, *Uṣūl al-Niẓam al-Ijtimāʿī fī al-Islām*, p. 21.

46   Ismail Hassani, *Naẓariyyat al-Maqāṣid*, p. 272.

47   Ibid., p. 430.

48   Ibid., p. 164.

49   Ibid., p. 169.

50   Ibid., p. 183.

51   Ibid., p. 185.

52   Ibid., p. 182.

53   Ibid., p. 188.

54   Ibid., p. 197.

55   Ibid., p. 200.

56   Ibid., p. 204.

57   ʿAllal al-Fasi, *Maqāṣid al-Sharīʿah al-Islāmiyyah wa Makārimuhā*, p. 219.

58   Ibid., p. 220.

59   Ibn ʿAshur, *Maqāṣid Al-Sharīʿah Al-Islāmiyyah*, p. 150.

60   Ibn ʿAshur, *Uṣūl al-Niẓām al-Ijtimāʿī*, p. 163.

61   Ibid., p. 139.

[62]   Ibn ʿAshur, *Uṣūl al-Niẓām al-Ijtimāʿī*, pp. 163-169.

[63]   Ibid., p. 170.

[64]   Ibn ʿAshur, Uṣūl al-Niẓām al-Ijtimāʿī, p. 177.

[65]   Ibid., p. 170.

CHAPTER 3

[1]   Abdallah Bin Bayyah, *Mashāhid min al-Maqāṣid* (Riyad: Dār Wajūh, 2010), p. 165.

[2]   Ibid. pg. 166.

[3]   Ibid., p. 166.

[4]   Ibid. p. 165-166.

[5]   Ibid., p. 165.

[6]   Ibid., p. 167.

[7]   Ibid., p. 140.

[8]   Ahmad al-Raysuni, *Naẓariyyat al-Maqāṣid ʿinda al-Shāṭibī*, p. 317.

[9]   Ibid., p. 16.

[10]   Ibid., pp. 271-282.

[11]   Ismail Hassani, *Naẓariyyat al-Maqāṣid ʿinda al-Imām Ibn ʿĀshūr*, p. 299.

[12]   Ibid.

[13]   Ibid., p. 333.

[14]   Ibid., p. 336.

[15]   Ibid., pp. 327-333.

[16]   Hasan Jabir, *Al-Maqāṣid al-Kulliyyah fī Daw' al-Qirā'ah al-Manẓumiyyah li al-Qur'ān al-Karīm* (Beirut: Dār al-Ḥiwār, 2011), p. 42.

[17]   Ibid., p. 84.

[18]   Ibid., p. 107.

[19]   Ibid., p. 99.

[20]   Ibid., p. 105.

[21]   Jasser Auda, *Maqasid as Philosophy of Islamic Law: A System Approach* (Herndon, VA: Islamic Institute of Islamic Thought, 1429 AH/2008 CE), p. xxviii.

[22]   Ibid., p. 46-49.

[23]   Ibid., p. 161.

[24]   Ibid., p. 171-174.

[25]   Ibid., p. 231-232.

[26]   Gamal Eldin Attia, *Naḥwah Tafʿīl Maqāṣid al-Sharīʿah*, (Herndon, VA: International Institute of Islamic Thought, 2001).

27   Ibid., p. 23.

28   Ibid., pp. 45-47.

29   Ibid., p. 51.

30   Ibid., pp. 120-122.

31   Ibid., p. 135.

32   Ibid. p. 122.

33   Ibid, p. 238.

34   Ibid., pp. 106-107.

35   Ibid., p. 122.

36   Abd al-Majid al-Najjar, *Maqāṣid al-Sharīʿah bi Abʿād Jadīdah* (Beirut: Dār al-Gharb al-Is-lāmī, 2008), p. 17.

37   Ibid., p. 15.

38   Ibid., p. 65.

39   Ibid., p. 68.

40   Ibid., p. 70.

41   Ibid., p. 85.

42   Ibid., p. 104.

43   Ibid., p. 112.

44   Ibid., p. 52.

45   Ibid., pp. 118-125.

46   Ibid., pp. 139-169.

47   Ibid., p. 184.

48   Ibid., pp. 24-35.

49   Ibid., p. 37.

50   Ibid., pp. 36-56.

51   Ibid., p. 55.

52   Ibid., p. 234.

53   Ibid., p. 21.

PART II

CHAPTER 4

1   ʿAllal al-Fasi, *Maqāṣid al-Sharīʿah al-Islāmiyyah wa Makārimuhā*, p. 47.

2   Ahmad al-Raysuni, *Muḥāḍarāt fī Maqāṣid al-Sharīʿah*, p. 103.

3   Translation from Abdullah Yusuf Ali, *The Meaning of the Holy Qur'an.*

4   Ibid.

5   Al-Shāṭibī, *al-Muwāfaqāt*, 1:32.

6   Ibid., 4:162.

7   Mustapha Tajdin, "Al-Naṣ al-Qur'ānī wa Mushkil al-Ta'wīl," *Islāmiyyat al-Maʿrifah* 4, no. 14 (October 1998): p. 25.

8   Yunus al-Sawalihi, "Al-Istiqrā' fī Manāhij al-Naẓr al-Islāmī: Namūdhaj al-Imām al-Shāṭibī fī al-Muwāfaqāt," *Islāmiyyat al-Maʿrifah* 1, no. 4 (April 1996): p. 89.

9   Ibid., p. 76.

10   Al-Shāṭibī, *al-Muwāfaqāt*, Vol. 1, p. 38.

11   Yunus al-Sawalihi, "Al-Istiqrā' fī Manāhij al-Naẓr al-Islāmī," p. 77.

12   Al-Shāṭibī, *al-Muwāfaqāt*, vol. 2, p. 297.

13   Al-Shāṭibī, *al-Muwāfaqāt*, vol. 2, p. 283.

14   Ibid.

15   Qutb Mustafa Sano, "Al-Mutakallimūn wa Uṣūl al-Fiqh: Qirā'ah fī Jadliyat al-ʿAlāqah bayn ʿIlmay al-Uṣūl wa al-Kalām," *Islāmiyyat al-Maʿrifah* 3, no. 9 (July 1997): p. 40.

16   Yunus al-Ṣawalihi, "Al-Istiqrā' fī Manāhij al-Naẓr al-Islāmī," p. 91.

17   Qutb Mustafa Sano, "Fī Muṣṭalaḥ al-Ijmāʿ al-Uṣūlī: Ishkāliyyat al-Mafhūm bayn al-Mathāliyyah wa al-Wāqiʿiyyah," *Islāmiyyat al-Maʿrifah* 5, no. 21 (July 2000): p. 83.

18   Ibn ʿAshur, *Maqāsid al-Sharīʿah al-Islāmiyyah,* pp. 6-7.

19   Ibid., p. 14.

20   Ibid., p. 23.

21   Ibid., p. 24.

22   Ibid., p. 148.

23   Ibid., p. 126.

24   Ahmad al-Raysuni, "Al-Naṣṣ wa al-Maṣlaḥah: Bayn al-Taṭbīq wa al-Taʿāruḍ," *Islāmiyyat al-Maʿrifah* 4, no. 13 (July 1998): p. 47.

25   Ibid.

26   Ibid., p 61.

27   Al-Shāṭibī, *Al-Muwāfaqāt fī Uṣūl al-Sharīʿah*, Vol. 2, p. 8.

28   Qays Mahmud Hamid, "Maqārabah Falsafiyyah Li Maqāṣid Al-Sharīʿah al-Islāmiyyah," in *Maqāṣid Al-Sharīʿah: Naḥū Iṭār Li al-Baḥth Fī al-ʿUlūm al-Ijtimāʿiyyah Wa al-Insāniyyah*, ed. Abdullah Muhammad al-Amin al-Naʿim (Damascus: Dār al-Fikr, 2009), p. 84.

29   Translator's note: The term *maṣāliḥ* and *maqāṣid* are often used interchangeably by some writers; or the term *maṣāliḥ* is used in reference to *maqāṣid*.

30   Ahmad al-Raysuni, *Muḥāḍarāt Fī Maqāṣid Al-Sharīʿah*, p. 67.

31 Ibid., p. 67.

32 Ahmad al-Raysuni, "Insāniyyat al-Insān Qabl Ḥuqūq al-Insān," in *Huqūq al-Insān Miḥwar Maqāṣid al-Sharī'ah*, edited by Ahmad al-Raysuni, Muhammad al-Zuhayli, and Muhammad Uthman Bashir (Doha: Wizārat al-Awqāf wa al-Shu'ūn al-Islāmiyyah, 1421 H./2002 C.E.), p. 53.

33 Al-Shāṭibī, *al-Muwāfaqāt*, vol. 2, p. 8.

34 Ibid., vol. 4, pp. 27-29.

35 Oath of condemnation. Disavowal of paternity by mutual oath of both spouses (resorted to by the husband in refutation of an accusation of *qadhf* by his wife, and by the wife in refutation of an accusation of adultery by her husband).

36 Falsely accusing someone of sexual misconduct.

37 Al-Shāṭibī, *al-Muwāfaqāt*, vol. 4, pp. 27-29.

38 Al-Raysuni, *Muḥāḍarāt fī Maqāṣid al-Sharī'ah*, p. 152.

39 Ibn 'Ashur, *Maqāṣid al-Sharī'ah*, p. 173.

40 It is important to note the term "the *actions* of the heart" in the Muslims' legacy writings, as it reflects the will of the person to be self-aware and critical toward feeling and thinking, and to try to purify this aspect of the human condition.

41 Taqī al-Dīn Aḥmad Ibn 'Abd al-Ḥalīm Ibn Taymiyyah, *Majmū' Al-Fatāwā al-Kubrā*, ed. Hasan Muhammad Makhluf (Beirut: Dār al-Ma'rifah, 1966), p. 234.

42 Al-Shāṭibī, *al-Muwāfaqāt*, vol. 4, p. 27.

43 Ibn 'Ashur, *Maqāṣid al-Shari'ah*, p. 51.

44 Al-Shāṭibī, *al-Muwāfaqāt*, vol. 2, p. 11.

45 Ibid.

46 Ibid.

47 Bin Bayyah, *Mashāhid Min Al-Maqāṣid*, p. 89.

48 Al-Raysuni, *Muḥāḍarāt Fī Maqāṣid Al-Sharī'ah*, p. 167.

49 Ibid., p. 170.

50 Abdul-Nur Baza, "Al-Maqāṣid al-Shar'iyyah bayn Mubda'a al-Ḥasr wa Da'wā al-Taghiyīr," *Islāmiyyat al-Ma'rifah* 10, no. 40 (April 2005): p. 113.

51 Ahmad al-Raysuni, *Naẓariyyat al-Maqāṣid 'inda al-Imām al-Shāṭibī* (Beirut: Al-Mu'assasah al- Jāmi'īyyah, 1992), p. 41.

52 Riyad Adhami, "Awlawiyyāt al-Aḥkām al-Shar'iyyah" (California: *Majallat al-Rashād*, 1995).

53 Ahmad al-Raysuni, *Naẓariyyat al-Maqāṣid*, p. 44.

54 Ibid., p. 359.

55 Ibid.

56   Ismail Hassani, "Al-Fikr al-Maqāṣidī wa Tarsīkh al-Fikr al-ʿIlmī," *Islāmiyyat al-Maʿrifah* 15, no. 57 (July 2009): p. 48-62.

57   Ahmad al-Raysuni, *Al-Kulliyyāt al-Asāsiyyah lil-Sharīʿah al-Islāmiyyah* (Rabat: Dār al-Imān; Cairo: Dār al-Islām, 2010), p. 56.

58   Ibid., p. 30.

59   Ibid., p. 56.

60   Ibid., p. 107.

CHAPTER 5

1   At this point of the book, we are forced to choose a generic equivalent to the term *nafs* in order not to implicate it with Greek or modern understandings to the self, character, soul, mind, and spirit.

2   Abdallah Bin Bayyah, *Mashāhid min al-Maqāṣid*, p. 79.

3   Ibid., p. 188.

4   Ibid., p. 189.

5   Ahmad al-Raysuni, *Naẓariyyat al-Maqāṣid ʿinda al-Shāṭibī*, pp. 17-18; Ahmad al-Raysuni, *Imam al-Shāṭibī's Theory of the Higher Objectives and Intents of Islamic Law*, Translated by Nancy Roberts (London: IIIT, 2005), p. xxxiv.

6   Ibid.

7   Translation from M.A.S Abdel Haleem, *The Qurʾan: A New Translation by M.A.S. Abdel Haleem* (Oxford: OUP, 2015).

8   ʿAllal al-Fasi, *Maqāṣid Al-Sharīʿah al-Islāmiyyah Wa Makārimuhā*, p. 80.

9   Ibid., p. 81-82.

10   Ahmad al-Raysuni, *Al-Kulliyyāt al-Asāsiyyah Lil-Sharīʿah al-Islāmiyyah*, p. 16.

11   See Tariq al-Bushri, "Manhaj al-Naẓar fī Dirasāt al-Qānūn Muqaranan bī al-Sharīʿah al-Islāmiyyah," *Islāmiyyat al-Maʿrifah* 2, no. 5 (July 1996): p. 39.

12   "Be tolerant and command what is right [*al-ʿurf*]: pay no attention to foolish people" (Qurʾan 7:199, Translation by M. A. S. Abdel Haleem).

13   ʿAllal al-Fasi, *Maqāṣid al-Sharīʿah al-Islāmiyyah wa Makārimuhā*, pp. 156, 201, 204.

14   Abd al-Majid al-Najjar, *Maqāṣid al-Sharīʿah Bi Abʿād Jadīdah*, pp. 84-107.

15   Al-Dehlawī, *Ḥujjat-Allah al-Bālighah*, vol. 2, p. 138.

16   Ibid., vol. 2, p. 137.

17   Ibid., vol. 2, p. 137-138.

18   "And [by] the soul and He who proportioned it. And inspired it [with discernment of] its wickedness and its righteousness". Quran 91:7-8; translation from *Sahih International*.

19   Ibn ʿAshur, *Uṣūl al-Niẓām al-Ijtimāʿī*, pp. 18-19.

20 Al-Fasi, *Maqāṣid al-Sharīʿah al-Islāmiyyah wa Makārimuhā*, p. 20.

21 Ibid., p. 9.

22 Ibid., p.66.

23 Ibid., p. 70.

24 Ibid.

25 Ibid.

26 Al-Dehlawī, *Ḥujjat-Allah al-Bālighah*, vol. 1, p. 111.

27 Ibid., vol. 2, p. 140.

28 Ibn ʿAshur, *Uṣūl al-Niẓām al-Ijtimāʿī*, p. 91.

29 Ahmad al-Raysuni, "Insāniyyat al-Insān Qabl Ḥuqūq al-Insān," in *Huqūq al-Insān Miḥwar Maqāṣid al-Sharīʿah*, edited by Ahmad al-Raysuni, Muhammad al-Zuhayli, and Muhammad Uthman Bashir, p. 39.

30 Abd al-Majid al-Najjar, *Khilāfat al-Insān bayn al-Waḥī wa al-ʿAql* (Doha: Kitāb al-Ummah, 2000), pp. 92-97.

31 Several scholars stressed this point, among which is Ṭaha Jabir al-ʿAlwani. However, it was the treatise of Ahmad Bassam al-Saʿi that elaborated this idea. See: Ahmad Bassam al-Saʿi, *Iʿādat Qirāʾat al-Iʿjāz al-Lughawī fī al-Qurʾān al-Karīm* (Herndon, VA: International Institute of Islamic Thought, 2012).

CHAPTER 6

1 Mohamed El-Tahir El-Mesawi, "Al-Taʿlīl wa al-Munāsabah wa al-Maṣlaḥah: Baḥth fī Baʿd al-Mafāhīm al-Taʾasīsiyyah li Maqāṣid al-Sharīʿah," *Islāmiyyat al-Maʿrifah*, no. 43 (2009), p. 52.

2 Hassani, *Naẓariyyat al-Maqāṣid ʿinda al-Imām Muḥammad ibn ʿĀshūr*, p. 438.

3 Mohammed Ibn Nasr, "Taʾsīl al-ʿUlūm al-Insāniyyah wa al-Ijtimāʿiyyah," *Islāmiyyat al-Maʿriffah* 11, no. 42-43 (January 2006): p. 119.

4 Taha Jabir al-Alwani, "Min al-Taʿlīl ila al-Maqāṣid al-Qurʾāniyyah al-ʿUlyā al-Ḥākimah," *Islāmiyat al-Maʿrifah* 12, no. 46-47 (January 2007): p. 5.

5 Ibid., p. 6.

6 Ibid., p. 6.

7 Ibid., pp. 16-17.

8 Taha Jabir al-Alwani, "Turāthunā al-Islāmī wa al-Maʿārif al-Insāniyyah wa al-Ijtimāʿiyyah," *Islāmiyyat al-Maʿrifah*, no. 42-43 (2006): p. 8.

9 Ibid., p. 9.

10 Adnan Zarzur, "Ibn Khaldūn wa Fiqhuhu al-Sunan," *Islāmiyyat al-Maʿrifah* 13, no. 50 (October 2007): p. 165.

11   Ibid.

12   Ibid., p. 166.

13   ʿAbd al-Raḥmān ibn Muḥammad ibn Khaldūn, *Al-Muqaddimah* (Sayda: al-Maktabah al-ʿAṣriyyah, 2010), p. 43.

14   Ibid., p. 38.

15   Ibid., pp. 263-264.

16   Abd al-Rahman al-Adrawi, "Al-Taṭbīq al-Maqāṣidī fī al-Manhaj al-Khaldūnī," *Islāmiyyat al-Maʿrifah* 13, no. 50 (October 2007): p. 177.

17   Ibid.

18   Hassan Shahid, "Shākilat al-Naẓar al-ʿIlmī bayn al-Shāṭibī wa Ibn Khaldūn: Maqarabah Minhajiyyah," *Islāmiyyat al-Maʿrifah* 15, no. 57 (July 2009): p. 89.

19   Abd al-Rahman al-Adrawi, "Al-Taṭbīq al-Maqāṣidī fī al-Manhaj al-Khaldūnī," p. 206.

20   Ibn Khaldūn, *Al-Muqaddimah*, Part 3, Chapter 26, p. 183.

21   Ibid., pp. 46-47.

22   Ibid., Part 3, Chapter 43, p. 263.

23   Adnan Zarzur, *Ibn Khaldūn wa Fiqhuhu al-Sunan*, p. 161.

24   Ibn Khaldūn, *Al-Muqaddimah*, Part 1, p. 92.

25   Ibid., pp. 427-428.

26   Ibid., pp. 497-480.

27   Ibid., p. 236.

28   Ibid., p. 527.

29   Ibid., p. 133.

30   Ibid., p. 126

31   Ibid., p. 116.

32   Ibid., p. 370.

33   Ibid.

34   Ibid., pp. 119-120.

35   Ibid., p. 174.

36   Ibid., p. 137.

37   Ibid., pp. 376-377.

38   Ibid., pp. 255-256.

39   Ibid.

40   Adnan Zarzur, "*Ibn Khaldūn wa Fiqhuhu al-Sunan*," p. 161.

41   Ibn Khaldūn, *Al-Muqaddimah*, p. 147.

42   Ibid.

43   Ibid., p. 176.

44   Ibid.

45   Ibid.

46   Ibid., p.177

47   Ibid.

48   Ibid., p. 178.

49   Ibid., p. 278.

50   Ibid., 217.

51   Ibid., p. 256.

52   Ibid.

53   Ibid., pp. 259-260.

54   Ibid.

55   Ibid., p. 373.

56   Ibid., p. 175.

57   Ibid., p. 184.

58   Ibid., p. 155.

59   Ibid., p. 181.

60   Ibid., p. 35.

61   Ibid., p. 143.

62   Ibid., p. 152.

63   Ibid., p. 151.

64   Ibid., p. 274.

65   Ibid., p. 275.

66   Ibid., p. 274.

67   Ibid.

68   Ibid., p. 148.

69   Ibid., pp. 263-264.

PART III

PREAMBLE

1   Mazen Hashem, "Maqāṣid al-Sharīʿah: Asʾilah fī al-Minhaj," in *Al-Dīn wa al-Ḥaḍārah: Ḥifẓ al-ʿUmrān Maqṣid Sharʿī* (London: Muʾassasat al-Furqān li al-Turāth al-Islāmī, 2018).

2   In the diagram, the inner core of religion is surrounded, first, by a circle representing the realm of the individual who has agency and who would act according to the guidance of religion and in light of its worldview. But the individual does not live in a vacuum, rather, persons operate in a social context interacting with each other where their joint efforts

create the reality in which they live; this was represented by the third layer in the diagram. However, social life needs and depends on economic activities, managing resources, providing rations, and supporting the society and its persons. The last circle represents polity and government, which among many of its functions pursue a collective agenda, provide necessary coordination, and secure protection. In sum, we have five circles representing the five *maqāṣid*: the radiating core of religion, the person the actor, the social habitat, the providence of the economy, and the coordinator state.

For the diagram to further reflect the dimensions of this theory, it should be viewed as five dimensional. Thus, the circles stand for spheres of various sizes, within which the activities pertaining to them take place. Each sphere has its own orbit that is connected to the center, by the gravity of seeking guidance from the teachings of Shariʿah. Additionally, let us bear in mind that this formation does not operate in isolation; rather, it is floating in the space of a particular location that has its own characteristics and input. Lastly, we can envision a fifth dimension representing the movement throughout time endowed by a historical memory and civilizational legacy of the Ummah.

CHAPTER 7

[1]   This is a reference to the following Qur'anic verse: "O mankind! We created you from a single (pair) of a male and a female, and made you into nations and tribes, that you may know each other (not that you may despise (each other). Verily the most honoured of you in the sight of Allah is (he who is) the most righteous of you. And Allah has full knowledge and is well acquainted (with all things)" (49:13, Translated by Yusuf Ali).

Bibliography

AbdelFattah, Saif. "Bayn Al-Nasaq Wa al-Manhaj:Al-Manẓūmah al-Fikriyyah Li Munā Abū al-Faḍl." In *Al-Taḥawwūl al- Maʿrifī Wa al-Taghiyīr al-Ḥaḍārī: Qirāʾah Fī Manẓūmat Fikr Munā Abū al-Faḍl*, edited by Nadia Mahmoud Mostafa, Saif AbdelFattah, and Majidah Ibrahim, 78–85. Cairo: Dār al-Bashar, 2011.

Abdullah, Muhammad al-Awad. "Al-Maḍāmīn al-Manhajiyyah Li Muqadimāt al-Shāṭibī Fī al-Muwāfaqāt." In *Maqāṣid Al-Sharīʿah: Naḥū Iṭār Li al-Baḥth Fī al-ʿUlūm al-Ijtimāʿiyyah Wa al-Insāniyyah*, edited by Abdullah Muhammad al-Amin al-Naʿim. Damascus: Dār al-Fikr, 2009.

Abul-Fadl, Mona. "Contrasting Epistemics: Tawhid, the Vocationist and Social Theory." *American Journal of Islamic Social Sciences* 7, no. 1 (1990): 15–39.

Adhami, Riyad. "Awlawiyyāt Al-Aḥkām al-Sharʿiyyah." *Majallat Al-Rashād*, 1995.

al-Adrawi, Abd al-Rahman. "Al-Taṭbīq al-Maqāṣidī Fī al-Manhaj al-Khaldūnī." *Islāmiyyat Al-Maʿrifah* 13, no. 50 (October 2007): 175–212.

al-Alwani, Taha Jabir. "Turāthunā Al-Islāmī Wa al-Maʿārif al-Insāniyyah Wa al-Ijtimāʿiyyah." *Islāmiyyat Al-Maʿrifah*, no. 42–43 (2006): 8.

Attia, Gamal Eldin. *Naḥwah Tafʿīl Maqāṣid Al-Sharīʿah.* Herndon, VA: International Institute of Islamic Thought, 2001.

Auda, Jasser. *Maqasid as Philosophy of Islamic Law: A System Approach.* Herndon, VA: International Institute of Islamic Thought, 2008.

Barazangi, Nimat Hafez. *Women's Identity and the Qur'an: A New Reading.* Gainesville, FL: University of Florida Press, 2004.

Baza, Abdul-Nur. "Al-Maqāṣid al-Sharʿiyyah Bayn Mubda'a al-Ḥasr Wa Daʿwā al-Taghiyīr." *Islāmiyyat Al-Maʿrifah* 10, no. 40 (April 2005): 77–124.

Bennabi, Malek. *Mushkilat Al-Thaqāfah.* Translated by Abdel-Sabour Shahin. Damascus: Dār al-Fikr, 1984.

Bin Bayyah, Abdallah. *Mashāhid Min Al-Maqāṣid.* Riyad: Dār Wajūh, 2010.

al-Dehlawī, Shah Walīullah. *Ḥujjat Allah Al-Bālighah.* Edited by Sayyid Sabiq. Beirut: Dār al-Jīl, 2005.

El-Mesawi, Mohamed El-Tahir. "Al-Taʿlīl Wa al-Munāsabah Wa al-Maṣlaḥah: Baḥth Fī Baʿḍ al-Mafāhīm al-Ta'asīsiyyah Li Maqāṣid al-Sharīʿah," no. 43 (2009): 52.

al-Fasi, ʿAllal. *Maqāṣid Al-Sharī'ah al-Islāmiyyah Wa Makārimuhā.* Beirut: Dār al-Gharb al-Islāmī, 1993.

Hamid, Qays Mahmud. "Maqārabah Falsafiyyah Li Maqāṣid Al-Sharīʿah al-Islāmiyyah." In *Maqāṣid Al-Sharīʿah: Naḥū Iṭār Li al-Baḥth Fī al-ʿUlūm al-Ijtimāʿiyyah Wa al-Insāniyyah*, edited by Abdullah Muhammad al-Amin al-Naʿim. Damascus: Dār al-Fikr, 2009.

Hasani, Ismail. "Al-Fikr al-Maqāṣidī Wa Tarsīkh al-Fikr al-ʿIlmī." *Islāmiyyat Al-Maʿrifah* 15, no. 57 (July 2009): 48–62.

———. *Naẓariyyat Al-Maqāṣid ʿind al-Imām Muḥammad Ibn ʿĀshūr.* Herndon, VA: International Institute of Islamic Thought, 1995.

Hashem, Mazen. "Contemporary Islamic Activism: The Shades of Praxis." *Sociology of Religion* 67 (2006): 23–41.

———. "Maqāṣid Al-Sharīʿah: As'ilah Fī al-Minhaj." In *Al-Dīn Wa al-Ḥaḍārah: Ḥifẓ al-ʿUmrān Maqṣid Sharʿī.* London: Mu'assasat al-Furqān li al-Turāth al-Islāmī, 2018.

———. "Muslim Friday Khutbas in America: Veiled and Unveiled Themes." Institute for Social Policy and Understanding, October 2009.

Ibn ʿAshur, Muhammad al-Tahir. *Maqāṣid Al-Sharīʿah al-Islāmiyyah.* Tunis: Maktabat al-Istiqāmah, 1946.

———. *Uṣūl Al-Niẓam al-Ijtimāʿī Fī al-Islām.* Tunis: al-Sharikah al-Tūnisiyyah li al-Tawzīʿ, 1985.

Ibn Khaldūn, ʿAbd al-Raḥmān ibn Muḥammad. *Al-Muqaddimah.* Sayda: al-Maktabah al-ʿAṣriyyah, n.d.

Ibn Khuzaymah, Muḥammad ibn Isḥāq. *Kitāb Al-Zakāt.* Beirut: al-Maktab al-Islāmī, 1980.

Ibn Nasr, Mohammed. "Ta'ṣīl al-ʿUlūm al-Insāniyyah Wa al-Ijtimāʿiyyah." *Islāmiyyat Al-Maʿriffah* 11, no. 42–43 (January 2006): 99–126.

Ibn Rushd al-Ḥafīd, Abī al-Walīd Muḥammad ibn Aḥmad ibn Muḥammad ibn Aḥmad. *Bidāyat Al-Mujtahid Wa-Nihāyat al-Muqtaṣid.* Edited by Muhammad Subhi Hassan al-Hallaq. Cairo: Maktabat Ibn Taymiyyah, 1994.

Ibn Taymiyyah, Taqī al-Dīn Aḥmad Ibn ʿAbd al-Ḥalīm. *Al-ʿUbūdiyyah.* Al-Iskandariyyah: Dār al-Imān, 2003.

———. *Majmūʿ Al-Fatāwā al-Kubrā.* Edited by Hasan Muhammad Makhluf. Beirut. Dār al-Maʿrifah, 1966.

Jabir, Hasan. *Al-Maqāṣid al-Kulliyyah Fī Daw' al-Qirā'ah al-Manẓumiyyah Li al-Qur'ān al-Karīm.* Beirut: Dār al-Ḥiwār, 2011.

al-Jawziyyah, Muḥammad Ibn al-Qayyim al-. *Iʿlām Al-Muwaqqiʿīn ʿan Rabb al-ʿĀlamīn.* Dammam: Dār Ibn al-Jawzī, 2002.

Karahanlı, Haldun. "Al-Tadāfuʿiyyah: Transcending the Imperial Concept Of 'Civilization': Recalling The Concept of Al-ʿUmrān." PhD diss., Ibn Haldun University, 2020.

Krämer, Gudrun. "Islamist Notions of Democracy." *Middle East Report* 183 (August 1993).

Mushawash, Salih ibn Tahir. *ʿIlm Al-ʿUmrān al-Khaldūnī Wa Athar al-Ru'yah al-Kawniyyah al-Tawḥīdiyyah Fī Ṣiyāghatihi.* Herndon, VA: International Institute of Islamic Thought, 2012.

al-Najjar, Abd al-Majid. *Khilāfat Al-Insān Bayn al-Waḥī Wa al-ʿAql.* Doha: Kitāb al-Ummah, 2000.

———. *Maqāṣid Al-Sharīʿah Bi Abʿād Jadīdah*. Beirut: Dār al-Gharb al-Islāmī, 2008.

al-Naʿim, Abdullah Muhammad al-Amin. "Itijāhāt Al-Naẓr Fī al-Taʾsīs al-Maqāṣidī Li al-ʿUlūm al-Ijtimāʿiyyah." In *Maqāṣid Al-Sharīʿah: Naḥū Iṭār Li al-Baḥth Fī al-ʿUlūm al-ʿUlūm al-Ijtimāʿiyyah Wa al-Insāniyyah*, edited by Abdullah Muhammad al-Amin al-Naʿim. Damascus: Dār al-Fikr, 2009.

al-Qarāfī, Shihāb al-Dīn. *Al-Iḥkām Fī Tamyīz al-Fatāwā ʿan al-Aḥkām Wa-Taṣarrufāt al-Qāḍī Wa-al-Imām*. Edited by ʿAbd al-Fattāḥ Abū Ghuddah. Halab: Maktab al-Maṭbūʿāt al-Islāmiyyah, 1967.

al-Raysuni, Ahmad. *Al-Kulliyyāt al-Asāsiyyah Lil-Sharīʿah al-Islāmiyyah*. Rabat and Cairo: Dār al-Imān and Dār al-Islām, 2010.

———. "Al-Naṣṣ Wa al-Maṣlaḥah: Bayn al-Taṭbīq Wa al-Taʿāruḍ." *Islāmiyyat Al-Maʿrifah* 4, no. 13 (July 1998): 47–65.

———. *Muḥāḍarāt Fī Maqāṣid Al-Sharīʿah*. Rabat and Cairo: Dār al-Imān and Dār al-Islām, 2009.

———. *Naẓariyyat Al-Maqāṣid ʿinda al-Imām al-Shāṭibī*. Beirut: Al-Muʾassasah al- Jāmiʿīyyah, 1992.

al-Raysuni, Ahmad, Muhammad al-Zuhayli, and Muhammad Uthman Bashir. *Ḥuqūq Al-Insān Maḥwar Maqāṣid al-Sharīʿah*. Doha: Wizārat al-Awqāf wa al-Shuʾūn al-Islāmiyyah, 2002.

Safi, Louay. "Islamic Law and Society." *American Journal of Islamic Social Sciences* 7 (1990): 177–91.

Sano, Qutub Mustapha. "Fī Muṣṭalaḥ Al-Ijmāʿ al-Uṣūlī: Ishkāliyyat al-Mafhūm Bayn al-Mathāliyyah Wa al-Wāqiʿiyyah." *Islāmiyyat Al-Maʿrifah* 5, no. 21 (July 2000): 45–84.

———. "Al-Mutakallimūn Wa Uṣūl al-Fiqh: Qirāʾah Fī Jadliyat al-ʿAlāqah Bayn ʿIlmay al-Uṣūl Wa al-Kalām." *Islāmiyyat Al-Maʿrifah* 3, no. 9 (July 1997): 37–70.

al-Sawalihi, Yunus. "Al-Istiqrāʾ Fī Manāhij al-Naẓr al-Islāmī: Namūdhaj al-Imām al-Shāṭibī Fī al-Muwāfaqāt." *Islāmiyyat Al-Maʿrifah* 1, no. 4 (April 1996): 59–91.

al-Saʿi, Ahmad Bassam. *Iʿādat Qirā'at al-Iʿjāz al-Lughawī Fī al-Qur'ān al-Karīm*. Herndon, VA: International Institute of Islamic Thought, 2012.

Shahid, Hassan. "Shākilat Al-Naẓar al-ʿIlmī Bayn al-Shāṭibī Wa Ibn Khaldūn: Maqarabah Minhajiyyah." *Islāmiyyat Al-Maʿrifah* 15, no. 57 (July 2009): 83–122.

al-Shāṭibī, Abū Isḥāq Ibrahīm. *Al-Muwāfaqāt Fī Uṣūl al-Sharīʿah*. Edited by Muḥammad ʿAbd Allāh Darrāz. Beirut: Dār al-Maʿrifah, n.d.

Tajdin, Mustapha. "Al-Naṣ al-Qur'ānī Wa Mushkil al-Ta'wīl." *Islāmiyyat Al-Maʿrifah* 4, no. 14 (October 1998): 7–29.

al-Thaʿālibī, ʿAbd al-Malik Ibn Muḥammad. *Fiqh Al-Lughah Wa Asrār al-ʿArabiyyah*. Beirut: Dār Maktabat al-Ḥayāh, 1999.

Zain, Ibrahim Mohamed. "Al-Istiqrā' ʿinda al-Shāṭibī Wa Manhaj al-Naẓar Fī Mudawwinātinā al-Uṣūliyyah." *Islāmiyyat Al-Maʿrifah* 8, no. 30 (October 2002): 27–60.

Zarzur, Adnan. "Ibn Khaldūn Wa Fiqhuhu Al-Sunan." *Islāmiyyat Al-Maʿrifah* 13, no. 50 (October 2007): 153–76.